Islam Encountering Globalization

One of the greatest dilemmas facing Muslims today is the fact that Muslim culture, which originated many centuries ago, is often seemingly incompatible with the culture of the modern Western world and the features associated with it – technological progress, consumerism and new electronic communication, all of which have the potential for a homogenizing effect on any culture. This book explores many key aspects of the globalization process, discussing how Muslim countries are coping with the encounter with globalization, as well as considering how the West is responding to Islam.

Ali Mohammadi is Reader in International Communication and Cultural Studies at The Nottingham Trent University. His recent publications are *Globalization and Recolonization: The Muslim World in the 21st Century,* with Muhammad Ahsan (Taha, 2002), *Iran and Eurasia,* co-edited with A. Ehteshami (Ithaca Press, 2000), *International Communication and Globalisation: A Critical Introduction* (Sage, 1997) and 'Electronic Empires: An Islamic Perspective', in *Electronic Empires* (Arnold, 1998).

RoutledgeCurzon Durham Modern Middle East and Islamic World Series 2

Islam Encountering Globalization

Edited by Ali Mohammadi

RoutledgeCurzon
Taylor & Francis Group

First published 2002
by RoutledgeCurzon
11 New Fetter Lane, London EC4P 4EE

Simultaneously published in the USA and Canada
by RoutledgeCurzon
29 West 35th Street, New York, NY 10001

RoutledgeCurzon is an imprint of the Taylor & Francis Group

© 2002 editorial matter and selection, Ali Mohammadi; individual
chapters, the authors

Typeset in Times by Taylor & Francis Books Ltd
Printed and bound in Great Britain by TJ International Ltd, Padstow,
Cornwall

British Library Cataloguing in Publication Data
A catalog record for this book is available from the British Library

Library of Congress Cataloging in Publication Data
A catalogue record for this book has been requested

ISBN 0–700–71731–5 (hbk)
ISBN 0–700–71732–3 (pbk)

Contents

Contributors

Muhammad Ahsan is a research analyst on Pakistan affairs at The Nottingham Trent University. His recent publications are 'Human Development Strategies and the Muslim World: A Multi-dimensional Approach' (*Journal of National Development and Security*, vol. 7, no. 3, 1999) and 'Education: 21st Century and Human Development in the Muslim World' (*Muslim Education Quarterly*, spring, vol. 16, no. 3, 1999).

Mike Featherstone is Professor of Sociology and Communications at The Nottingham Trent University. He is founding editor of *Theory, Culture and Society* and the *TCS* book series. He is co-editor of the journal *Body and Society*. He is author of *Consumer Culture and Postmodernism* (1991) and *Undoing Culture: Globalization, Postmodernism and Identity* (1995) and has edited and written numerous books on social theory and globalization.

Fred Halliday is Professor of International Relations at the London School of Economics. His recent books include *Islam and the Myth of Confrontation* (I. B. Tauris, 1996), *Revolution and World Politics* (Macmillan, 1999) and *Nation and Religion in the Middle East* (Saqi, 2000). His books have been translated into Arabic, Persian, Turkish and Indonesian.

Karim H. Karim is an Assistant Professor in the School of Journalism and Communication, Carleton University, Ottawa, Canada. His most recent publication is *Islamic Peril: Media and Global Violence*, (Black Rose, 2000), which won the Canadian Communication Association's Robinson Book Prize.

Charles Kurzman is Associate Professor of Sociology at the University of North Carolina. His most recent book is *Liberal Islam: A Sourcebook* (Oxford University Press, 1998).

viii *Contributors*

Peter G. Mandaville is Lecturer in international relations at the University of Kent at Canterbury. His research interests include transnational Muslim politics, non-Western political theory and the philosophy of community. He has published in journals such as *Millennium* and *Review of International Studies*.

Ali Mohammadi is Reader in International Communication and Cultural Studies at The Nottingham Trent University. His recent publications are: *Globalization and Recolonization: The Muslim World in the 21st Century,* with Muhammad Ahsan (Taha, 2002), *Iran and Eurasia* co-edited with A. Ehteshami (Ithaca, 2000), *International Communication and Globalisation: A Critical Introduction* (Sage, 1997), and 'Electronic Empires: An Islamic Perspective', in *Electronic Empires* (Arnold, 1998).

Mahmood Monshipouri is Professor of Political Science at Quinnipiac College, Hamden, Connecticut. His most recent book is *Islamism, Secularism and Human Rights in the Middle East* (Lynne Rienner, 1998).

Manuchehr Sanadjian is Senior Lecturer in Social Anthropology in the Faculty of Leisure and Tourism, Buckinghamshire Chilterns University College. His recent article 'An Anthology of "the people". Place, Space and "Home": Reconstructing the Lur in South-Western Iran', is published in *Social Identities* (vol. 2, no. 1, 1996).

Preface

For the first time since the establishment of the Organization of Islamic Countries (OIC) in 1969 in Rabat, Morocco, Iran became the host to fifty-five Muslim countries in Tehran in October 1997. President Khatami addressed the leaders of Islamic countries as well as the Secretary-General of the United Nations. It was a great achievement for the Iranian government to be able to bring all the Muslim leaders and representatives in a single *shi'ah* country to discuss the unity of the Islamic world and the problems which are obstacles to progress in the Islamic world. President Khatami argued that the first and the most agonizing pain was that once upon a time the Muslim world was in the forefront of knowledge, human thought and civility, and he posed the question 'what has happened?'. In the last few centuries, he argued, we have been weak, under-developed, and static in terms of philosophical modes of thought, and furthermore there is a lack of questioning of ourselves about why we are stuck and not able to move forward. Every civilization in the world is a response to human enquiry into the nature of existence – if a civilization does not allow this questioning, which is fundamental to human nature, then that civilization is doomed. Now is the right time to recognize the necessity for us to address this issue because we need to know and understand why Western culture has been so successful and how it has influenced us. We need to ask ourselves, why have we not been able to progress? President Khatami went on to argue that the present post-Cold War world system, based on majority rule rather than the previous bipolar system of superpowers, provides an opportune moment for the Muslim countries to play a constructive and active role in shaping the future of the world in the twenty-first century. Since its inception the achievement of the OIC has not been significant. President Khatami also suggested that the prosperity of the Muslim world depends on the continuity of peace and tranquillity between Muslim and non-Muslim countries. In order to achieve a permanent peace, he argued, there is a need for discussion to define the role of OIC for the security and development of Muslim countries. This is crucial, not only for the well-being of Muslim people, but also for further consolidation and cooperation among the Muslim countries in all fields, including the political, economic, cultural and social spheres. It should be noted that one of the greatest dilemmas for Muslims today is that our culture springs from a civilization whose era ended many centuries ago, and our lives are now influenced by a new civilization which demands a culture compatible with it. This is the reality of our world today. What we need to do to is to open the door to research and dialogue in order to find ways of living with honour which are in keeping with our Islamic identity. Western civilization, based on the idea of progress and thus technological innovation, is changing traditional ways of life and creating more dynamic and exciting styles of living. Consequently we need to adapt our culture to the new way of life which is emerging rapidly with the advent of electronic communication and the expansion of the information society. The globalization of the consumer market has penetrated Western and non-Western societies; consumer culture has an homogenizing effect beyond the control of any one nation; and as consumer worlds become alike everywhere, eventually the minimization of cultural differences becomes inevitable.

The dynamics of the 1990s were very different to the post-industrial periods of the 1960s and 1970s as the extraordinary changes in communication technologies have caused the compression of time and space. The rapid diffusion of the fax machine as the fastest mode of communication overcame the bottleneck of postal development in less developed countries; the influence of computer technology in finance and telecommunication systems and the rapid change of INTELSAT policy towards the South pushed most of the developing world into a new era of information technology. Now at the beginning of twenty-first century, many Islamic countries are still confused about their encounter with modern communications, as well as with a Western culture which is expanding the force of capitalism in a global form with alarming speed.

In many ways, the rapidly changing media environment of the 1990s looks set to alter non-Western cultures more radically than ever before. However, I think that the nature and the direction of this change are drastically different to those at the advent of industrialisation. In order to examine the contentious issue of globalization processes and their impact on the Islamic world, this volume has been organized around various aspects of the globalization process and of Muslim countries' encounters with it, as well as considering how the West is responding to Islam.

The first chapter focuses on the term 'globalization' and how it is defined by a range of theorists. This chapter carefully examines the argument of each chapter of the book and the process of Islamic reaction to, or adoption of, globalization. It also considers the possible ground for the construction of a genuine global public sphere.

Chapter 2 examines the nature of discussion between Muslim states and Western countries which raises two concerns: first, alarmism, meaning the perception of a threat from Islam by both Western and non-Muslim countries; and second, simplification, whereby most Muslims are labelled as terrorists or most terrorists are labelled as Muslims. Instead of this simplistic dichotomy of either fearing or hating Muslims, the author concludes that we need to respect and understand Islam in order to avoid Islamophobia, Eurocentrism and stereotyping from both sides.

Chapter 3 discusses use of the internet and the ways in which Muslims around the world engage with communication networks. The process of globalization through electronic communication is seen as providing a worldwide fellowship, not for remooring modernity but for creating space for the spiritual solidarity of the *ummah* as a challenge to the dominant materialistic model of globalization.

Chapter 4 examines the ways in which the impact of global communications and information technology on various forms of one particular tradition, Islam, has led both to the imagining of new political communities and to the re-imagining of traditional categories of social and religious solidarity.

Chapter 5 carefully examines how globalization energizes the moral force of human rights, and concludes that the Muslim world has no choice but to negotiate the basis for a global civil society.

Chapter 6 explores the major differences between Islamic and Western approaches to the concept of human rights, and suggests various ways of minimizing the differences between the two views.

Chapter 7 suggests that the 'rights' discourse is not fundamentally different to religious discourse, and argues that just like automobile or population control, the concept of human rights was invented in the West, packaged as universally applicable and exported to the rest of the world. The chapter identifies four global processes: first, the adoption of rights; second, the growth of a secular class; third, the acceleration of international communications and electronic media; and fourth, disillusionment with the Islamist project. All these processes provide the ground for a 'rights discourse' in the Islamic world.

Chapter 8 argues that the articulation of game, as a set of rules governing the relationship between participants and their competition, within a particular social and cultural context, allows for the examination of a major area of the exercise of power within the relationship between represented/representatives. This relationship is examined in detail through an analysis of the popular response in Iran to the World Cup football tournament.

Chapter 9 offers a case study of Pakistan, and examines how the concept of security has changed in recent years. Security is no longer limited to the military power of a country but extends to socio-economic issues. It is estimated that Muslim countries spend over $70 billion every year on defence. Instead, they could save a substantial part of this expenditure by creating an organization for their common security.

Chapter 10 is centred on sociological distinctions between tradition and ideology, with special emphasis on the issue of globalization and Iran. It concludes that the central step of political development, that is the transition to ideological politics, has yet to be permanently taken in Iran.

Ali Mohammadi

Acknowledgements

I would like to thank all the contributors, especially Mike Featherstone at the TCS centre for his introduction to such an important topic, and John Tomlinson, head of CRICC, for his encouragement and useful discussion. Thanks also to Frances Banks, English and Media Studies secretary, for her kind support of this book.

I should also like to thank Sara Mohammadi for her sincere help and editorial support. Finally, I would like to dedicate this volume to my mother and to my children, Sara and Leili.

1 Islam encountering globalization

An introduction

Mike Featherstone

Globalization is rapidly joining other stock social science terms such as society, class and culture to become a highly contested concept. Although the term global can be traced back in the English language for over 400 years, according to the *Oxford English Dictionary* the term globalization, along with the related terms globalize and globalizing, seems to have first come into use in the 1960s, largely in economic contexts (Waters 1995: 2). In economics and management literature, the first use seems to have been Levitt's paper on the globalization of markets published in 1983 (Dicken 1998: 15). In sociology Roland Robertson was one of the first to use the term in the early 1980s (see Robertson 1985; 1992a; 1992b; Robertson and Lechner 1985). In media and cultural studies, Marshall McLuhan's (1960) use of the term 'global village' in his book *Understanding Media*, published in 1960, was a significant influence. Yet these academic usages can hardly have prepared us for the way in the 1990s the term rapidly became part of the everyday vocabulary not only of academics and business people, but circulated widely in the media and everyday life.

The term globalization now has developed an immediate intelligibility for wider publics, which other recent academic terms, such as postmodernism, postmodernity and reflexive modernization, have never been able to attain. The root 'global' seems to possess a self-evident quality in its suggestion of not only the expansion of the scope of our social relations to the planetary limits, but also in the way it points to the spatial integration of the world through increased communication and trade. It suggests that we are becoming pulled together into a global society and in the process of developing a global culture through intensified communication. It suggests a process of integration together into a common humanity. Planetary space seems to be shrinking, with 'planet earth' now seen as finite and vulnerable and in need of protection from the consequences of human exploitation.

But, perhaps most strongly in the popular imagination, globalization has become associated with the integration of the global economy, a process which on the level of the nation-state is seen by many to inevitably cause social, cultural and political deregulation and disintegration. The current phase of globalization, then, is associated with marketization, something which some also see as leading to the 'emptying out of culture', the weakening and dilution of local cultures. Yet it can also be argued that in the short run at least, this can lead to an upsurge of interest in culture. Cultures decline, but culture is everywhere. This is evident in contemporary business practices through the popularity of spatially dispersed, disaggregated, post-Fordist forms of production which, along with niche marketing, increases the need to be aware of the particularities of different regional and local markets across the globe.[1] We can also point to intensified communication, especially through cheaper and quicker telecommunications, along with the expansion of satellite television, the internet and the new digital media, which are leading to more voices talking – what has been referred to as the 'global babble' (see Featherstone 1995).

One dominant meaning of globalization, then, is built around marketization and economic deregulation to permit the freer flow of money, raw materials, information and commodities across national borders (Appadurai 1990). A perspective which is often accompanied by an implicit or explicit evolutionism: that the social dislocations which result from the spread of the market are the inevitable price of progress. They produce changes which in the long term will necessarily be beneficial for humanity. This universalizing logic is even stronger when combined with technological optimism, as we find in the current wave of enthusiasm for 'the new economy'. Here the digital and internet economy is seen as rewriting the rules of economic life and ushering in, according to the internet magazine *Wired*, 'a 25 year long boom' (Schwartz and Leyden 1997). From this perspective, those who resist globalization are castigated with the blameword 'tradition', and seen as irrationally clinging to obsolete and negative values which stand in the way of the extension of human freedom and happiness.

Yet at a time when the US economy has enjoyed an unprecedented period of growth, with much of this attributed to globalization and the development of the new information economy, the discontents about the negative effects of globalization have been growing to the extent that in many parts of the world globalization has become a negatively loaded term. It has become associated with the destructive effects of the extension of the market: the reduction of tariff and trade barriers, the deregulation of local protectionism, the mobility of capital, the flight of corporations to the most profitable worldwide locations, the break-up and downsizing of companies, the emergence of new forms of sovereignty with the expansion of global financial markets. If the above economic processes can be characterized as 'globalization-from-above', then it is a characteristic of the last few years that the pressure has been building up for some form of global politics and resistance, or the exploration of 'globalization-from-below' (Falk 1999: ch. 8).

This was something which was dramatically played out in front of global television audiences viewing the WTO (World Trade Organization) talks in Seattle in late November 1999. A motley alliance of protesters and environmental groups from various parts of the world were in Seattle to denounce the negative effects of global deregulation of trade, especially in relation to its impact on jobs, local identities and the conservation of nature[2] (St Clair 1999: 88). The protests and running street battles with the police were repeated a few months later in front of world political and business leaders at the prestigious World Economic Forum Conference, in Davos, February 2000. Such protests point to the first attempts to open up a global public sphere or global civil society, to highlight the question of the excluded, the victims of the new inequalities, the new global North/South divide, what some have referred to as a form of 'global apartheid'. A world in which one fifth is rich and four fifths are poor (Falk 1999: 14).[3]

Optimists might see these first steps towards a global public sphere as eventually leading to the development of institutions which seek greater accountability from multinational corporations and global elites (Lasch 1996), along with greater democratic representation for those excluded from the new forms of sovereignty such as financial markets (Latham 2000; Sassen 2000). Something which can be seen as throwing out stepping stones towards an eventual global state which would move towards the monopoly of the means of violence and taxation.[4] At the same time we have to be aware that movements towards a genuine global public sphere would have to be critical of the Western origins.[5] A multicultural global public sphere would need to be dialogical, not only in terms of content, through encouraging interchanges between different civilizational traditions, but also in form, by interrogating and respecting a range of different cultural notions of the public, citizenship, representation, human rights and democracy. A concept of the public sphere which is based upon symbolic hierarchies which uncritically derive from Eurocentric notions is inadequate for this task. We need to take into account the perspective of those who seek to critically deconstruct the universal claims of such globalizing discourses by regarding them as forms of 'globalized localism', a perspective from which the universal is seen as merely the view of the dominant particular, writ large (see Featherstone 1991; 1995).

The challenge is to develop a genuinely global human rights based upon respect and conservation, which acknowledges the integrity of different traditions and civilizations, not just in a defensive sense, but through their dialogical potential. Many people in the West assume that given the global success of the science and technology and the democratic forms of citizenship which were developed in the Western Enlightenment during the eighteenth century and became identified with progress, the only problem is how to generalize these forms to everyone. Yet if we want a genuine human rights which is respected in different parts of the world, we need to go beyond notions of human rights solely based on the 'globalized localism' of the Western form. As long as this tradition sees itself as universal, other civilizational traditions will feel excluded. The famous United Nations Declaration of Human Rights of 1948 was drafted without the participation of the majority of the peoples of the world (Santos 1999), a point emphasized in various ways by Ali Mohammadi, Charles Kurzman and Mahmood Monshipouri in their chapters in this volume in their discussions of Islamic human rights. Here one also thinks of Mahmood Monshipouri's point that the West has often used human rights arguments to justify hostile policies towards governments with which it fundamentally differs, while turning a blind eye to rights questions in countries which are seen as essential to its strategic interests.

It can be argued that a genuine global human rights is only possible on the basis of a dialogue between different civilizational traditions. Yet the danger of this approach is that the world becomes reified into the construction of tradition operative at the current point in time. It also depends upon the power struggles within particular nation-states by politicians, clerics and intellectuals, to become guardians of tradition, to appropriate and define the content of cultures and civilizations. The potential for cross-cultural dialogue has to work in the opposite direction and operate through the acceptance that all cultures are incomplete and partial. All cultures are not fixed, but are in process. In this sense one of the central tasks of our time is the translation of human rights from globalized liberalism, the freedoms of the marketplace, into a genuinely cosmopolitan project based upon inter-cultural dialogue (see Featherstone 2000b; 2000c; Robbins 1998).

This project, and subsequent inter-civilizational dialogues, could well mean not just the limitation, but the extension of human rights. As Karim H. Karim, Peter Mandaville and a number of other contributors to this volume point out, in the Islamic notion of *ummah*, the worldwide Muslim community, we have an emphasis upon the collective rights of groups. It can be argued that the notion of *ummah* is significant at this particular juncture in making us aware that a genuine global integration process must take into account the view that not just individuals but groups, ranging from ethnic minorities to humanity as a whole, have rights to solidarities along with collective obligations. In short, a global public sphere needs to operate with some broader notion of global community, and Islamic thought has an important contribution to play in bringing about a fuller version of human rights.

It can also be added that the interrogation of other civilizational traditions can be equally productive in extending our notion of human rights. From the perspective of the Hindu tradition of *dharma*, we can see the limitations of the Western notion of human rights, which emphasizes that we only grant rights to those who perform duties. Yet because nature does not perform any duties, it does not deserve any rights. Also important here is the concept of *ahimsa*, the Hindu ideal of non-violence, which means 'not-forcing' and actively engaging in compassion. From this perspective, when we engage in production and consumption patterns which mean we take more than we need we engage in violence (Shiva 1999). This is not just an ethical principle, but can be seen as a cautionary self-interested principle too, because to avoid taking more than you need in the absence of full knowledge can preserve us from many unknown dangers. In addition, future generations have no rights under the Western scheme. Yet it can be argued that we are in debt to previous generations, and to nature, which provides the grounds which make the world our field of possibilities. Likewise we have an interest in taking the role of the other, in anticipating the needs of future generations and keeping this chain of transmission intact.

This suggests that if each tradition is prepared to recognize its own incompleteness and weaknesses, there is the basis for a cross-cultural dialogue which could be highly productive in opening up wider participation in the formation of a global public sphere, and for starting the process of outlining some of the foundations for a genuine global citizenship. Such a perspective depends upon respect and tolerance and has clear ethical implications, in terms of the obligations and duties people should have towards others, groups, future generations and nature.

When we look at actually existing Islamic societies, as Ali Mohammadi points out in his discussion of 'religion versus ideology in Iran', there is often the lack of the basis for a public sphere of political debate based upon participation and literacy. Retraditionalization, anti-modernization and Islamization are clearly potent sentiments which can be mobilized by particular groups such as the clergy in Iran. Yet it is increasingly difficult to police and control global communications, and the current phase in Iran is one in which there are active attempts to explore the implications of globalization and a more active civil society. For some the new global processes, such as the intensified flows of information and people around the world, have led to a break or rupture in the process of globalization.

Appadurai (1996), for example, argues that since the 1970s the electronic media and mass migration have become 'massively globalized'. Intensified migration results in the deterritorialization of the imagination and the potential to construct diasporic public spheres.[6] He argues that while classical modernization theory was firmly attached to the nation-state, globalization has shrunk the distance between elites, and broken many of the links between work and family life through migration. As the mass media become dominated by the electronic media and depend less and less on the capacity to read and write, and link people across national boundaries, audiences are able to develop diasporic public spheres, which are the key vehicles of a postnational political order through their capacity to link together workers, students, activists and refugees along with various social movements, NGOs, etc.

Diasporic public spheres form the basis for postnational imagined communities. Here Appadurai (1996) builds on the work of Benedict Anderson (1991), who pointed out the importance of the construction of an imagined community through the mass media in the formation of nationalism. If Anderson emphasized the importance of 'print capitalism', Appadurai stresses 'electronic capitalism' and points to the role of film, television, video and the internet with their post-symbolic imagistic communicative forms. Hence postnational imagined communities are deterritorialized, yet permit people to communicate over distance. The Sikh taxi-driver in Chicago can listen to a temple speech from India on cassette while driving, the Pakistani worker in Los Angeles can watch videos of religious movements in Pakistan. Distant people see themselves as having a stake in each other's lives, as we find in the case of Bosnian Muslims who were under pressure from Islamic forces in Saudi, Sudan and Egypt, and who felt they had a legitimate stake to reconstitute Bosnian Islamic identity more in line with their own perspectives.

Appadurai's postnational imagined communities, then, point the way towards a postnational public sphere. But his vision is very different from those like Habermas who want to emphasize the potential of the public sphere for developing rational forms of communication based upon the acknowledgement of the better argument. Rather, for Appadurai, the new image-based forms are more rhetorical and a long way from the alleged rational arguments of philosophers. The dogmas of nationalism, fundamentalism and Balkanization can also be seen as gaining sustenance from these global processes (Mestrovic 1994). The speed of communication, the ease and rapidity of interchanges, also favours a pace of dialogue which is different from that of the slow deliberative efforts of philosophers. Yet this does not mean that they lack critical potential. Hence, as Mandaville argues in his chapter in this collection, the internet has the potential to allow Muslims to participate in the imagined community of the *ummah*, to build or re-imagine a virtual *ummah* which nets together Muslims and also acts as a platform for Islamic ideas on the global stage.

But it should also be understood that the new communications technologies make possible a complex and contradictory set of effects. The ease of information exchange through e-mail and the internet, despite the efforts of some Islamic states to impose censorship, may not simply lead to the importation of Western ideas. It may lead to new articulations, as we find with the development of specifically Islamic notions of human rights which may be encouraged by ruling elites, who have to address rights questions to counter accusations of rights abuses from the West and redirect potential protest at home. The internet also, as Karim H. Karim points out in his chapter, makes available web-based religious resources which have a critical potential in de-monopolizing knowledge, in taking it out of the hands of clerics and other guardians. There is a potential here for developing critical hermeneutics on the part of various groups and publics who can question dogmatic and literalist readings of religious texts. Although the internet is driven by the new global economy, the 'dotcom' 'click and purchase' logic, it cannot be reduced solely to this aspect. We also need to investigate the ways in which the internet is reconstituting the archive and collective memory by widening public access to information formerly under the close surveillance of various official guardians and gatekeepers (Featherstone 2000a).

This potential for the development of an active global public sphere must be set against the triumph of global marketization and the rise of the much heralded 'network society' (Castells 1996a; 1996b; 1998). It is too early to assume the triumph of global economics, especially when the first signs of a global politics, the development of various forms of global publics and protest movements, the expansion of INGOs (international non-government organizations) and the development of a host of cross-sector flexible alliances are beginning to emerge. These movements need not simply be seen as the resistance of culture and tradition to the expansion of the market and technology. Rather, the active ways in which culture is continually reconstituted through technology must be considered too. The danger is in conceiving this process in a simple zero-sum game, or equilibrium balance. The problem with the level of complexity we experience in the current phase of globalization is conceptually handling and modelling such seemingly contradictory expanding processes – the expansion of global marketization and the expansion and visibility of participation in global public sphere activities.

As Fred Halliday argues in his chapter, we should be cautious about over-simple stereotypes which assume a unitary identity for the West, or for all Muslims. This not only fuels Islamophobia, but also does an injustice to the internal differentiation of Muslim societies, the struggles between secularizing and conservative religious forces within different states/societies. The danger of such approaches is that they work with a static or reified notion of culture: the world is composed of separate cultures which sit apart from each other as distinct islands. Whether it is civilizational theories such as those of Samuel Huntington (1997), or the emergence of 'jihad vs. McWorld' as suggested by Benjamin Barber (1996), the world is seen as originating with compartmentalized units. The standard unit of historical analysis tends to be the nation-state or region, a partial view which has also been encouraged by the rise of area studies. As Bergesen (1990) notes, this amounts to a form of methodological individualism, in which the separate units of the world are seen as primarily working out their own fates and only slowly coming to influence each other in the last couple of centuries. Rather, Bergesen wants us to adopt a form of methodological collectivism and focus on the underpinning structures and links which form a common ground which makes the reaction and ideology of separation possible.[7]

Hence it can be argued that one of the acts of cultural forgetting committed by those who have discovered globalization as the dominant sign for the present age, is to obliterate the memory of a human world which has practically always been connected. This holistic perspective on global history is developed by André Gunder Frank in his book *ReORIENT: Global Economy in the Asian Age* (1998).

Gunder Frank argues that the world system goes back much farther than the 500-year European-based system, which Wallerstein and others saw as the origin of the modern economy. Rather, there was a single interconnected world economic system based upon Asia, in which China was dominant from the eighth century onwards (although, as Frank argues, the origins of the system can be traced back millennia before this). Hence for Gunder Frank there were not several separate regional world economies, but one world economy in which Europe played a relatively minor role until the sixteenth century, when South American gold and silver enabled Europeans to begin to trade with East Asia on more equal terms; these precious metals were the only commodities Asians desired from Europe, given Asian superiority in manufacturing. Europe did not assume hegemony until the early nineteenth century.

There are several implications to be drawn from Gunder Frank's work which influence our view of the past and current phase of globalization. First, in the phase of European and Western ascendancy over the past two centuries, there was a rewriting of world history to produce the myth of origins of modernity in the West, the 'European exceptionalism' arguments we find in Marx, Weber and others. The symbolic hierarchies which equated modernity and progress with the superior West and tradition, indolence and inactivity with the exotic and inferior East (Orientalism) were a product of this phase. In the current phase, in step with the shift of global power balance away from the West, we find many attempts to excavate this process and delve into the counter-memories which have become obliterated; here we think of postcolonial theorists such as Said, Spivak, Bhabha and others (see Venn 1999; Friedman 1994; 1999 for a critique). This analytical, deconstructive and critical phase could well be followed by a more synthetic, systematizing phase, in which the new scholarship which is currently excavating the various regional histories, gives rise to a process of re-conceptualization and development of new theories and models; theories and models which challenge some of the Western classifications of knowledge and generate new classifications and syntheses.

Second, it can be argued that the approach of Gunder Frank has wider practical implications for the global public sphere. If a global sphere depends upon a dialogue between participants from different cultural and civilizational traditions, it is only by acknowledging a fuller and fairer account of global history that a movement forward can be made. Part of this process also means pointing out the stakes in the shifting relationships between separation and connection, dependency and recognition of independence. Recently there has been a revival of interest in Hegel's master/bondsman dialectic, especially in the notion of recognition (Sakai 1989; Sakamoto 1996; Fraser forthcoming; Yar forthcoming). It can be argued that only by recognizing the identity of the other, which itself is a product of the past the other has experienced, which is intertwined with one's own past, that one can attain greater freedom and the capacity to develop one's identity. Recognition of the other points towards respect, and the capacity to rethink the same/other dichotomy in us all. It points to the importance of counter-memories and counter-histories, the need to become aware of the grounds upon which the current phase of globalization has been constructed. It involves an acknowledgement of the interdependencies and power balances we have necessarily been, and still remain, locked into – something which can also be seen as necessary grounds for the construction of a genuine global public sphere.

Notes

1   Hence many transnational firms adopt the Japanese strategy of *dochakuka*, a farming term, referring to the capacity to grow what is best suited on the land in question, which became adopted by business. This is the basis of the more familiar academic terms 'glocalism' and 'glocalization' (Robertson 1995). On the rise of culture and the formation of transnational intercultural management skills in business education, see Trompenaars (1993).

2   The group of French farmers was led by José Bové, the sheep farmer from south-west France who had made a personal protest against McDonaldization by burning down a McDonald's restaurant, an act of protest which won the praise of French president Jacques Chirac, who shared his concerns and desire to stand against American hormone-treated beef.

3   For some this process of exclusion is not to be seen as just between the West and the rest, but as something which economic globalization is bringing home to Western societies in a dramatic way. Hence some predict we are heading for the '20/80' society (Martin and Schumann 1997). The top 20 per cent will be 'creatives', the symbol analysts, the information and knowledge specialists, in the upper corporate levels. The 80 per cent majority will have low-paid service work, McJobs, or have to go on government schemes, or will be under-employed and unemployed (Reich 1992; see also Bauman 1998).

4   There are currently a number of proposals for global taxation such as the Tobin tax, to regulate the estimated $1.5 trillion a day flows of hot money around the world's financial markets. The Tobin tax would be a small 0.05 per cent tax on financial transactions which would raise billions of revenue for public works, and in the words of Tobin, a former Nobel prize winner for economics, 'throw some sand into the wheels of the global financial markets' (Henderson 1999; Patomäki 2000).

5 Habermas' (1999) concept of the public sphere has been the subject of much debate and discussion (see Calhoun 1992; Featherstone 2000b; see also the latter for a discussion of the related concept of global citizenship).
6 *Contra* Appadurai, it should be noted that only 1.5 per cent of the global labour force works outside their own country, and that over half of this total is in the Middle East and sub-Saharan Africa (Mulgan 1998: 55).
7 Bergesen's (1990) debt here is to Durkheim (the underlying non-contractual aspects of contract) and Simmel (the culture underlying the economy and the internally integrative aspects of social conflicts between groups).

References

Anderson, B. (1991) *Imagined Communities*, revised edn, London: Verso.

Appadurai, A. (1990) 'Disjunction and Difference in the Global Cultural Economy', *Theory, Culture and Society*, vol. 7, 2–3, reprinted in M. Featherstone (ed.) *Global Culture*, London: Sage.

——(1996) *Modernity at Large: Cultural Dimensions of Globalization*, Minneapolis: University of Minnesota Press.

Barber, B. (1996) *Jihad vs. McWorld*, New York: Ballantine Books.

Bauman, Z. (1998) *Globalization: the Human Consequences*, Cambridge: Polity Press.

Bergesen, A. (1990) 'Turning World-System Theory on its Head', in M. Featherstone (ed.) *Global Culture*, London: Sage.

Calhoun, C. (ed.) (1992) *Habermas and the Public Sphere*, Cambridge MA: MIT Press.

Castells, M. (1996a) *The Information Age, Volume 1: The Rise of the Network Society*, Oxford: Blackwell.

——(1996b) *The Information Age, Volume 2: The Power of Identity*, Oxford: Blackwell.

——(1998) *The Information Age, Volume 3: The End of the Millennium*, Oxford: Blackwell.

Dicken, P. (1998) *Global Shift: Transforming the Global Economy*, 3rd edn, London: Chapman.

Falk, R. (1999) *Predatory Globalization: A Critique*, Cambridge: Polity Press.

Featherstone, M. (1991) *Consumer Culture and Postmodernism*, London: Sage.

——(1995a) *Undoing Culture: Globalization, Postmodernism and Identity*, London: Sage.

——(2000a) 'Archiving Cultures', *British Journal of Sociology*, special issue on the Millennium, vol. 51, no. 1, January 2000.

——(2000b) 'The Global City, Information Technology and Public Life', in C. Davis (ed.) *Identity and Social Change in Postmodern Life*, Baltimore: Johns Hopkins University Press.

——(2000c) 'Globalization and the Problem of Ethics in a Multicultural World', paper delivered to the 'Merging Mosaic? Facing the Ethical Challenge of the Global Community' conference, College Women's Association of Japan, Tokyo, mimeo.

12   *Mike Featherstone*

Frank, A. G. (1998) *ReORIENT: Global Economy in the Asian Age*, Berkeley: University of California Press.

Fraser, N. (forthcoming) 'Recognition', *Theory, Culture and Society*.

Friedman, J. (1994) *Cultural Identity and Global Process*, London: Sage.

——(1999) 'The Hybridization of Roots and the Abhorrence of the Bush', in M. Featherstone and S. Lash (eds) *Spaces of Culture: City, Nation, World*, London: Sage.

Habermas, J. (1989) *The Structural Transformation of the Public Sphere*, Cambridge: Polity Press.

Henderson, H. (1999) *Beyond Globalization: Shaping a Sustainable Global Economy*, West Hartford: Kumarian Press.

Huntington, S. (1997) *The Clash of Civilizations and the Remaking of World Order*, London: Simon and Schuster.

Lasch, C. (1996) *The Revolt of the Elites*, New York: Norton.

Latham, R. (2000) 'Sovereignty', *Theory, Culture and Society*, vol. 17, no. 4.

Levitt, T. (1983) 'The Globalization of Markets', *Harvard Business Review*, May-June, 92–102.

Luhmann, N. (1998) *Observations on Modernity*, Stanford: Stanford University Press.

McLuhan, M. (1960) *Understanding Media*, London: Routledge.

Martin, H-P. and Schumann, H. (1997) *The Global Trap*, London: Zed Books.

Mazlish, B. (1993) 'Global History in a Postmodern Era', in B. Mazlish and R. Buultjens (eds) *Conceptualizing Global History*, Boulder: Westview Press.

Mestrovic, S. G. (1994) *The Balkanization of the West*, London: Routledge.

Mulgan, G. (1998) *Connexity: Responsibility, Freedom, Business and Power in the New Century*, London/New York: Vintage.

Patomäki, H. (2000) 'The Tobin Tax', *Theory, Culture and Society*, vol. 17, no. 4.

Reich, R. (1992) *The Work of Nations*, New York: Vintage.

Robbins, B. (1998) 'Introduction: Actually Existing Cosmopolitanism', in P. Cheah and B. Robbins (eds) *Cosmopolitics*, Minneapolis: University of Minnesota Press.

Robertson, R. (1985) 'The Relativization of Societies: Modern Religion and Globalization', in T. Robbins, W. C. Sheppherd and J. McBride (eds) *Cults, Culture and the Law*, Chico: Scholars Press.

——(1992a) 'Globality and Modernity', *Theory, Culture and Society*, vol. 9, no. 2, 151–61.

——(1992b) *Globalization*, London: Sage.

——(1995) 'Glocalization: Time-Space and Homogeneity-Heterogeneity', in M Featherstone, S. Lash and R. Robertson (eds) *Global Modernities*, London: Sage.

Robertson, R. and Lechner, F. (1985) 'Modernization, Globalization and the Problem of Culture in World-Systems Theory', *Theory, Culture and Society*, vol. 2, no. 3, 103–17.

Santos, Boaventura de (1999) 'Towards a multicultural conception of Human Rights' in *Spaces of Culture: City, Nation, World*, edited by Mike Featherstone and Scott Lash, Sage, London.

St Clair, J. (1999) 'Seattle Diary', *New Left Review*, no. 238, 81–96.

Said, E. W. (1978) *Orientalism*, Harmondsworth: Penguin.

Sakai, N. (1989) 'Modernity and its Critique: The Problem of Universalism and Particularism', in H. Harootunian and M. Myoshi (eds) *Postmodernism and Japan*, Durham NC: Duke University Press.

Sakamoto, R. (1996) 'Japan, Hybridity and the Creation of Colonialist Discourse', *Theory, Culture and Society*, vol. 13, no. 3.

Sassen, S. (1999) 'Electronic Space and Power', in M. Featherstone and S. Lash (eds) *Spaces of Culture: City, Nation, World*, London: Sage.

——(2000) 'Electronic Space and Sovereignty', *Theory, Culture and Society*, vol. 17, no. 4.

Schwartz, P. and Leyden, P. (1997) 'The Long Boom', *Wired*, July, 115–22.

Scott, A. (1997) 'Introduction', in A. Scott (ed.) *The Limits of Globalization*, London: Routledge.

Shiva, V. (1999) 'Diversity and Democracy: Resisting the Global Economy', *Global Dialogue*, vol. 1, no. 1.

Trompenaars, F. (1993) *Riding the Waves of Culture: Understanding Cultural Diversity in Business*, London: Nicholas Brearley.

Waters, M. (1995) *Globalization*, London: Routledge.

Venn, Couze (1999) 'Narrating the Past Colonial', in *Space of Culture,city,nation,World*, Edited By Mike Featherstone and Scott Lash, London: Sage.

Yar, M. N. (forthcoming) 'The Politics of Recognition', *Theory, Culture and Society*.

2   West encountering Islam

Islamophobia reconsidered[1]

Fred Halliday

An anxiety of our times: 'Islam' versus the 'West'

No subject in contemporary public discussion has attracted more confused discussion than that of relations between 'Islam' and the 'West'. Whether it be the discussion of relations between Muslim states and non-Muslim countries, or that of relations between non-Muslims and Muslims within Western countries, the tendency has *on both sides* been, with some exceptions, towards alarmism and simplification. Alarmism has concerned the 'threat' which, from one side, 'Islam' poses to the non-Muslim world, and on the other, which the 'West' poses to Muslims. Non-Muslim simplification involves many obvious issues: terrorism – as if most Muslims are terrorists or most terrorists are Muslims; the degree of aggressiveness found in the Muslim world and the responsibility of Muslims for this; the unwillingness of Muslims to allow for diversity, debate and respect for human rights. It is not only the sensationalist media, but also writers with an eye to current anxieties of the reading public, such as V. S. Naipaul and Samuel Huntington, who reinforce such misrepresentation. Muslim simplification is itself two-sided: on the one hand, a stereotyping of the 'West', on the other the assertion of a unitary identity for all Muslims, and of a unitary interpretation of text and culture.

The core simplification involves these very terms themselves: 'the West' is not a valid aggregation of the modern world, and lends itself far too easily to monist, conspiratorial, presentations of political and social interaction; but nor is the term 'Islam' a valid shorthand for summarizing how a billion Muslims, divided into over fifty states, and into myriad ethnicities and social groups, relate to the contemporary world, each other or the non-Muslim world. To get away from such simplifications is, however, virtually impossible, since both those opposed to 'Islam' and those invoking it adhere to such labels. Moreover, as much of this literature shows, those who are most intent on critiquing standard Western prejudices about the Muslim world, themselves fall back on another set of simplifications. Instead of fearing or hating anti-Muslim stereotypes, we are now invited to respect, understand or study 'Islam'.

Islamophobia, Eurocentrism, stereotyping

Recent literature on the West and Islam ranges across several aspects of this question, and illustrates some of the pitfalls that arise. The Runnymede Trust report (1997) and the Wilton Park report (Browning 1998) identify misinterpretations, above all in the West, of the Muslim world and advocate a more tolerant, informed relation to the Muslim world. They reflect an approach derived on the one hand from race relations and, on the other, from inter-faith dialogue. They both set current frictions in the context of the long historical relations between Muslims and the Christian world, both identify the role of the media in reinforcing stereotypes, and both advocate greater discussion between communities. Most significantly, perhaps, they accept the term 'Islam' as a denomination of the primary identity of those who are Muslims; they avoid discussion of the diversities within Muslim societies, on ethnic grounds or on the interpretation of the Muslim tradition and on its application to the contemporary world.

A volume by Bobby Said, a sociologist writing in a Nietszchean-Foucauldian vein, strikes a less emollient note (Said 1997). Said seeks to provide a critical 'conceptual narrative' of how the Western world has come to identify an Islamic threat. He sees the category 'fundamentalism' not primarily in terms of the social or political factors that occasion it within specific Muslim societies, but rather as a Eurocentric response by the West as its hitherto undisputed domination of the Muslim world is challenged. Eurocentrism, the bane of so much analysis of the region, is, he argues, not so much a product of a historical Western hegemony, but a response to the threat which the decentering of the West now poses to that hegemony: it is a sign of decline, not of enduring power.

Islamism is, in this context, something to be welcomed, the return of the repressed, a rejection by Muslims of Western domination. Said excoriates those in the Muslim world – be they the liberal modernizers of the eighteenth and nineteenth centuries, or the Kemalists of the twentieth – who have tried to learn from the West and so modernize their societies. Said also denies the argument that Islamism contains another variant of radical Western discourse, seeing this as another form of hegemonic denial: those who have argued this – Aziz al-Azmeh, Sami Zubaida, myself – come in for a spirited attack. Islamism is a discursive construct that rejects the West, a form of modernity that is non-Western.

In contrast to these three works, which treat 'Islam', for the purposes of their argument at least, as a unitary object, and Muslims as a single community, there are other works that stress the diversity of Muslim societies, and of non-Muslim responses to them. Two works edited by Kai Hafez, a scholar at the Orient Institute in Hamburg, examine the different historical and modernist interpretations of Islam, and the different interactions of Muslims with the West. *Der Islam und der Westen* covers political thought, the status of women, terrorism and economics, together with the foreign policies of specific Muslim countries – Iran, Algeria, Turkey, Bosnia, the Palestinians, Central Asia and Pakistan (Hafez 1997). *Islam and the West in the Mass Media* provides a subtle, and disaggregated, account of the coverage of the Muslim world, relating it to different strategic priorities (e.g. the enormous disproportion in regional coverage), to the distortions contained with the media of Muslim world, and to the broader changes of globalization (Hafez 1999).[2] It includes an informative chapter by Elizabeth Poole, on British press coverage of Muslims.

In a study of Turkey by Hugh and Nicole Pope we get analysis of an actually existing Muslim society (Pope and Pope 1997). Turkey exemplifies many of the general issues in this debate, illustrating as it does the tensions of modernity, not least those between a secular state and an Islamist opposition, and between the Turkish state and the equally Muslim but politically secular Kurdish opposition. Their assessment of the contemporary Turkish scene has drawn strong attack from those who associate them with a trend known as 'the second republic': by this is meant those who wish to lessen the hostility of the state to Kurdish and Islamist opposition, by, for example, permitting the wearing of the headscarf or *turban* in universities, and granting an element of autonomy to the Kurdish regions.

To read a concrete study is a breath of fresh air. Here Islam ceases to be a monist abstraction and becomes something specific and diverse in terms of belief, history, culture, literature, symbol, and political and economic force. Thus, in marked contrast to Iran, the Turkish Islamists try to invoke the monarchical, Ottoman past in their favour. On the other hand, the Alevi Shi'ite minority is staunchly secular – for fear of the Sunni Islamist majority. The Kurdish parties have shunned Islamism – the PKK is as secular as you can be – yet many Kurds vote for the Islamists. As elsewhere, all is not as it appears: in the Turkey of the 1980s, as in Algeria, Pakistan, Egypt and the Israeli-occupied Palestinian lands, the state indulged in promoting Islamism as a means of isolating the left, only to find its client had slipped the leash. Turkey matters not only because it is the symbol of the secular/religious conflict in the Muslim world, but also because it shows how, in a variety of ways, other forms of interest identify and interact with religion. The Popes' analysis, like that in the two volumes edited by Hafez, enables us to get away from the stereotypes of confrontation and piety that too often afflict this subject.

The international dimensions

Similar dangers, and a similar need for clarification, apply to this question when it is transferred to relations between states and societies. Indeed, few subjects have in recent years provoked as much controversy and attention, and so little clear thought, as that of the international relations between the Islamic and Western worlds. On both sides a welter of historical, cultural and even psychological generalization has sought to define an overall, and usually conflictual, relation between the two. Items selected from history, or politicians' speeches, or newspaper headlines, are adduced as proof of an enduring hostility. Solemn and well intentioned statements by more moderate leaders on both sides have sought to redress the balance by a stress on common values and common interests. There is, it seems, no end to the rhetoric of confrontation. A rhetoric that, for all its falsity, runs the risk of becoming a self-fulfilling prophecy.

Two books on this subject are exemplars of, respectively, *how* to discuss and *how not* to discuss this question. The work by Fawaz Gerges, Professor of International Affairs and Middle East Studies at Sarah Lawrence College, New York, is, like his earlier work *Superpowers in the Middle East* scholarly, measured and relevant (Gerges 1999). The central term in his analysis, as in his earlier work, is 'specificity' – the breaking down of what is presented as a single political process, into different ideas, interests, phases and policies. The US, he shows, has not, and has never had, a single policy towards Islamist states and movements, or towards 'Islam'. It has pursued a flexible set of approaches based not on culture or religion at all, but on strategic and economic interests. The work by Alexandre del Valle, the pseudonym of a right-wing French writer, is the opposite. It is a rant that treats the Islamic threat as part of an all-out offensive against European peoples and values, and one moreover that is orchestrated by the USA (del Valle 1997). Both Islam and the USA are joined in a cultural offensive against Europe; Michael Jackson and McWorld on one side, radical Islamic movements on the other, have one goal, the destruction of the European nation-state. This 'Islamoyankee' offensive rests, he argues, on a spiritual affinity between Protestantism and Islam.

Gerges (1999) sets out to answer two interrelated questions. First, he lays out a set of general questions about the role of attitudes to Islam in US foreign-policy making, and seeks to use this to cast light on the formation of foreign policy as a whole. Here he distinguishes between two strands in US foreign policy, a confrontationist and an accommodationist. He suggests that, despite strong historical and popular antipathy to the Muslim world, it is the accommodationist which has prevailed. The key moment he indentifies is the speech by the then Assistant Secretary of State for Near Eastern Affairs, Edward Djerejian, in June 1992. In this speech Djerejian laid out what became for the Bush, and later the Clinton, administrations its policy – one that eschews any general labelling of Islam, or Islamists, and seeks to find a policy, flexible as far as each country is concerned, that is consistent with other, material, interests.

The second part of Gerges' books takes four case studies of US policy towards Islamism itself – one case where Islamists have been in power (Iran) and three cases where Islamists have been in the opposition (Algeria, Egypt, Turkey). While he rightly shows the depth of US hostility to Iran, he also brings out the extent to which the Iran debacle led policy-makers in Washington to seek another policy, one that would avoid such confrontations in the future. This more flexible policy has indeed alarmed some, in Israel and also Europe, who want a harder line. With regard to each country where there has been Islamist opposition, Gerges shows that the US has, while maintaining support for the state, sought to encourage dialogue with more moderate opposition forces, sometimes to the irritation of the local state itself.

This book is persuasive and important – both as an account of policy-formation in regard to important parts of the Muslim world, and as a cogent corrective to the kinds of generalization that have become common in this field. It is not to derogate from its importance to suggest some ways in which, inevitably within the confines of one work, a degree of selection has occurred. It can be argued that Gerges both overstates the problem, by laying too much stress on *historic* American attitudes to Islam, which one may doubt are any more an obstacle or any more bigoted than those towards, say, China, Japan or Latin America, and understates the impact of recent history. While the cases discussed are important, no discussion of this topic can be satisfactory without analysis of the two most explosive of all *recent* issues in US/Islamic relations, Palestine on the one hand, and Afghanistan on the other. In the former a range of attitudes which are hostile to Muslims and deny their legitimate national claims has endured. This is not so much for historical reasons, as because it has been promoted by a one-sided sympathy for Israel, and suitably fuelled by terroristic actions and rhetoric by Palestinians themselves (secular as much as Islamist, it must be said). In Afghanistan, the reverse has occurred. Here, in the 1980s, for reasons of Cold War opportunism, the most retrograde Islamist forces were armed and incited by Washington, in what was the CIA's largest ever covert operation. Indeed, the main chapter of US/Islamist relations has been one of retrograde collusion.

Gerges, in his search for a more intelligent and flexible policy, also runs the risk, as reasonable people do, of understating the problems involved. On the Islamist side, he tends, as do all critics of US foreign policy from within, to understate the depth of animosity from without. There is in the Muslim world widespread and deeply felt hatred of the USA, now fuelled by globalization, the IT revolution and, since his book went to press, the US missile attacks on Sudan and Afghanistan in August 1998. This may make any reasonable accommodation by even the most sensible and well informed US foreign policy-makers very difficult. No one could have got it 'right' with Khomeini, and the same goes for his successors, including Ossama bin Laden. On the other side, while Gerges endorses the 'accommodationist' approach, he also urges the US to do more to insist on universal human rights and democratic standards. But, as Gerges recognizes, the problem with the accommodationist approach is that it tends to avoid discussion of internal politics, and tends towards a relativist view of values. In a context where all robust promotion of human rights, let alone humanitarian military intervention, is seen as a form of imperialism, this poses major difficulties. I hasten to add that I do not have answers to these questions.

The work by Alexandre del Valle posits, of course, the opposite case: America's conflicts with Islam are just a fake, designed to cover up what is a common strategy. The Iran-Libya Sanctions Act, for example, is a fraud, designed to keep European firms out of the Middle East, while US firms, through dummy companies, take the pickings. The assault on Serbia is part of a nefarious alliance between Turkey and the USA to implant Islamic states in Europe. The campaign against Iraq is similarly, an assault on an independent Arab state enjoying, as his book makes clear, much sympathy in France. All of this coincides with the 'third expansion' of Islam – after that of the

Arabs in the seventh century, and the Turks in the sixteenth. The distinction between 'Islam' and 'Islamist' is false – the two are one. Islam is an enemy of European civilization, just as the USA is, a society formed by the riffraff of Europe and a group of Puritan renegades. This apparently demented outlook is more common than might at first sight appear. If nothing else, it shows that conspiracy theory is not the prerogative of extreme American nativist, or Middle Eastern Islamist, groups.

The issues discussed in these two books, contrasting in style as they may be, are not going to disappear. Fuelled by the misuse of history and culture on both sides, and intertwined with very real issues of wealth, oil, security and national independence on the other, they promise to be central to the discussion of international relations for a long time to come. All the more need, therefore, to welcome the kind of measured, informed, analysis provided by Fawaz Gerges and to be on guard against the flow of nonsense proffered by del Valle.

Modernism and variety

So much for a corrective to prevailing accounts of this issue, in its domestic and international dimensions. To identify conflicts between Muslims and non-Muslims and to challenge misunderstandings is not, however, sufficient to explain such tensions or to identify how to resolve them. It is here that some of the conciliatory coverage, exemplified in the Runnymede and Wilton Park reports, may be open to question. Too often political and humanist good intentions seem to have got the better of sociological analysis. In the first place, there is the question of historical context. It is tempting, but misleading, to link contemporary hostility to Muslims to the long history of conflict between 'Islam' and the West. Bobby Said does this – 'the return of the repressed' – without evidence. It is even more mistaken to ascribe contemporary hostility to 'Islam', to the end of the Cold War, although some commentators seem to think they are clever by doing so. This presupposes something, for which there is little evidence; that modern society, 'the West', needs an enemy.[3] One has to apply to this prejudice, and indeed to the study of prejudice in general, the same sociological critique that is applied to other ideologies: the perennialists *will* argue that such ideologies are permanent, be they Islamophobia or anti-Semitism. But a modernist reading is also possible and more plausible.

The past provides a reserve of reference and symbols for the present but it does not explain it. The Ottoman siege of Vienna in 1683 or the crusades do not explain current politics, they are used by them. A modernist interpretation, with regard to this prejudice as with regard to others, also offers more hope, the possibility of change. If, rather from being embedded in the collective psyche or national character of Western society, negative attitudes to Muslims are more contingent, then it is more likely that something can be done. Here the analysis in the Runnymede Report of the media runs the risk of overstating its case. For if in the *national* British press there is still much that is distorting, this is less so in the local and regional press. Coverage of Muslims in, say, Birmingham or Cardiff, has changed over the years, in response to education and political protest. Therefore, for modernist reasons, the situation is not as fixed as might appear.

To this historicization can be added the pertinence of national differences on both sides. On the European side, as the Hafez volumes bring out, there are significant differences of emphasis, prejudice and engagement, depending on the colonial histories, the geographical location and the composition of the immigrant community. The issues of conflict within Western societies vary: Rushdie in the UK, the headscarf in France, Turkish/Kurdish rivalry in Germany, anti-Arab racism in the USA. Equally, the relation of different Muslim societies to the Western world is distinct. Secular nationalism, and communism, have provided as much resistance as has Islamism. Alliance and cooperation have been as prevalent as conflict: the Kaiser sought to lead Muslims in World War I; the Soviet Union backed *jihad* and national liberation from the 1920s to the 1970s; the CIA funded the Afghan *mujahidin* in the 1980s.

To the diversities of history can be added the diversities of identity. All those who are Muslims certainly consider Islam as part of their identity. They respect the five injunctions of Islam, they practice the rituals of life in an Islamic way, they celebrate Muslim festivals and they call their children by Muslim names. Equally importantly, and central to this issue, they experience a degree of common identity with Muslims who are oppressed elsewhere, be this in Palestine, Bosnia or Kashmir. Yet these commonalities of faith, practice and solidarity are not the whole story. Islam may, in some contexts, be the prime form of political and social identity, but it is never the sole form and is often not the primary one. Within Muslim societies, divisions of ethnicity matter much and often more than a shared religious identity, and this is equally so in emigration. There is no lack of difference between genders and classes, between those with power and wealth and those without. No-one can understand the politics of, say, Turkey, Pakistan or Indonesia, on the basis of Islam alone. Despite the rhetoric, Islam explains little of what happens in these societies.

The claim of a shared Muslim identity is, therefore, a distortion if this is meant to imply the primacy of such an identity. It is equally a distortion if it implies a common, or given, interpretation of that tradition. Perhaps the great disservice which invocations of 'Islam', of community and of tradition, indeed of the whole communitarian and identity rhetoric of today, does is to distort the degree to which what is presented as 'Islam', or any other religion, is itself diverse and changing. The claim of fundamentalisms, indeed of all, be they religious or nationalist elites, who claim to be interpreters of the perennial, is that they are representatives of a given: therein lies authority. But such is never the case. This is well explained in the essays in *Der Islam und der Westen*, and is the core of the modernist account of Islamism and Islamic thought. Bobby Said vigorously rejects a monist interpretation of Islam, but he offers no specific, researched, analysis of what Muslim thinkers have said or of their concepts. Indeed, his very rejection of reformers such as al-Afghani and Abduh would seem to imply the aspiration for a similar essentialist, and unchanging, view of Islam.

What this implies for the study of Muslim societies, and for the study of Muslims in Western Europe, is an analysis of 'Islam' that is much less general and less absolute than has often been the case, and as is claimed by representatives, often patriarchal, sectarian and self-appointed, of Muslim societies. On the one hand, what is presented as 'Islam' may well be one, but by no means the only, possible interpretation. Aziz al-Azmeh has shown well, for example, in *Islam and Modernities* how the apparently given symbol of Islamism, *shariah* law, is itself a modern creation and liable to many, contingent, interpretations: there is no one *shariah* which Islamists can invoke. The *taliban* interpretation of the place of women in society, or of the ban on images of the human figure, is but one interpretation, and very much a minority view. Similarly, the view of fundamentalists about the impropriety of Muslim women in the West training to be doctors or engineers is one, but very much a minority, view.

The mistake of those opposed to anti-Muslim prejudice has been to accept, *as the one true Muslim answer*, particular, and often conservative versions of that tradition.[4] Even more so, the identification of Muslims with supporters of terrorism or fundamentalist groups is a distortion. A work like that of the otherwise judicious Gilles Kepel, *Allah in the West* (Kepel 1997), misrepresents the Muslims of the UK, France and the USA as if they are, in large measure, adherents of the Bradford Council of Mosques or of the Black Muslims. In a more extreme vein, Sheikh Omar Bakri Mohammad of *al-Mohajirun* was to claim in January 1999, during the controversy over British subjects being arrested in Yemen, that in every mosque in Britain and the Middle East young men were receiving military training.[5] Allah *is* in the West, but in different forms.

Most challenging from an analytic point of view is the analysis of the intersection of identities. It is easy to visit a Muslim country or study an immigrant community, and present all in terms of religion. But this is to miss the other identities – of work, location, ethnicity – and, not least, the ways in which different Muslims relate to each other. Anyone with the slightest acquaintance with the inner life of the Arabs in Britain, or of the Pakistani and Bengali communities, will know there is as much difference as commonality.[6] The repeated feuds over sites of worship – common to Muslims, Hindus, Sikhs and Jews – testify to the intrusion of other, secular factors and to different interpretations of the tradition. The analytic challenge is to identify how the tradition and religion are shaped, how the modern is presented as the traditional, and how other factors of ethnicity, class and sect play a role.

There may be, therefore, occasions on which 'Islam' is the main or sole identity, not least when people are attacked on that basis, but such occasions are rare. 'Islam' tells us only one part of how these peoples live and see the world: and that 'Islam' may vary greatly. To take the most divisive international issue of the 1990s: if there can be an Islamic solidarity with Saddam Hussein, there can also be one with the countries Iraq has attacked, Iran and Kuwait, just as there is a strong Islamic opposition by Iraqis to Saddam's regime.

Islamophobia or anti-Muslimism

Such historicization and disaggregation is relevant to the issue of what to term prejudice against Muslims[7]. That there is such a thing, as denoted by the term 'Islamophobia', is undoubtedly true. Recent examples in the British press are not hard to find.[8] Elsewhere we can see similar trends: in Denmark the People's Party has made such hostility central to its programme;[9] in 1998 Hollywood produced an alarmist film, *The Siege*, focusing on Islamic terrorism – in marked contrast, be it said, to its indulgent treatment of Irish republicanism. Nor is this specific to the Christian or Jewish worlds. Perhaps the most striking instance of hostility to Muslims today is to be found in India. The BJP ran for re-election in 1997 on three anti-Muslim issues: rebuilding the temple at Ayodhya; removing separate legal codes for Muslims; and ending the special status of Kashmir. Other policies, renaming Bombay after a Hindu goddess and rewriting history books, follow a similar logic.

The positing of a continuous, historic, past of confrontation may not only be historically inaccurate but may ascribe cause to religion, an eternal factor, when other, more contingent and contemporary causes, may be at work. It also misses the point about what it is that is being attacked. 'Islam' as a religion *was* the enemy in the past – in the crusades or the *reconquista*. It is not the enemy now. Islam is not threatening to win large segments of Western European society to its faith, as communism did, nor is the polemic, in press, media or political statement, against Islamic faith. There are no books coming out questioning the claims of Muhammad or the Koran. The attack now is not against *Islam* as a faith but against *Muslims* as people, the latter grouping together all, especially immigrants, who might be covered by the term. Equally, the 'Islamophobic' attack is against states which may be amongst the most secular in the world, as Saddam Hussein's is. If we take the study as one of negative stereotyping, of what in German is called the *Feibild*, the enemy image, then the enemy is not a faith or a culture, but a people. Hence the more accurate term is not 'Islamophobia' but 'anti-Muslimism'.

The use of the term 'Islamophobia' may also convey two other misleading associations. One is that the term reproduces the distortion, already discussed, that there is one Islam – that there is something out there against which the phobia can be directed. This serves not only to obscure diversity, but also to play into the hands of those, within the Muslim communities, who wish to reply to this attack by offering their own, selective, interpretation of the tradition, be this on women, rights of free speech, the right to renounce religion or anything else. 'Islamophobia' indulges conformism and authority within Muslim communities. One cannot avoid the sense, in regard to work such as the Runnymede Report, that the race relations world has yielded, for reasons of political convenience, on this term.

The use of 'Islamophobia' also challenges the possibility of dialogue based on universal principles. It suggests, as the Runnymede and Wilton Park reports do, that the solution lies in greater dialogue, bridge-building and respect for the other community, but this inevitably runs the risk of denying the right, or possibility, of criticisms of the practices of those with whom one is having the dialogue. Not only those who, on universal human rights grounds, object to elements in Islamic tradition and current rhetoric, but also those who challenge conservative readings from within, can more easily be classed as Islamophobes.[10] The advocacy of a dialogue, one that presupposes given, homogeneous, communities places the emphasis on understanding the 'other', rather than on engaging with the ways in which communities, national and religions, violate universal rights. The danger in these reports is that they are defined, if not monopolized, by representatives of religious bodies and community organizations who apply to them the conventions of inter-faith dialogue.[11] The churches have a role, in educating their own people about the faith, but also in the everyday lives and political grievances of other faiths, Muslims included. This cannot and should not be at the expense of a critical examination of how these religions treat their members.

'Islamophobia' may also have confusing practical results. The grievances voiced by Muslims in any society may relate directly to religious matters – of school curriculum, dress, diet, observance of ceremonial days. But much of what is presented as the Islamic critique of the West has little or nothing to do with religion. It is secular, often nationalist, protest and none the less valid for that. Support for Palestine, denunciations of Western hegemony in the oil market, solidarity with Iraq, opposition to Soviet involvement in Afghanistan, denunciations of cultural imperialism and protests at double standards on human rights are all part of the 'Muslim' indictment of the West, but are not necessarily religious in content, or specific to the Muslim world. The Chinese denunciation of Western human rights interference, on the grounds that it violates sovereignty, is the same as the Iranian. It has little to do with belief, and a lot to do with political power in the contemporary world. Similarly, within Western society, issues of immigration, housing, employment, racial prejudice and anti-immigrant violence are not specifically religious. The British term 'Paki' can, in a racist attack by white youth, as easily denote a Hindu, a Sikh or a Christian from Tamil Nadu as it can a Muslim.

Nor should the international implications of all this be overlooked, not least because they so directly affect the level of dialogue within Western societies. Violations of human rights, in the name of religion or secular power, are found in many Muslim societies. The analysis within the West of attitudes to Islam, and of renderings of Islamic tradition, cannot be divorced from what is going on *within Muslim societies themselves*. Here horrendous violations of human rights are being committed, against Muslims, in the name of religion. The fight against fundamentalism is not, as Bobby Said presents it, between the West and the Muslim world, but within the Muslim world itself. The briefest acquaintance with the recent history of Iran, Afghanistan, Pakistan, Egypt or Algeria would bear this out. Those who protest the loudest about such violations are inhabitants of these countries, that is Muslims themselves. Their protests are framed in universal terms, and demand a universal response.[12] This is as true for political prisoners, trade unionists, journalists and women, as it is for representatives of ethnic groups within Muslim countries who are denied recognition and group rights. There are, as in any discussion of human rights, difficult issues here relating to accuracy of information, approach and impartiality. But to deny their right to make these protests, on the grounds that there can only be one Muslim voice, or that their invocation of universal principles violates tradition, is a paradoxical conclusion for those who begin by protesting at non-Muslim discrimination against Muslims. 'Islamophobia', like its predecessor 'imperialism', can too easily be used to silence critics of national states and elites.

A return to universalism

Underlying much of this discussion, and policy debates, is the question of how far we are able to apply universal categories, of analysis and ethics, to different religious and political communities.

Current fashion has it that this is no longer possible, or desirable. Huntington on the right, and Bobby Said on the left would, in their own ways, agree. So too would Islamists, and their anti-Muslim opponents in the West. Yet it may be that all is not quite so relative as it appears. In the first place, much of the political language of protest and difference is itself part of a universal vocabulary. This is as true for the universal invocation of rights, as it is for the universal, and very modern, principles of sovereignty and national independence. Contrary to Bobby Said, I would sustain the modernist argument that much of Khomeini's rhetoric, like that of Islamists elsewhere, is derived from a modern and a Western populist and revolutionary vocabulary. Despite the fact that Islamists reject aspects of the modern world, they are grappling with similar problems and use similar instruments, of which the modern state, and the resources of the modern economy, are central. One of the most striking, and original, assertions of this universalism has come from the President of Iran, Mohammad Khatami: he argues from a shared reason and a shared cultural and intellectual interaction for the possibility of common values. Khatami, elected with a 70 per cent majority in May 1997, took office in August of that year. In the ensuing period he has tried to reorientate Iran's politics, within the country and in relations with the outside world. At home he has set a new tone, calling for respect for the law, the democratization of politics and an active role for women in society. With regard to the West, not least the USA, he has called for dialogue and for a lessening of the hostility built up over decades. He has continued to criticize Israel's denial of Palestinian statehood, but has denounced terrorism and stated that Iran will accept a solution acceptable to the Palestinians themselves. No one can be sure Khatami will prevail. His advent to power, and visit to the UN, do, however, mark something dramatically new in Iranian politics, with implications for the Middle East, Central Asia and the Islamic world as a whole. He is a new man, with a new voice.

Khatami presents himself as a man of learning. He says that the most important room in his house is the library. His ideas can be gleaned from his speeches as candidate and President and from two books.[13] The first, *Fear of the Storm* (*Bim-i Mouj*) is a collection of five essays published in 1993; the second *From the City-World to the World-City* (*As Donya-yi Shahr ta Shahr-i Donya*), published in 1994, is a study of Western political thought, from Plato to contemporary liberalism, an argument for democracy and freedom, and for open dialogue between civilizations. Written in broad philosophical terms, with judicious hints at what the contemporary practical implications might be, these works represent something which, for Iran and Islamic thinking as a whole, is a break with the tenor of much recent fundamentalist work. In place of an outright rejection of the non-Muslim, and the West, there is a call for knowledge of the other and for mutual enrichment. There is criticism of the West, but no recourse to nativist demagogy. In place of claims that all the solutions to the world's problems are to be found in the core texts of Islam, or any other religion, there is an openness to change, and to secular ideas. In many ways Khatami, by going beyond the dogma of fundamentalism, reaches back to an earlier tradition in Islamic thought, one that prevailed from the late nineteenth century through to the first decades of this century, which is more liberal, and modernist, both in its interpretation of the Islamic tradition and in its attitude to the West. Such thinkers as Jamal al-Din al-Afghani, Muhammad Abduh, Ali Abd al-Razzaq, Qasim Amin and Muhammad Iqbal represented this trend. They wanted to remain Muslims, in religion and culture, but to learn from the West.

It has been easy, amidst the clamour of recent years, to present fundamentalism as *the* voice of the Muslim world: it is not, and never was. What the fundamentalism of the past two decades and more has tried to drown out within the Islamic world is not just non-Islamic, Western, imperialist thinking, but also alternative religious and cultural traditions within the Islamic world. This goes for the modernism of the earlier decades but also for the lyrical, often hedonistic and critical, literature of earlier centuries that is central to Iranian culture. Khatami's work is a rejection of this dogma: the very title of his collection of essays, *Fear of the Storm*, is from the medieval Persian hedonistic poet Hafez; and his range of interest, from Plato and Aristotle, to Locke and Rousseau, denies any theological exclusion. Above all his work stands out by its tone. He rebukes those who rely on a rejection of the West and on a ranting search for enemies, counter-revolutionaries and conspiracies.

Four themes stand out in his work above all else. In the first three of the five essays comprising *Fear of the Storm*, Khatami discusses different thinkers in contemporary Islam who have tried to shape their teachings to meet the challenges, social and political, of the modern world: Khomeini, the leader of the Iranian revolution until his death in 1989; Morteza Motahhari, a theologian assassinated by an extremist group just after the revolution; and Mohammad Baqr Sadr, the Iraqi leader who was executed by Saddam in 1980. The fourth essay, entitled 'Hopes and Fears', addresses the question of how Muslims should relate to the West. The fifth, 'Our Revolution and the Future of Islam', provides a broad account of civilizations.

Khatami argues that there are three broad kinds of Islam: reactionary, eclectic, and pure (*irtijai, iltiqati, nab*).[14] The reactionaries argue against the participation of women in politics, and deny that anyone other than the clergy can play a political or social role. They also imposed a narrow-minded cultural policy, going so far as to try to ban music and sport from television. Eclectic Islam refers to those who are not really Muslims at all but have concealed their goals under Islamic garb.

Sources within the Islamic tradition are deployed by Khatami to give substance to this 'true' Islam. One is the work of the mediaeval thinker al-Farabi (870–950 AD). Al-Farabi was born in Central Asia, studied in Syria and Egypt, and taught in Aleppo. He was one of the key links between non-Muslim and Muslim thinking, reaching back to Plato and Aristotle, and having, in his turn, influence on St Thomas Aquinas. His concept of *al-madinah al-fadhila*, 'the virtuous city', sought to integrate the thought of Plato and Aristotle within the framework of Islamic political thinking. In a neo-Platonist trend, already strong within the thinking of his time, he developed a threefold categorization of the intellect: the active, the potential and the acquired. The import of this was clear: human beings, albeit subject to divine will and the authority of holy texts, could develop their ideas, making independent interpretations and judgements on issues of the day.

This classical legacy has, in modern times, been put to particular use by thinkers within Shi'ite Islam, not only in Iran but in other areas of innovative Shi'ite thinking, notably Iraq and Lebanon. Khatami's respect for the Iraqi Baqr Sadr is matched by that for the Lebanese Musaq Sadr, to whom he is also related, and who disappeared, after being abducted apparently by Libyan agents, in 1978. Here the central concept, one far less prominent amongst Sunni thinkers, is that of *ijtihad*, or independent judgement. For Sunnis, the 'door of *ijtihad*' has in large measure been closed; for the Shi'ites of the Usuli school, originating in the early nineteenth century, the opposite is the case. The founder of the Usulis, Shaikh Murtaza Ansari (died 1864), is another of Khatami's inspirations. The Usulis stress independent judgement, and the authority of the *mujtahid* or authority for *ijtihad*. So strongly has this developed over the past two centuries that a new caste system has developed, with, at the top, the rank of *ayatollah* – a creation of the early twentieth century. It was the hierarchy that emerged from Usuli thinking which, at the end of the nineteenth and in the first decade of the twentieth century, provided the core for resistance to foreign, British and Russian, encroachment on Iran, and to resistance to the autocracy of the Shah.

The origins of modern Iranian politics lie in this period, with the Tobacco Boycott of 1891–2 and the Constitutional Revolution of 1905–11. They provide a nationalist historic point to which all later Iranian political leaders, religious and secular, can refer. There is therefore both religious and nationalist meaning in this reference: Khomeini exercised *ijtihad* in arguing that there could, despite the disappearance of the Prophet's successor, be an Islamic government. Khatami seeks to exercise it in advocating his new, more open approach to modern problems and non-Muslim ideas.

There is, however, another current in Khatami's thinking that runs across this modernist interpretation: that of *irfan*, literally 'cognition', but meaning here Shi'ite mysticism. *Irfan* is an informal, non-scholastic approach to Islam that was denounced by many earlier Shi'ite *mujtahids*; but Khomeini was strongly influenced by it, and it informed both his other-worldliness and denunciation of material goods, and his broad, apparently detached and lofty, at times perceptive, at times cruel, attitude to everyday politics. He once said that economics was a subject fit for donkeys. Significantly, Khatami, himself a strong rationalist, has drawn attention to this streak in Khomeini's thinking. Indeed, in *Fear of the Storm* he characterizes Khomeini with three titles: 'a Mujahid jurisprudent, a revolutionary mystic, and a statesman immersed in moral values'. An Iranian audience would not need to be told what this allusion to *irfan* meant. On the one hand, it signifies a particularly Persian mystical tradition, one that even more than Shi'ism itself, sets Iran apart from the rest of the Muslim world; on the other hand, in his carefully chosen words, Khatami can be read as seeking to shield Khomeini from charges relating to his record in practical politics. It is his spirituality, and willingness to interpret the tradition in the light of contemporary concerns, that Khatami wishes to underline.

This attitude to the Islamic past coexists in Khatami with an open attitude to Western thinking. Time and again in his books and speeches he stresses the need for dialogue between civilizations. He gives this historical weight, showing how Islam and Western thought have interacted, but also contemporary salience, by criticising the goal of shutting off a country like Iran from the outside world. With the mass of the population under twenty years of age, and intently interested in what the outside world has to offer, from the more to the less salubrious, this is no abstract position. Opponents of Khatami rave about *tahajum-i farhangi*, 'cultural aggression', and have imposed a formal ban on satellite dishes. What some Iranians term the 'silent sexual revolution' now underway in the country, is, along with fascination with satellite TV and consumer goods, an index of the erosion of these barriers.

Opposition to openness is precisely what Khatami sees as part of 'reactionary Islam'. Khatami's argument is, however, predominantly a positive one. 'True' Islam has nothing to fear from contact with the outside world: 'The cultural strategy of a dynamic, vibrant Islamic society cannot be isolation'.[15]

This more open cultural perspective is linked to a broad theory of civilizations, developed in the fourth essay of *Fear of the Storm*. In an argument that will be as unwelcome to Samuel Huntington as to fundamentalists – Islamic, Christian, Jewish, Hindu or neo-Confucian – he rejects the idea of discrete, separate, cultural entities: 'Unless they are completely unaware of each other's existence, civilizations ordinarily affect and transform one another....The give-and-take among civilizations is the norm of history'.[16] Equally, civilizations are entitled to no permanent domination. For the past four hundred years, Western civilization has dominated the world but, in its heyday, so did Islam. If this forces us to recognize signs of a growing crisis of the West, it even more so precludes any claims about the return of Islamic dominance. Perhaps most surprisingly in the prevailing Middle Eastern intellectual context, where religious invocation is common amongst clergy and intelligentsia alike, Khatami ascribes the fate of civilizations not to any divine element but to two more worldly factors – the dynamism of the human mind, and the emergence of new needs in human society.

The West is in crisis, he argues, and the failure of Marxism was one further chapter in the onset of this crisis. In the final part of *From the City-World to the World-City* he writes in tones strangely redolent of some trends in postmodernism. 'The manifest weakening of its inner strength' is evident in the West's increasing inability to provide answers to new questions and in a growing lack of confidence in the ability of Western civilization to produce a desirable future. Science, and the scientific method, have lost their unquestioned authority. 'Science is no longer a panacea which can provide a point of reference and cannot provide an absolute answer to the restless human soul'.[17] But there is also a crisis in the society of revolutionary Iran. Unless Iran is able to find a way of providing an answer to the problems it faces, reconciling religion with the pressures of the modern world, it will succumb to Western domination.

Khatami develops his view of the West at length in *From the City-World to the World-City*. This is a study of Western political thought, bringing out above all the growth of ideas of freedom and of rights. After chapters on Aristotle, Plato and medieval Christian thought, he comments favourably on the emergence of secular reason in the Renaissance, and John Locke's concept of liberty. He also discusses the development and flexibility of liberalism. Since liberalism has been a term of abuse in revolutionary Iran, associated as it has been with pro-Western intellectuals, if not agents of the CIA, this calm and sympathetic assessment is all the more striking. He complains that scholars in Iran have been deprived of adequate and reliable information on the basis of which they could make an informed judgement.

At times in his writing, Khatami talks of the 'West' as an undifferentiated whole, as if it is one single force from which everything else, from liberal values to capitalism and imperialism, issues. This is one of the stocks-in-trade of so much critical Third World and nativist writing on the 'West'. But in the final chapter of *From the City-World* Khatami recognizes that the values he most admires are not the product of some unitary 'West', but the result of struggle within the West, and have been achieved at high cost. Among the values he mentions are 'freedom', 'limits on the power of rulers', 'constitutional government' and the finding of 'human, measurable and practical solutions' for implementing these values. The key to any overcoming of stereotypes about 'East' and 'West' is precisely such a disaggregation.

Khatami has less to say in his two books and speeches about what all this means for practical, political life. Yet throughout his philosophical and historical work he reiterates the need for any civilization, or philosophic system, to respond to the needs of his time. There is, indeed, enough to indicate what he believes can and should be done, to meet the double crisis he identifies, of Western civilization on the one hand, and the Islamic revolution in Iran on the other. In the spirit of Western liberalism and al-Farabi alike, Khatami insists on three political values above all. One is freedom itself: he is clear, as are many other leading figures in Iran, on the need to allow political parties to form; equally he insists on the need for a free press. Second, he advocates enforcement of the rule of law, and of constitutional government: the first upheaval of twentieth century Iran was the revolution for a constitution in 1905–11, and there is in Iran today a constitution which, if properly applied, can form the basis for the consolidation of democracy. Third, he advocates a concept of 'civil society', meaning by this, in a strict sense, a set of independent social associations acting in public life, and, more broadly, active participation of the people in politics, and the subordination of government to their will.

These general ideas were spelt out in more detail in his inauguration speech on 4 August 1997.[18] The duties of the President include safeguarding the official religion, serving the people, desisting from autocracy, and protecting the freedom and dignity of individuals and the rights of the nation. He quoted the words of Imam Ali, the Prophet Mohammad's son-in-law, fourth Caliph, and first Imam, or leader, of Shi'ite Islam:

> Do not praise me, so that I can fulfil the rights that are left unrealized and perform the obligations that are left undone. Do not address me the way despots are addressed, and do not avoid me as the ill tempered are treated. Do not approach me with an air of artificiality, and do not think that I find the truth offensive. I do not want you to revere me. He who finds listening to complaints difficult will surely find administration of justice even more so. Therefore, do not hesitate in telling the truth or in advising me on matters of justice. I am neither above fallibility nor am I immune from error in my conduct, unless God safeguards me from the self, over which He commands more control than I.[19]

In this inaugural address, Khatami appealed to the judiciary and the executive to establish a society based on the rule of law and on the latter to promote and consolidate the principle of accountability. There was little in his speech about obedience to religion and much about the rights of the people and the need for them to participate. In international affairs, he emphasized the need for 'a proud, prosperous and independent Iran' and for a dialogue among civilizations. Within Khatami's own work there are, however, questions that must remain unresolved until the test of practice is met. Khatami has supported the creation of political parties, but the how and the when, and the limits that will be imposed, remain unclear. He supports greater public activity by women, but has, as yet, been silent on specific discriminations to which women are subjected, in dress and in law. He is open to Western ideas, but has been critical in his work of secular intellectuals and of secularism in general. His attitude to Western political thought is positive, but some might wonder whether this admiration for the philosopher-king Plato is so desirable. He wishes to make a break with the dogma of the revolutionary past, yet continues to appeal, in his own rationalist and independent rendering, to the legacy of Khomeini. Whatever the obstacles and ambiguities, few can doubt the importance of the success or the failure of his liberalizing venture – for Iran, for the Middle East as a whole and for a Muslim world torn between an indecisive modernism and an assertive fundamentalism.

Conclusion

The simplifications of demagogues and cultural essentialists on both sides need, therefore, to be corrected. The modern world is *not* shaped by monolithic cultural blocs. Nowhere is this modern context more important than in regard to the fissure that, perhaps more than any other, separates most Muslims from their Muslim fellow-citizens and Muslim states from the West, namely the inequality of rich and poor in the contemporary world. Islamism is a form of protest – political and discursive – against external domination, just as Islamist movements within these societies are protests against social and political power that excludes them from power. It is important, however, and a point postmodernist friends of resistance too easily forget, to note that the Islamists are far from being the first to contest the inequalities of modernity. Nationalism on the one hand, and socialist, populist and communist movements on the other, have long contested Western hegemony. The twentieth century was one of relentless denial of Western hegemony, long before Khomeini and the FIS appeared on the scene.

The problems are, however, not only whether such a challenge can succeed, but also whether, in posing such a challenge, other violations of rights may not occur. Power relations, and distortions of truth and history, may occur within protest movements as much as in relations between these movements and their oppressors. Hence the false salvation offered by those who, out of well intentioned ecumenism, or partisan engagement, seek to remove the possibilities of critical dialogue with regard to those who invoke religious discourse. The alternative to the clash of civilizations need not be the mutual indulgence of communities. It may, on the contrary, enable a universal argument and struggle.

Notes

1 This chapter is based on materials published in earlier form in *Ethnic and Racial Studies* (vol. 22, no. 5, September 1999), *Journal of Islamic Studies* (vol. 11, no. 2, April 2000) and *New Republic* (5 October 1998).

2 An English translation of this text is to be published by E. J. Brill.

3 The Runnymede Trust Report (1997: 8) lends credence to this.

4 For a cogent critique of how well-meaning British politicians have colluded in such conservative renderings of Islam, see Caroll (1997).

5 Interview on the BBC *Today* programme, 12 January 1999.

6 I have tried to explore this in my study of the first Muslim community in the UK (Halliday 1992).

7 I have argued the case at greater length in Halliday (1996). For an alternative, and itself dissident, approach see Banton (1998).

8 Thus two front pages – the *Daily Mail* (22 February 1996) on the decision of the Minister of Education, Gillian Shephard, to permit separate religious education for Muslims in Birmingham: 'Shephard Gives Way on Segregation. Moslems Win Their Separate Lessons'; and the *Sun* (24 November 1998) on a British woman who abandoned her children on holiday: 'Worst Mum in World. She Dumps Kids in Turkey to Run Off with Arab Lover'.

9 *International Herald Tribune*, 17 November 1997.

10 For an account of the policing of women in British Muslim communities by young males, and of their hostility to those who question their authority, see Alibhai-Brown (1998).

11 Membership of the Runnymede Commission gives striking evidence of this, in those who were included and those whose voices were not heard: Women Against Fundamentalism, dissident Muslims and sympathetic but secular critics of both camps. The report also ties itself into a knot (p. 60) by arguing for an extension of the blasphemy law. Would they ban the Koran which argues, *inter alia*, that Christ was not the son of God, that he was not crucified, and that he did not rise from the dead? All these propositions would be considered blasphemous by Christians.

12 See the regular reports of *Women Living Under Muslim Laws*, and the documents of Amnesty International and Human Rights Watch: Said is silent, and arguably complicit, on such issues.

13 I have based the following on two versions of Khatami's work rendered into English. *Hope and Challenge: The Iranian President Speaks*, published by the Institute of Global Cultural Studies at Binghampton University and edited by Parviz Morewedge and Kent Jackson, is comprised of chapters 4 and 5 of *Fear of the Storm*, a speech on the information world, his inaugural address, and quotes from other speeches. The second set of materials comprise a part translation and summary of *Fear of the Storm* and *From the City-World to the World-City* by Dr Farhang Jahanpur of

the BBC Monitoring Services. There are significant differences in vocabulary between the two sets of translations: where there is a choice I have tended to favour the Jahanpur rendering.

14 *Hope and Challenge*, 51, translates *iltiqati* as 'diluted', but 'eclectic' is more precise.
15 *Hope and Challenge*, 47.
16 *Hope and Challenge*, 2–3.
17 Jahanpur translation, 10.
18 *Hope and Challenge*, 69–86.
19 *Hope and Challenge*, 74–5. The sayings and other speeches attributed to Ali collected in a work entitled *Nahj al-Balagha* or 'The Way of Eloquence' have served as a model for Arabic in a manner comparable to the use of the speeches of Cicero for Latin.

References

Alibhai-Brown, Y. (1998) 'God's own vigilantes', *Independent*, 12 October.

Banton, M. (1998) 'Islamophobia: A Critical Analysis', *Dialogue*, December.

Browning, D. (1998) *Building Bridges Between Islam and the West*, Wilton Park Paper 138.

Carroll, L. (1997) 'Muslim Women and "Islamic Divorce" in England', *Women living under Muslim laws*, Dossier 19, October.

del Valle, A. (1997) *Islamisme et les Etats Unis: Une Alliance Contre l'Europe*, Lausanne: L'Age d'Homme.

Gerges, F. (1999) *America and Political Islam: Clash of Cultures or Clash of Interests?*, Cambridge: Cambridge University Press.

Hafez, K. (ed.) (1997) *Der Islam und der Westen: Anstiftung Zum Dialog*, Frankfurt am Main: Fischer Verlag.

——(1999) *Islam and the West in the Mass Media: Fragmented Images in a Globalizing World*, Cresskill: Hampton Press.

Halliday, F. (1992) *Arabs in Exile: Yemen Migration in Urban Britain*, London: I.B. Tauris.

——(1996) 'Anti-Muslimism in Contemporary Politics', *Islam and the Myth of Confrontation*, London: I. B. Tauris.

Kepel, G. (1997) *Allah in the West: Islamic Movements in America and Europe*, Cambridge: Polity Press.

Morewedge, P. and Jackson, K. (eds) *Hope and Challenge: The Iranian President Speaks*, Binghampton University: Institute of Global Cultural Studies.

Pope, N. and Pope, H. (1997) *Turkey Unveiled: Ataturk and After*, London: John Murray.

Runnymede Trust (1997) *Islamophobia: A Challenge for Us All*, London: Runnymede Trust.

Said, B. S. (1997) *A Fundamental Fear: Eurocentrism and the Emergence of Islamism*, London: Zed Books.

3   Muslim encounters with new media

Towards an inter-civilizational discourse on globality?

Karim H. Karim

This chapter discusses uses of the internet and the world wide web by Muslims, in the contexts of tradition, modernity, and globality. Electronic networks have become symbols of a technological civilization that has extended itself around the planet. The traditional world views of Muslims have often been identified in dominant Western discourses as being against modernity and its expressions of globality. However, the social-intellectual aspects of the 'Islamic piety model', which is quite distinct from the anti-modernist manifestations of militant Islamism, offers an alternative approach to modernity. Its emphasis on a transcendent view of knowledge, a frontierless fellowship, a humanism founded on religious faith, and an economic framework that gives priority to social justice and social ethics, (Pasha and Samatar 1997), offers a particular way of conceptualizing human progress.

The non-materialist ethos of the Islamic piety model, which represents the world view of 20 per cent of the world's population, serves as a foil for the economically and technologically deterministic models of progress that have tended to create vast disparities between the haves and the have-nots at national and global levels. The dominant discourses on modernity and globality are mainly anchored in Western history, and have been largely shaped according to the priorities of market-centred neo-liberalism. In many parts of the world (including the industrialized West), the centrifugal tendencies of globalization appear to be inspiring a centripetal resurgence of national and communal identities (Karim 1997: 77–9). An inter-civilizational discourse on these issues would allow for alternative constructions of human progress, which could enable an authentic globalization that is inspired by the experience and ideas of all humanity, as well as responding to its diverse needs and values.[1] Such a discourse may be increasingly possible as people of various backgrounds engage in horizontal, inter-continental communication with each other via online networks which are relatively less hierarchical and centrally organized than the mass media (Karim *et al.* 1998). This form of communication, while limited to those who have access to online services, also has advantages over the mainly one-to-one telecommunications services such as the telephone or the fax. In addition, whereas inter-civilizational discourse is already carried out among societal elites such as diplomats, academics, journalists, artists and others whose professional or financial status permits such interactions, online networks enable more continual contact for a broader cross-section of society.

The current socio-political turmoil experienced by several Muslim societies is partly a reaction to forms of Westernization that may be considered inimical to indigenous values. Some of the expressions of such turmoil, including religious dogmatism, philosophical conservatism, and the repression of minorities, would seem to go against the grain of the traditional Islamic piety model. The focus on the restrictive and punitive aspects of Muslim law, as opposed to its overall purpose of providing a societal context for spiritual and material growth, appears to manifest the use of religion for personal and group politics. Conversely, the elites in some Muslim-majority states have aligned themselves with dominant models of modernization and globalization, adopting a neo-liberal view of progress and aspiring to become members of the transnational elite. Therefore, while proposing that the Islamic piety model could form part of an inter-civilizational discourse on globalization, I remain aware of the internal tendencies in Muslim societies that serve as barriers to its promotion.

Given the increasingly significant place of diasporas in the context of globalization (Appadurai 1996), this discussion will consider the role of diasporic Muslims in inter-civilizational discourse. While the place of indigenous Muslim minorities living in various countries and that of minorities in states with Muslim majorities is also important, the focus of the present study are migrant Muslim diasporas. The latter appear to have significant access to online technologies, and are using them to communicate within Muslim communities and with others.

Tradition and modernity

Tradition has often been viewed as being the polar opposite of modernity. According to Daniel Lerner's *The Passing of Traditional Society: Modernizing the Middle East* (1958), an influential work of its time, adherence to tradition was an obstacle in attaining modernity.

Modernization, as used here, is synonymous with Westernization. Lerner insisted that in the Middle East, tradition, in the form of Muslim cultures and religion, had to be surpassed as modernization involved 'the infusion of "a rationalist and positivist spirit" against which, scholars seem agreed, "Islam is absolutely defenceless"' (Lerner 1958: 45).[2] Lerner's book not only influenced subsequent work on development communication, for instance Wilbur Schramm's *Mass Media and National Development* (1964), but it also served as a pillar for thinking about development in general through the 1960s and the early 1970s. Smith (1970: 14) speculated that secularism in its 'humanistic-pragmatic' form would sweep through Muslim-majority countries. Lerner's views were also embraced by certain Arab social scientists such as Hisham Sharabi, who wrote that 'in the contemporary Arab world Islam has simply been bypassed' (Sharabi 1966: 26).

This kind of thinking has had to be reassessed in the light of the *ulama*-led Iranian revolution in 1979, and the rise of militancy among Islamist groups in various other countries. Use of 'small media', such as audio cassettes and traditional communications networks, enabled the efficient dissemination of messages to large numbers of people, who had lost faith in the state-controlled mass media (Sreberny-Mohammadi and Mohammadi 1994; Mowlana 1979). Such innovative uses of communications systems appears to be a clear example of the spirit of experimentation characteristic of Lerner's modernized individual; but here she/he was linking traditional communications networks with contemporary technology to attain her/his aims. The methodology of Lerner's study of the mass media in Turkey, Lebanon, Egypt, Syria, Jordan and Iran appears to have been tainted by an ideological framework shaped by the Cold War and by cultural imperialism.[3] These biases rendered the proponents of his approach blind to the continuing significance of indigenous cultures, even as Muslims and other peoples in developing countries gradually adopted the accoutrements of a technological society.

The social theorist John B. Thompson (1995) has revisited Lerner's work in his discussion of the relationship between media and modernity. While Thompson does not subscribe to the view of a linear progression from tradition to modernity, he finds value in Lerner's notion of 'the mobile personality' of the modernized individual who, in contrast to the traditional person, is 'distinguished by a high capacity for identification with new aspects of his environment' (Lerner 1958: 49). This was due to their faculty of empathy with the larger society, which was the result of going beyond the face-to-face world of daily interaction to the larger world presented by the mass media. Lerner suggested that this capacity made the modern person an active participant in society (as a cash customer, radio listener, voter) and the mass media, described as 'the mobility multiplier', facilitated such participation (Lerner 1958: 52). Experience and knowledge that previously could be gained mainly through travel were seen as expanded by mediated perception. Lerner implied that the media transmit messages in value-free and benign manners around the globe, resulting in the formation of a unitary and progressive 'world public opinion' (Lerner 1958: 54). This made the traditional person, whom the author constructed as shunning rationality and innovation, more open to experimentation as they entered modernity. Such changes in attitude would lead to the breakdown of locally based, traditional structures of power and authority, since the new points of reference were not local, face-to-face ones but national and global. However, Thompson (1995) suggests that tradition does not disappear in the process of modernization, but that it is 're-moored' in new contexts.

Human beings have an innate need to make sense of the world around them and of their place in it. This is done by giving value and meaning to objects and relationships. Thompson asserts that the discourses of technological society merely provide their own sets of meanings that exist alongside the long-standing cultural and religious value systems (Thompson 1995: 192). In the West, and many of its former colonies, contemporary legal and constitutional systems are partially based on ideas derived from the Bible. The Christian calendar and festivals guide the rhythms of what are otherwise secular societies. The media, which Lerner said would unravel tradition, have actually been significant participants in the weaving of threads of Western religious traditions into the fabric of contemporary life. Not only are Christian ceremonies, festivities, dramaturgy, music and discourse a substantial part of media content, but basic 'Judaeo-Christian' notions of right and wrong, good and evil, and self and other are echoed in entertainment as well as in news production (Silk 1995).

Thompson holds that, just as the media are infused with elements from tradition, tradition is also changed by the media. He suggests that society has become deritualized, depersonalized and delocalized, primarily through a decreasing dependence on face-to-face communication (Thompson 1995: 195–7). As the cultivation of traditional values and beliefs becomes increasingly reliant on the symbolic cultural and religious content borne by media products (books, films, etc.), the need for the enactment of ritual in congregational, face-to-face settings diminishes. Also, because the transmission of tradition becomes dependent on mediated forms of communication, it becomes detached from the people with whom one interacts on a day-to-day basis. Despite the broadcasting of religious content, mediated froms of communication can, at best, only provide for a 'non-reciprocal intimacy at a distance' (Thompson 1995: 197). The rootedness of traditions in particular spatial locales also weakens as the mass media obviate the need to maintain bonds through face-to-face interactions. Thompson does indicate, however, that these processes are not uniform and unambiguous, and that there are varying degrees of the deritualization, depersonalization, and delocalization of tradition that result from mass media use. He also maintains that the de-localization of traditions allows them to be re-moored in other contexts and re-embedded in social life in new ways, which 'does not necessarily render them inauthentic, nor does it necessarily spell their demise' (Thompson 1995: 202). These ideas are evaluated below in the context of Muslim uses of online media, together with a consideration of the re-mooring, not only of tradition, but also of modernity, and, by extension, of globality.

Re-mooring modernity

In *Jihad vs. McWorld*, Benjamin Barber refers to an 'exceptionalist thesis' which marks out Islam and its followers as standing outside (and even against[4]) global trends of social, political and technological modernization:

> Islam creates an exceptional set of circumstances that disqualify Islamic countries from becoming democratic and fates them to an eternal struggle against the Enlightenment and its liberal and democratic children.
>
> (Barber 1995: 208–9)

Similarly, Naipaul (1991) identifies Muslim societies as unfit for what he calls the 'universal civilization', and Huntington (1996) pits them against the West in his prognosticated 'clash of civilizations'. The vital contributions of Muslim scholars to the growth of knowledge in the medieval era, and the attempts by a series of modernizers since the nineteenth century to engage Western philosophy from Quranic perspectives (Fakhry 1983), generally go unacknowledged by Western commentators.

Theorists who share the views of Barber, Naipaul and Huntington seem to remain unaware of the contemporary discussions among Muslims on Islam, modernity and postmodernity. Azmeh (1993) states that the revivalist Islamist movement manifests a break with crucial aspects of the Muslim tradition, and should be seen as a characteristically modernist phenomenon that draws on themes commonly encountered in the discourse of romantic populism and subaltern nationalism. However, Ahmed (1992) says that if modernism meant the pursuit of Western education, technology and industrialization immediately following de-colonization, then the current return to traditional Muslim values and a rejection of modernism by some Muslims is a feature of postmodernity. Rather than being limited to the varying contingencies of modernity and postmodernity in their material contexts, Azim Nanji has sought to move the debate to what is termed 'intellectual modernity':

> Intellectual modernity...ought not to be seen as a totalizing discourse, but as a perspective, as a set of tools of comprehension which unlock creativity and release the potential for a constructive dialogue with the community in its contemporary environment.
>
> (Nanji 1991: 222)

Such an approach would not be dependent on others' conceptions of modernity, but would help determine paths of development appropriate to the needs and values of Muslims themselves.

The Muslim concept of *ummah*, the worldwide Muslim community, is providing a basis for contemporary Muslim discussion on globality. Mowlana (1996) contrasts an 'Islamic community paradigm' with the 'information society paradigm' proposed by Western governments in order to promise a Utopian future that would be brought about by the use of new technologies. As opposed to the instrumental rationality and market-based logic of the latter, the 'Islamic community paradigm' would be guided by principles of social justice and of an ethical system informed by Islam. Mohammadi (1998) suggests the formulation of an 'Islamic cultural strategy' to protect Muslim identities from the homogenizing effects of globalization. This would be achieved through a redefinition of knowledge according to Islamic epistemology, which, in contrast to Western intellectual traditions, draws on revelation as well as on the tangible universe.

Pasha and Samatar (1997) approach Islam's relationship with modernity and globality by proposing a two-pronged framework which echoes the thinking of a number of other Muslim scholars:

> First, we situate 'globality', as a feature of modernity, in a more interactive framework – as the product of a long historical

exchange between different cultures, including elements that draw their inspiration from the Islamic civilization. Second, we treat Islamic piety as an integral part of an alternative vision of modernity.

(Pasha and Samatar 1997: 187–8)

Globalization has been described as 'the *intensification* of worldwide social relations which link distant localities' (Giddens 1990: 64, emphasis added). Thompson (1995: 150) traces the origins of globalization to the expansion of trade in the late (European) Middle Ages, although the intercontinental land and sea networks established by Muslims to link themselves with their neighbours in Asia, Africa and Europe had even earlier origins. Pasha and Samatar (1997: 192) draw attention to the long-standing inter-civilizational dialogue between Christendom and Muslims by challenging what the historian Marshall Hodgson has criticized as the 'presentist' readings of modernity. Their approach attempts to surpass the global/local dualism through an understanding of civilizational relations in a more horizontal framework that avoids the reinforcement of the North/South hierarchies. Rather than being relegated to the margins of the world, as a local, anti-modernist particularism which will be swept away by the 'universal civilization', Islam emerges in this perspective as a challenge to the Western elites' political and corporate hegemony. It becomes a participant, representing one fifth of humanity, in an inter-civilizational discourse on globalization.

Pasha and Samatar see Islamic piety as an alternative construction of modernity that is cognizant of non-materialist dimensions of progress and their place in an ethical social formation. They criticize the reactive tendencies among some Muslims for being fixated on opposition to modernity and for disregarding the traditional roles of Islamic piety in renewal and affirmation, as well as in conducting inter-civilizational dialogue (Pasha and Samatar 1997: 195). These authors view the social expression of Islamic piety to be in the form of a covenant that guides ethical conduct in the social, economic, and political aspects of life. Therefore, 'citizenship' for the members of the *ummah* is founded, not on juridical or contractual bases, but on a 'more durable and sacrosanct sources' (1997: 196). Islamic piety 'registers a mobilizing tendency to move large populations to seek a better world, to put materialism in its proper place, and/or to negotiate a new relationship with modernity' (197). In this way, tradition interacts with modernity in a dialectical fashion rather than being its irreconcilable nemesis.

Pasha and Samatar suggest that Islamic piety offers a way to deal with the aspects of modernity and globality that lead to hedonism, narcissism and consumerism.

The role of Islamic piety in providing an alternative vision of the future cannot be dismissed on the mere basis that its use in funda-mentalist discourse resurrects anti-modernist sentiments. In stressing the pitfalls of materialism, piety compels a language of propriety and pushes towards a humanization of the world. It quali-fies the arrogance of reason with a gentle reminder that ultimately the content of any civilization rests on its capacity to organize social life on the foundations of justice and equality – above all, on humility. Islam does not propose an anti-rationalism, but empha-sizes tempering rationalism to serve human need and dignity

(Pasha and Samatar 1997: 200).

Islamic piety offers, therefore, a social-intellectual way of dealing with the effects of globalization that create blocs of haves and have-nots and privilege only Western, secular perspectives of rationalism. The challenge for Muslims, according to Pasha and Samatar, is to avoid slipping into the monastic or the zealous interpretations of their religion as they engage with globality. And the reciprocal task for the West 'is to recover memory and history, acknowledge the diversity of the Islamic *ummah*, and strive toward a solidarity based on mutual recognition and respect' (Pasha and Samatar 1997: 200).

Islamic piety becomes a practical mode for 'globalization-from-below' to deal with 'globalization-from-above', which Richard Falk identifies as reflecting 'the collaboration between leading states and the main agents of capital formation (quoted in Pasha and Samatar 1997: 190). The latter type of globalization is characterized by a relentless push for accumulation driven by a consumerist ethos, whose protago-nists are transnational capital and political elites, together striving for the functional integration of national structures and cultural tastes into a mode of planetary uniformity. Conversely, globalization-from-below highlights the dysfunctional and degenerative consequences of global-ization-from-above, 'by pointing to a corrosion of autonomy, individual and group efficacy, a weakening of the local bases of mate-rial sustenance, and the diminution of ecological values and the breakdown of cultural foundations' (quoted in Pasha and Samatar 1997: 190). In this view, transnational networks of non-state actors work to highlight the threats to the environment, to democratic free-doms, and to human rights.

A key aspect of globalization-from-below is constituted in the activities of diasporic groups. Diasporic connections are becoming increasingly significant in the light of what is viewed as the diminishing importance of national borders and the growing global links between non-state actors. Whereas Appadurai (1996: 18) is somewhat premature in declaring the imminent 'end of the era of the nation-state', what he calls the 'transnations' of diasporic communities do appear to be significant aspects of globalization processes. In some ways, the notion of *ummah* located around the planet but united in certain basic beliefs, prefigures the globalized nature of diasporas. Muslim diasporic transnations (linked by sect, ethnicity, national origin, and/or political alliances) straddle several continents, maintaining contact with each other through various media including mail, telephone, fax, and digital broadcasting satellites (Mohammadi 1998), and the internet. Muslim diasporic transnations use these technologies, which are part of the top-down globalization's infrastructure, to develop alternative communication flows running along networks that support a globalization-from-below. In some cases, such networks counter the restrictions placed by governments in countries with Muslim majorities, for example the Kurdish MED-TV and the Muslim television company Ahmadiyya International (Karim 1998).

According to postcolonial theorists Homi Bhabha and Abdul JanMohammed, the immigrant diasporic community in the West becomes the site of the cultural border between the country of origin and the country of residence. Bhabha (1994) writes about the integral place of newcomers ('postcolonials') in the Western state, the hybridity of cultures engendered by migration, and the 'third space' that opens up beyond the binary oppositions of national and ethnic identities. The discourses of minorities challenge majoritarian claims of cultural dominance, the notions of a homogeneous people in a nation-state, and the supremacy of any one group's history over another. Bhabha links the Western state with the immigrant through the shared past of colonialism. He suggests that '[t]he Western metropole must confront its postcolonial history, told by its influx of postwar migrants and refugees, as an indigenous or native narrative *internal to its national identity*' (Bhabha 1994: 6). In an era of intensified globalization, the Western state is faced not only with the consequences of history, but also with the contemporary value that the transnational nature of its diasporic minorities has to offer (Bhabha 1994: 213). The evolving national identity of the individual Western state in the globalized environment becomes vitally linked, therefore, with that of its newest citizens, whom it is forced to deal with by virtue of their very presence in its midst:

colonial and postcolonial texts do not merely tell the modern history of 'unequal development' or evoke memories of under-development. I have tried to suggest that they provide modernity with a modular moment of *enunciation*: the locus and locution of cultures caught in the transitional and disjunctive temporalities of modernity.

(Bhabha 1994:251)

We see here a re-mooring of modernity to a wharf on which is found not only the past and current contingencies of the West but also those of other peoples, upon whose histories, social structures, economic development, and modernities the West has impinged. Such a perspective enables us to view the use of communications technologies by Muslims as expressions of modernity which are not necessarily inconsistent with their tradition. These expressions may even, in some cases, be at the cutting edge of global culture.

The internet in countries with Muslim majorities

Even in a country like Canada, which has the cheapest monthly internet subscription rates in the world (Karim *et al.* 1998: 12), a large part of the population is without ready access to the internet. Canadian statistics show that the probability of a person's online access decreases if they live in a household with a low income, are over fifty-five years old, do not have a post-secondary education, are not familiar with English, live outside a major urban centre, are not enrolled in an educational institution, or are not employed (Karim *et al.* 1998: 14–17). The measurement of internet access is still in its early stages, and widely differing figures are sometimes provided by various sources, even in countries with fairly sophisticated means of statistical surveying. Assessments about data are made more complicated by the endemic hype-driven reporting about the worldwide growth of information and communications technologies (ICT), which often leads to the inflation of figures. Internet access in countries with Muslim majorities appears to be growing at varying rates. Some governments have substantial restrictions against the use of ICT, and accurate information for most states is difficult to obtain due to the fast-changing access to online services. The available data (see Table 3.1 below) only list *access*[5] to the internet through subscriptions with internet service providers (ISPs). Actual numbers of users may be four times higher than the subscription figures indicate (DITnet: *www.ditnet.co.ae*).

Table 3.1   Internet subscriptions in Muslim-majority countries*

Country	Number	Source	Date
Afghanistan	N/K		
Albania	N/K		
Algeria	500	SANGONeT	Jan. 1998
Azerbaijan	N/K		
Bahrain & Saudi Arabia	46,538	DIT Group	Jan. 1998
Bangladesh	7,000	Nando Techserver	Sept. 1997
Bosnia-Herzegovina	N/K		
Brunei	N/K		
Djibouti	400	SANGONeT	Jan. 1998
Egypt	61,021	DIT Group	Jan. 1998
Egypt	20,000	SANGONeT	Jan. 1998
Eritrea	300	SANGONeT	Jan. 1998
Gambia	150	SANGONeT	Jan. 1998
Guinea	300	SANGONeT	Jan. 1998
Indonesia	80,000	Indonesia IT	May 1998
Iran	N/K		
Iraq	N/K		
Jordan	20,213	DIT Group	Jan. 1998
Kazakhstan	N/K		
Kyrgyzstan	N/K		
Kuwait	42,350	DIT Group	Jan. 1998
Lebanon	43,828	DIT Group	Jan. 1998
Libya	N/K		
Malaysia	600,000	Jaring Network	Jan. 1998
Mali	400	SANGONeT	Jan. 1998
Mauritania	100	SANGONeT	Jan. 1998
Morocco	6,000	SANGONeT	Jan. 1998
Niger	200	SANGONeT	Jan. 1998
Nigeria	1,000	SANGONeT	Jan. 1998
Oman	20,888	DIT Group	Jan. 1998
Pakistan	N/K		
Palestine	N/K		
Qatar	17,295	DIT Group	Jan. 1998
Senegal	2,500	SANGONeT	Jan. 1998
Somalia	N/K		
Sudan	300	SANGONeT	Jan. 1998
Syria	N/K		
Tajikistan	N/K		
Tunisia	3,500	SANGONeT	Jan. 1998
Turkmenistan	N/K		
Turkey	600,000	NUA Est	May 1997
United Arab Emirates	88,552	DIT Group	Jan. 1998
Uzbekistan	N/K		
Yemen	2,426	DIT Group	Dec. 1997

Source: Compiled from data listed by Nua Internet Surveys (*www.nua.ie*)

Note: *A Muslim-majority country is defined here as one with a Muslim population of 50 per cent or more.

The Malaysian government's aggressive policy to develop ICT appears to have resulted in high rates of internet access.[6] The Jaring Network's January 1998 study yielded the rounded-out figure of 600,000, which constituted around 3 per cent of the Malaysia's population. This seemed to show unusually steep growth rates when compared to an October 1998 survey by International Data Corporation, which had cited 137,436, i.e. 0.7 per cent of the population (Nua Internet Surveys: *www.nua.ie*).[7] Indonesia, which has a much larger population, was estimated to have 80,000 connections in May 1998. The economic downturn in South-East Asia has led to a drastic decrease in national information technology budgets, and forecasts for growth in ownership of personal computers have been reduced (Bickers 1998).

Some Arab countries are experiencing a boom in growth rates for internet subscriptions. The rate of 17,295 for Qatar, shows that access was available to 3.1 per cent of Qataris in January 1998, up from 1.51 per cent in July 1997. A similar rise was noted in the United Arab Emirates, up to 2.99 per cent from 1.47 per cent. Kuwait also saw a growth from 1.51 per cent to 2.15 per cent. The figures for Bahrain and Saudi Arabia, which are lumped together by the DIT Group, were less spectacular (0.19 per cent to 0.23 per cent).

Saudi Arabians have access to the world wide web primarily through university email accounts and through ARAMCO. The government has already given its go-ahead for the introduction of the internet in the kingdom. At the moment (November 1998), only intense negotiations among Saudi Arabian IT and telecommunications companies are holding up its availability. All analysts expect the number to hit the roof when Saudi Arabia finally comes online (DITnet: *www.ditnet.co.ae*).

There are wide variations in the data for Egypt. Whereas SANGONeT reported only 20,000 in January 1998, DIT Group found 61,021 connections (up from 35,520 in its July 1997 survey), which, in this the largest Arab country, accounts for only 0.09 per cent of the population. However, some of the technical aspects for growth potential appear to be present. Egypt has a relatively high number of ISPs (26) compared to other Arab countries, and according to the Intel Corporation, it 'has the second "fastest growing" market for personal computers in the world' (ArabiaTech 1998a).

Although 'after Israel, Iran was the second country in the Middle East to link up to the internet in 1992' (Arabshahi 1996), the conditions for domestic use were still undergoing a major government review in mid-1998 (ArabiaTech 1998b). Information about the number of subscribers is hard to come by; one 1996 estimate indicated that 'at least 60,000 people have in one way or another used internet services' (Arabshahi 1996). Nevertheless, 'access is limited to government organisations and those with special permission, such as journalists from the state-run media' (ArabiaTech 1998b). Universities also have connections. For those who have access, use is slowed down by the low-capacity telephone lines on which the networks run. Officials conduct random checks 'to ensure users do not use bad language or transmit unfavourable political messages' and a government review on the internet was also studying ways of 'preventing its possible detrimental effects' (ArabiaTech 1998b). Although the review was to include an examination of the usefulness of the internet to Iran, recent history has shown that the conservative members of the Iranian leadership have not been receptive to new technologies that enable cross-border communications.[8]

In absolute numbers, Turkey seems to have the same number of internet subscribers (600,000) as Malaysia, but this makes up only 1 per cent of its population. While there is significant activity in Turkish online chat groups, possibilities for discussion of public affairs are limited. In June 1998, a Turkish teenager was given a ten-month suspended jail sentence for posting comments which were deemed anti-police on a daily chat forum hosted by Turknet, a local ISP (Reuters 1998). Three Malaysian netters fared worse in August 1998 when they were arrested and jailed indefinitely, under the Internal Security Act, for spreading false information about race riots in Kuala Lumpur (Hiebert 1998). Since the Malaysian government is seeking massive foreign investment in its Multimedia Supercorridor project it has, on the one hand, promised a 'hands-off' approach to electronic content with the exceptions of illegal or offensive materials while, on the other hand, it has restricted the direct reception of satellite broadcasts (Smeltzer 1997: 44–6). Before the Saudi Arabian government granted its first ISP licenses, it attempted to ensure that 'sufficient measures have been taken to prevent the transmittal of pornographic or politically sensitive material over the Net' (Nua Internet Surveys: *www.nua.ie*). World wide web services in Arab countries appear to be heavily business-oriented, with strong encouragement from the transnational information technology industry to move towards electronic commerce. Web sites seem to predominate in the areas of computing and electronics, banking, consulting and tourism. A growing number of online versions of newspapers are also available.

As a group, countries in sub-Saharan Africa have the least access to the internet. They are handicapped by major infrastructural problems such as poorly developed telephone systems and the lack of computing hardware (Thapisa 1996: 76). With the exception of Senegal and Nigeria, Muslim-majority countries in this region do not have more than 400 internet subscribers each, according to current data. Given that Nigeria's population in 1991 was 88.5 million, the 1,000 internet access points are far from sufficient for the country's needs. Senegal, with a much smaller population (8 million in 1991), has been making efforts to enhance its computer-based technologies. In 1988 it became the first African country to have access to CD-ROM equipment (Richer 1996: 296), and had 2,500 internet subscribers in January 1998. Senegal appears to have played a role in the development of the information technology policies of the Francophonie, the international organization of Francophone countries (Richer 1996: 296), and also at the inter-African level of technological development. The 'Dakar Declaration on the Internet and the African Media', signed by media organizations, non-governmental organizations and educational institutions from west, central and southern Africa, as well as from Europe and the US, stresses the fostering of information pluralism, human rights, civil society and international cooperation (Dakar Declaration 1997).

It appears ironic that those in Muslim society with the fewest means for electronic communication seem to be the most concerned about the democratic uses of the internet. Governments around the world have attempted to bring a measure of regulation and control over online technologies. Whereas the concerns about content in developed states have been mainly about pornography and incitements to hatred, the focus in several developing countries has also included discussions that challenge the national *status quo*. The primary use of the internet in most Muslim-majority countries appears to be by government organizations and by business. Although there is some use by research and academic institutions, open debate on political issues is generally discouraged. There is not sufficient access to the internet in countries with Muslim majorities to suggest that its use has supplanted face-to-face interaction. Therefore, it seems too early to test Thompson's (1995) contention that the use of media technologies in these contexts is aiding deritualization, depersonalization and delocalization.

In Malaysia, the Muslim-majority country with the greatest per capita access to the internet, information policy theorist Tengku Mohammed Azzman Shariffadeen has suggested that this is a technology that 'has come closest to the human mind and the human spirit' (Shariffadeen 1992: 1). Shariffadeen has attempted to discuss Malaysia's ICT policies within an Islamic framework:

development in the Islamic sense, even in the context of science and technology, refers to the attainment of spiritual progress and perfection, of which the natural world is the environment provided for man to prove himself. Ultimately, scientific enquiry, the application of technology and man's attempt to improve himself in development, are acts of worship in understanding his mission towards his Creator and the...[manner] in which it should be fulfilled. Knowledge is the key element in development, but this knowledge must be transcendent linking human understanding to its Ultimate Source and thus attain the power to guide man to correct understanding and subsequently, legitimate action.

(Shariffadeen 1992:9)

Such an approach to the use of the new communications technologies could provide for an integrative practice of national development that would 're-moor modernity' to other than merely material concerns. However, those Malaysians who support this perspective appear to have a difficult challenge within a global policy and corporate environment, one which does not seem to appreciate the non-material aspects of technological endeavour. This task is especially arduous given that the Malaysian government and businesses are eager to attract investors and high-technology firms from the West. The latter's primary interests appear to be the exploitation of the potential of Malaysia's proximity to enormous Asian markets for their products rather than the application of metaphysical concepts related to knowledge and development to their work. Nevertheless, Shariffadeen's words provide a rare rationalization of ICT policy from an Islamic piety perspective, contributing to the articulation of a counter-discourse to globalization-from-above.

Diasporic Muslim networks on the internet

The most innovative and far-reaching uses of the internet among Muslims appear to be carried out by diasporic communities, which have mostly resulted from inter-continental migrations over several generations. Several of these global communities[9] are communicating with each other using online services such as e-mail, Usenet, Listserv, and the world wide web. These technologies are especially appropriate for the far-flung 'transnations', since they are cheaper to operate compared to the mass media, and they generally operate in horizontal networks rather than in a linear, hierarchical way. Due to the greater access to internet resources in the West than in developing countries, those members of diasporas who are resident in North America, Europe and Australia have more opportunities to utilize this global medium for their purposes.[10] While the mere use of contemporary technology is not an indication of modernity, the varied applications of electronic networks by Muslim diasporas provide examples that contradict Lerner's (1958) model which presented tradition and modernity as being polarized. Thompson's (1995) notion of the re-mooring of tradition with the use of contemporary media may offer a revision of Lerner's views, but Thompson provides a limited range of empirical evidence to support his ideas. Examples from diasporic Muslim uses of new communications technologies present an opportunity to test Thompson's hypothesis about the deritualization, depersonalization and delocalization of traditional structures effected by media use.

One of the key problems with Thompson's construction of deritualization (1995: 195–6) is that it appears to reduce the role of ritual in physical gatherings to merely maintaining traditional practices. This disregards the ontologically based meanings of the religious ceremonies for those who perform them. In fact, the primary aspect of rites for believers is their spiritual efficacy. Thompson's functionalist view of ritual proposes that its regular repetition in face-to-face settings 'is the only way of securing temporal continuity' (1995: 195) and that, with the fixation of symbolic content of ritual in media materials, the maintenance of tradition over time can be separated from the continual re-enactment of rites. Thompson attributes the decline of church attendance to the availability of religious materials in books and films.

Scans of websites containing Muslim religious materials indicate a growing corpus of information relating to scripture, ritual, doctrine, theology, history, literature and current events. These are in textual, graphic, pictorial, audio, and video formats. Among the sites from which audio recitations of the Quran, the Islamic holy book, can be accessed include: 'Radio Al-Islam' (*islam.org/radio*) based in California; 'The Quran' (*www.the-quran.com*) operated from Vancouver; and a British-based site (*www.unn.ac.uk*). The ability to *hear* the text of the primary Islamic scripture is of special significance to Muslims, since in Islamic belief it was initially recited by the Prophet Muhammad as he received it through divine revelation. Events in the Muslim calendar are tracked in various sites, providing timely information to the faithful on congregational gatherings and ritual practices (e.g. times for prayer and fasting). In addition to information about the holy month of Ramadan, offered in several web documents, certain sites also have materials on practices of specific groups like Sufi orders,

Ismailis, Ithna Aasharis and Ahmadis. The 'Naqshbandi Sufi Way' (*www.naqshbandi.org*) site, based in California, carries a video file of a 'live Naqshbandi dhikr' (*dhikr* is a form of Islamic worship). The 'Moharram' site (*www.vcan.com/moharram*), operated from Mumbai, India, offers audio versions of the congregational *Majlis* held during the Muslim month of Muharram, by Shia Ithna Aashari adherents in Mumbai's Moughal Masjid. Beliefs and rituals are also discussed in electronic discussion groups, participation in some of which is open only to members of particular Muslim groups through designated passwords.[11]

Whereas broadcasts of Quranic recitations and other Islamic rituals have been carried out for decades on radio and television, the world wide web allows the playing of recordings at the convenience of the user, who could be anywhere in the world where she/he has access to the web. Therefore, this technology, which has become an icon of global modernity, is being used by Muslims (among followers of various faiths) to practice their religious traditions. While Thompson (1995) suggests that the fixation of symbolic content of ritual in material media content can diminish the need to maintain tradition, it is difficult to establish if this is the case in Muslim contexts. On the contrary, the availability of web-based religious resources seems to offer the diasporic faithful, especially those who may be isolated from their communities and live in places where the mass media do not provide information on their ritual practices, the means to remain in touch with their religious traditions. The religious calendars and listings of upcoming events on websites and their mention in electronic discussion groups, may also provide the information as well as the incentive to participate physically in congregational gatherings. However, substantial field studies and surveys would have to be conducted before one could establish whether or not deritualization is occurring among diasporic Muslim groups due to their accessing of religious materials through computer-based technologies.

Thompson also maintains that 'to the extent that the transmission of tradition becomes dependent on mediated forms of communication, it also becomes detached from the individuals with whom one interacts in day-to-day life – that is, it becomes *depersonalized*' (Thompson 1995: 196). He suggests that for media-dependent adherents, the tradition itself gains a certain autonomy from those individuals who may be actually responsible for transmitting it from one generation to another. In this way, even Christian 'televangelists', such as Billy Graham, while succeeding in 'repersonalizing' tradition, have not enabled personalized interactions with the individual believer.

Websites run by Muslim diasporic groups often carry information about the past and current activities of their respective religious leaders in text, audio, pictorial and video formats. Among other items, the 'What's New' file of the 'Naqshbandi Sufi Way' site tracks the activities of the group's shaykhs reciting Quranic verses, leading religious ceremonies, providing explanations on doctrinal issues, making polemical statements to counter criticism of the order, visiting various countries, and meeting leaders of other religions (*www.naqshbandi.org/whatnew.htm*). 'F.I.E.L.D' (*globale.net*), an un-authorized Ismaili site operated from Canada, contains files on the activities, speeches and interviews of the Ismaili *imam*, the Aga Khan. Thompson's notion of depersonalization through the media would seem to apply here if one were to disregard particular Muslim beliefs about the profound spiritual relationship between the disciple (*murid*) and the guide (*murshid*), which is viewed as transcending barriers of distance (Schimmel 1975: 206). The history of sections of Muslim groups who, in various periods, have been separated from their religious leaderships (*shaykhs*, *pirs*, *imams*) by physical or polit-ical borders for centuries has demonstrated their ability to rejoin the respective community once the obstacles have been overcome (Daftary 1998). The latter is especially true in the present time of easier travel and the lifting of border restrictions after the collapse of the Soviet Union. In many cases, the isolated sections of respective Muslim communities only had dated printed materials as guides to their religious traditions. The reintegration of these communities appears to belie Thompson's notion about the long-term effects of media depersonalization on adherents of a particular tradition.

Thompson also says that the rootedness of traditions in particular spatial locales weakens as the mass media remove the need to maintain bonds through face-to-face interactions (1995: 197). In this context he offers the example of migrant populations whose traditions in new lands are sustained through media content. Online networks are offering unparalleled opportunities for diasporas to reconstitute the community to a limited extent in cyberspace. There is a growing body of literature on 'virtual communities' or 'cybercommunities' comprising those individuals who intereact regularly via online technologies (see Jones 1997). Apart from communicating via e-mail, chat groups and Usenet with members of the inter-continental *ummah*, Muslim dias-poric netters are also locating long-lost friends and relatives through inquiries via these services.

The notion of community among Muslims, whether at the level of the *ummah*, which constitutes all adherents of Islam, or at the sub-levels, such as *madhhab*, *firqa*, *tariqa*, *jamat* or *ikhwan*, has long included a non-localized horizontal relationship. (Ibn Khaldun, the Muslim proto-sociologist, theorized about group solidarity of various kinds as early as the fourteenth century.) The idea of a global community is therefore not novel to those individuals who are attempting to use online networks to actualize an Islamic ideal of frontierless groupings of Muslims extending around the world. In addition to providing a broad range of files on information related to the Sufi order led by Shaykh Muhammad Hisham Kabbani, the Naqshbandi Sufi Way site's hypertext links also connect to Naqshbandi sites in Europe, and to other sites on Sufism and on Islam in general (*www.naqshbandi.org*). Similarly, members of the Khoja Ithna Aashari community (with origins in India) have websites inter-linking their diaspora in Tanzania and the United Kingdom as well as carrying 'News from the Shia World' (*www.world-federation.org*).

The wide range of newsgroups and chat groups also allows Muslims to actualize communal links electronically. However, experience has shown that an electronic discussion group only seems to be able to support coherent and relevant discourse on an ongoing basis for a limited number of participants. My own tracking of the newsgroup 'Ilm Net', which is administered from Winnipeg, Canada, indicated that most of the active members tend to be from North America. Dissatisfied with the Canada and US-centred nature of discussions, UK participants expressed a desire to form their own network. Thus the spatial locale in which netters are situated seems to matter even though they 'meet' in cyberspace. The Council of American-Islamic Relations (CAIR) has attempted to mobilize American Muslims primarily in the United States through its Listserv mailings and its website (*www.cair.com*). Its primary area of activity is to report discrimination against Muslims and conduct a media watch function, following up any perceived injustice by communicating its concerns to those deemed responsible (media, government officials, politicians) and encouraging the individuals on its mailing list to do the same. Such activities in cyberspace (in addition to those carried out by various US Muslim organizations in 'real life') appear to create solidarity among American Muslims[12] in the US national context, reinforcing the notion of a distinct community within the larger *ummah*. Thus, while diasporic Muslims may lose strong attachments to their previous locales, the community is reconstituted in another territorial locus.

It may appear from this that these migrant communities are re-mooring their traditions in alternative, electronic 'spaces' through processes of de- and re-localization, as Thompson (1995) suggests. However, even though the conditions of group communication dynamics using online networks allow interaction mainly at local levels, the ultimate reference point for religious community among Muslims generally remains the global *ummah*. The intercontinental linkages of the Naqshbandi and Ithna Ashari serve as examples of the continuing desire to sustain and perhaps even strengthen global connections using new communications technologies. By bringing this historically valorized notion of worldwide fellowship to the process of globalization, through electronic communication, modernity and glob-alization are re-moored. The ideas of spiritual solidarity attached to the planetary sisterhood/brotherhood of the *ummah* challenges from below the dominant materialistic model of globalization in which transnational linkages emphasize relations based on exchange value.

Conclusion

Pasha and Samatar (1997) suggest that the Islamic piety model could have a central place in an inter-civilizational dialogue on globality between Muslims and the West. But such a *dialogue* merely between two civilizations would be uncharacteristic of the history of Muslims, which is a record of interaction with a variety of peoples. Apart from the European, African, Indian and Chinese civilizations and non-Muslim minorities with whom Muslims have been engaged in the past, there are also opportunities to participate in a more multilateral discourse that is inclusive of the indigenous peoples of the Americas, Australasia and Oceania. Contemporary conditions enable the bringing forth of insights into modernity from all the cultures and intellectual traditions of the world. A horizontal inter-civilizational discourse, without engaging in cultural relativism, could de-link modernity from Eurocentric and elitist biases (Amin 1989), and re-moor it to sets of diverse world views through lateral, global interaction. The Islamic piety model, representing the ethos of a billion people, can potentially provide a stream of ideas and practice for the betterment of humankind.

As an alternative construction of modernity, it offers a frame-work which values ethical, non-materialist aspects of progress. Its long-standing concept of global community, *ummah*, presents contemporary thinking with an example of worldwide solidarity based on ties other than those of exchange value. With the failure of Marxism's notion of proletariat-based opposition to capitalism, such solidarity can offer an alternative for countering the socially destructive facets of corporate globalization such as rampant consumerism. The Islamic piety model's particular view of knowledge, which underlines its transcendent value, also has the potential to make important contributions to current thought about 'information society' that tends to reduce knowledge to commodity.

However, the dominant discourses of globalization-from-above are currently pushing aside the Islamic piety model, even in Muslim-majority countries. The evidence to date shows that the policies of many of these states are being aligned with the agenda of powerful Western governments and transnational corporate interests. Additionally, democratic discourse via new communications technologies is often disallowed by the governments in Muslim-majority states, as in many other developing countries. While there is occasional voicing of the Islamic piety model in the context of national and community development, it is muffled, on the one side, by the chorus of those supporting dominant discourses on globalization, and on the other by that of the anti-modernist Islamists.

Nevertheless, there does remain hope that diasporic Muslim groups working in alliance with their co-religionists in Muslim societies, as well as with people of other backgrounds, can engage in inter-civilizational discourse on globalization. Their present use of online networks provides opportunities for the development of such a discourse, since they are generally able to overcome the barriers faced by the hierarchical and centrally controlled communication channels of the mass media. Whereas the closed discussion networks allow for intra-community communication, the discussions on public networks like Usenet (e.g. *alt.religion.islam*) seem to show the growth of inter-cultural and inter-religious discourse. Although these discussions sometimes disintegrate into name-calling, they are also providing occasions for mutual understanding.

The nature of the web theoretically allows for open access to the contents of various sites for all users, with opportunities in many sites for feedback via e-mail. However, it appears that the communicative potential of such technologies has not been fully exploited. An example of an innovative use of the web-based technology in order to develop an interactive, global discourse is the Napf project. Described as an 'intercultural multimedia project' (*www.hof3.ch*) and based in Napf, Switzerland, it enables artists in various locations around the world to contribute video narratives coordinated according to common themes, camera placements and time period. It is designed to produce an ongoing electronic interaction based on personal expressions of life observed by participating artists (including those of diasporic backgrounds) who are located in Switzerland, Egypt, the United Kingdom, Australia, Japan, the United States of America, Brazil, Bosnia-Herzegovina and the Ukraine. This showcasing of local environments by individuals in a transnationally coordinated mode makes for a unique experiment in how this medium can be used to enhance inter-civilizational and inter-cultural discourses:

> We are creating a panorama at the end of the century and are trying to correct the image of how this world is mediated by television-news. During this one year we are not observing the global centers, or its events and noises but instead twelve places on this world where everyday life happens.
>
> (*www.hof3.ch*)

Such preliminary efforts may be far from developing a fully fledged bottom-up challenge to transnational elites, but they do seem to indicate the potential for re-mooring modernity and globality.

Notes

1 This notion of inter-civilizational discourse is drawn from Jürgen Habermas' conception of 'communicative action' that challenges and rivals the state and the economy in the coordination of life (Habermas 1987).
2 These views appear to echo the proposition of Enlightenment philosophers who posited rationalism as a necessary characteristic of modernity.
3 Rohan Samarajiwa has shown that Lerner's work was part of broader research secretly funded by the Office of International Broadcasting of the US State Department, and was carried out for the Voice of America – a key player in the Cold War (Halloran 1997: 33). Lerner's ethnocentric attitude towards Muslims can also traced to certain academic traditions of orientalism (Said 1978).
4 For a discussion of how Barber essentializes a perceived opposition of Islam to modernity through his use of the term *jihad*, see Karim (1996).
5 For a discussion on the difference between access to and use of online services see Karim *et al.* (1998).
6 Central to Malaysia's ICT policy is the development of the 'Multimedia Supercorridor'.
7 These figures are far below those for Canada, the United States and some Nordic countries, which had the highest percentages of national populations with internet access at between 25 and 30 per cent in the same time period (Nua Internet Surveys: *www.nua.ie*).
8 In 1994, the Islamic Council Assembly banned the import, manufacture and use of satellite dishes (Mohammadi 1997: 88). Nevertheless, diasporic Iranians have made a broad variety of materials available on the web, including the writings of controversial Iranian writers such as Abdol Karim Soroush (*www.seraj.org*).

9 Apart from Muslims resident in Muslim-majority and Western countries, there are substantial minority Muslim populations in non-Western countries; for example, India has around 100 million Muslims – more than in most Muslim-majority states.

10 Since ICT access data is not collected by religion, it is virtually impossible to ascertain how many diasporic Muslims use online services.

11 Heated debates on various points of belief occur in some of these electronic discussion groups (Cohen 1997). There are also ongoing discussions on Islam by Muslims with non-Muslims on public Usenet newsgroups. Additionally, Muslims interact in a variety of areas via online services with other members of their respective ethnic and cultural groups who may belong to other religions.

12 American Muslims, as with Muslims in many other Western countries, also include those who are not from immigrant backgrounds.

References

Ahmed, A. S. (1992) *Postmodernism and Islam: Predicament and Promise*, London: Routledge.

Amin, S. (1989) *Eurocentrism*, New York: Monthly Review Press.

Appadurai, A. (1996) *Modernity at Large: Cultural Dimensions of Globalization*, Minneapolis: University of Minnesota Press.

ArabiaTech (1998a) 'Egypt Tops Arab PC Markets', 19 November, *www.arabia.com*.

——(1998b) 'Iran Reviews the Global Picture', 29 June, *www.arabia.com*.

Arabshahi, Payman (1996) 'The Internet in Iran: A Survey', last updated 1 October, *www.Iranian.com*.

Azmeh, A. (1993) *Islams and Modernities*, London: Verso.

Barber, B. R. (1995) *Jihad vs. McWorld*, New York: Times Books.

Bhabha, H. (1994) *The Location of Culture* London: Routledge.

Bickers, C. (1998) 'Reality Bytes', *Far Eastern Economic Review*, 19 March, 27.

Cohen, R. (1997) *Global Diasporas: An Introduction*, Seattle: University of Washington Press.

Daftary, F. (1998) *A Short History of the Ismailis*, London: I. B. Tauris.

'Dakar Declaration on the Internet and the African Media' (10 July 1997) *Devmedia*

DITnet (1998) 'Internet Boom: Double Digit Growth Rates for Internet Users in the Middle East', accessed 25 November, *www.ditnet.co.ae*.

Fakhry, M. (1983) *A History of Islamic Philosophy*, New York: Columbia University Press.

Giddens, A. (1990) *The Consequences of Modernity*, Cambridge: Polity Press.

Habermas, J. (1987) *The Theory of Communicative Action*, 2 vols, Boston MA: Beacon.

Hallaron, J. (1997) 'International Communication Research: Opportunities and Obstacles', in Ali Mohammadi (ed.) *International Communication and Globalization*, London: Sage, 27–47.

Hiebert, M. (1998) 'Reality Bytes', *Far Eastern Economic Review*, 27 August, 17.

Huntington, S. (1996) *The Clash of Civilizations and the Remaking of World Order*, New York: Simon and Schuster.

Jones, S. G. (1997) *Virtual Culture: Identity and Communication in Cybersociety*, Thousand Oaks: Sage.

Karim, K. H. (1996) 'Internecine Conflict and Planetary Homogenization: The Only Two Games in the Global Village?', *Islam in America*, vol. 3, no. 2, 10–17.

——(1997) 'Relocating the Nexus of Citizenship, Heritage and Technology', *The Public: Journal of the European Institute of Culture and Communication*, vol. 4, no. 4, 75–86.

——(1998) 'From Ethnic Media to Global Media: Transnational Communication Networks Among Diasporic Communities', *SRA Reports*, Ottawa: Canadian Heritage.

Karim, K. H., Smeltzer, S. and Loucheur, Y. (1998) 'On-line Access and Participation in Canadian Society', *SRA Reports*, Ottawa: Canadian Heritage.

Lerner, D. (1958) *The Passing of Traditional Society: Modernizing the Middle East*, Illinois: Free Press.

Mohammadi, A. (1997) 'Communication and the Globalization Process in the Developing World', in Ali Mohammadi (ed.) *International Communication and Globalization*, London: Sage, 67–89.

——(1998) 'Electronic Empires: An Islamic Perspective', in Daya Kishan Thussu (ed.) *Electronic Empires: Global Media and Local Resistance*, London: Arnold.

Mowlana, H. (1979) 'Technology versus Tradition: Communication in the Iranian Revolution', *Journal of Communication*, vol. 29, no. 3, 107–12.

——(1996) *Global Communication in Transition: The End of Diversity?*, Thousand Oaks: Sage.

Naipaul, V. S. (1991) 'Our Universal Civilization', *New York Review of Books*, vol. 38, no. 3, January, 22–5.

Nanji, A. (1991) 'Contemporary Expression of Islam in Buildings: What Have We Learned?', in Hayat Salam (ed.) *Expressions of Islam in Buildings*, Geneva: Aga Khan Trust for Culture, 219–25.

Nua Internet Surveys (1998) 'How Many Online?', accessed 25 November, *www.nua.ie*.

Pasha, M. K. and Samatar, A. I. (1997) 'The Resurgence of Islam', in James H. Mittleman (ed.) *Globalization: Critical Reflections*, Boulder: Lynne Rienner, 187–201.

Reuters (1998) 'Turkish Police React to Online Dissent', 5 June, *www.arabia.com*.

Richer, S. (1996) 'The Phenomenon of Information Highways in the Francophonie', *International Information and Library Review*, vol. 28, 289–301.

Said, E. (1978) *Orientalism*, New York: Vintage Books.

Schimmel, A. (1975) *Mystical Dimensions of Islam*, Chapel Hill: University of North Carolina Press.

Schramm, W. (1964) *Mass Media and National Development*, Stanford: Stanford University Press.

Shariffadeen, T. M. A. (1992) 'Information Technology and the Malaysian Development Paradigm', paper presented at the Kongres Menjelang Abad 21: Islam dan Wawasan, 3 July, Kuala Lumpur, Malaysia.

Sharabi, H. (1966) 'Islam and Modernization in the Arab World', in J. H. Thompson and R. D. Reischauer (eds) *Modernization of the Arab World*, Princeton: D. Van Nostrand, 26–33.

Silk, M. (1995) *Unsecular Media: Making News of Religion in America*, Chicago: University of Illinois Press.

Smeltzer, S. (1997) 'Government Responses in the Information Society: A Comparative Analysis of 6 Asian Countries', *SRA Reports*, Ottawa: Canadian Heritage.

Smith, D. E. (1970) *Religion and Political Development*, Boston: Little, Brown.

Sreberny-Mohammadi, A. and Mohammadi, A. (1994) *Small Media and Big Revolution*, Minneapolis: University of Minnesota Press.

Thapisa, A. P. N. (1996) 'The Impact of Global Information on Africa', *Internet Research: Electronic Networking Applications and Policy*, vol. 6, no. 1, 71–8.

Thompson, J. B. (1995) *The Media and Modernity: A Social Theory of the Media*, Cambridge: Polity Press.

4 Reimagining the *ummah*?

Information technology and the changing boundaries of political Islam

Peter G. Mandaville

This chapter discusses the role of information technology in the Islamic context and examines how the proliferation of information technology (IT) is likely to affect the ways in which the political community is imagined in Islam. Will global networks and computer-mediated communication (CMC) enable Muslims to approximate more closely to the *ummah*, the traditional model of the Islamic world community? Much of the recent literature in sociology and cultural studies suggests that the spread of IT and CMC will lead to the emergence of new forms of community (Jones 1995), but attention is rarely given to the question of how traditional notions of community are mediated and refigured through sustained contact with new technologies of communication. The complex processes commonly referred to under the rubric of globalization can serve to reify these changes, making them potentially available to much larger, and often geographically widespread, audiences. This chapter will explore some of these issues and attempt to assess the extent to which IT could provide the catalyst for a reformation of Muslim discourse. In short, we shall be inquiring as to the future of Islam in the context of globalized information technologies.

'The field [of globalization], if not controlled', warns Abu-Lughod (1991), 'can degenerate into what we might call "global-babble"'. Her preference is for an approach which tries to 'capture the ambiguities and nuances of the concrete, as they are embedded in the lives of people'. (Abu-Lughod 1991: 131). The purpose of this chapter, then, is to examine the ways in which the impact of globalized communications and information technology on various forms of one particular tradition, Islam, has led both to the imagination of new political communities and to the reimagination of traditional categories of social and religious solidarity. Our exploration of the nexus between Islam and information technology will proceed as follows. After

examining the original connotations attached to the notion of the
ummah, some observations will be made as to the complex and often
contradictory sociological implications of contemporary globalization.
The discussion will then move on to highlight the salient issues
surrounding the digitization and communication of Islamic knowledge, and the religious politics which this activity can engender. In
order to developing the model of globalization as outlined in this
chapter, two case studies involving encounters between Islam and IT
are explored. Muslim diaspora activity on the internet is characterized
as an instance of 'globalizing the local', and the controversial appearance of the internet in the Gulf is assessed as an example of 'localizing
the global'. The concluding section returns to the question of information technology as a catalyst for recreating traditional models of
community in Islam. Drawing on evidence presented throughout the
chapter, it will be argued that the phenomenal rise of globalized IT
does as much to challenge the *ummah* as to reconstitute it.

The origins of the *ummah*

How did the first Muslim community, the original *ummah*, come to be
constituted at Medina (then known as Yathrib) during the seventh
century, and what did this community look like? Note that this earliest
period of Islamic history is particularly salient because the normative
models which developed in these years eventually came to form the
basis of Islamic law (*shari'a*). The authoritative deeds and dictums of
the Prophet Muhammad (the *sunna*) have, along with the Quran itself,
come to constitute the two primary sources of scriptural authority in
Islam. The traditions of Muhammad's companions and their
supporters in Medina have also been recorded, interpreted, and coded
as sources of jurisprudence (*fiqh*), which carry an almost mythical
warrant even today. In contemporary Muslim discourses, the themes,
events, and personages of these years continue to be important points
of reference and sources of inspiration. This story begins, however,
with a decisive social rupture that occurred in Arabia over a thousand
years ago: the *hijra*.

The migration of persecuted early Muslims from Mecca to Medina,
the *hijra*, has become an enduring symbol in Islam, with a resonance
that can still be heard in the names of various twentieth-century
Islamist movements ranging from *al-Takfir w'al-Hijra* in Egypt to the
diasporic *al-Muhajiroun* ('the emigrants') in London. In this sense the
hijra has taken on a significance much wider than the specific historical event itself. It has come to symbolize deliverance from oppression

and the condition of pre-Islamic ignorance known as *jahiliyya*. In this sense the *hijra* represents the institution of a new social paradigm in which 'the good life' accrues from submission to the will of a single divine source. As Ira Lapidus puts it:

> For Muslims the [*hijra*] has come to mean not only a change of place, but the adoption of Islam and entry into the community of Muslims. The *hijra* is the transition from the pagan to the Muslim world – from kinship to a society based on common belief.
>
> (Lapidus 1988: 27)

In theory then, the *hijra* represented an idiomatic shift with regard to the manner in which community was to be 'imagined' (Anderson 1991). Social cohesion based purely on clan and kin was seen as a source of constant strife and feuding, whereas a 'community of believers' could strive to transcend this base tribalism in the name of a greater unity. In Islam, the core doctrine of *tawhid* (unity of and in God) reflects this concern. For those who participated in the first migration, then, it was not the relatively short geographic separation between Mecca and Medina which mattered, but rather the much more dramatic (and, one would imagine, initially disorienting) split with their tribal kin-groups. These affiliations had been the crux and core of social solidarity in Arabia for centuries, and to leave them behind in the name of a new religion signified a major break with traditional practice.

The social environment which the Prophet and his followers found in Medina was significantly different from the one they had left behind in Mecca. The ruling elites of their native city had all come from a single tribe, the Quraysh, an autocratic family subdivided into several clans which wielded varying degrees of political influence. Medina, on the other hand, did not have a single hegemonic tribe, nor did it possess a clear hierarchy of clan organization. Its politics were instead dominated by disputes among various competing factions and ethnic affiliations. Medina was also home to a large Jewish community as well as a number of other Arab groupings. It was this unstable social atmosphere that actually provided Muhammad with the opportunity to settle in Medina. Facing increasingly intense persecution in Mecca because of his religious beliefs, he managed to convince the dissenting factions of Medina to enter into an alliance with him and his followers, and to accept his arbitration in settling their various disputes.

The *ummah* or world community of Muslims had, therefore, its initial incarnation in this group which accompanied Muhammad on the *hijra* in 622. It is difficult for the modern commentator to discern exactly what was implied by the term *ummah* in the context of Medinan society.[1] As it occurs in both the Quran and other primary source material from the period, we may understand the *ummah* as referring to a wide range of social groupings – anywhere from Muhammad's closest followers on one end of the scale, to all living creatures on the other.[2] The etymology of the word is also ambiguous. The instinctive tendency has been to relate it to the Arabic word *umm* which means 'mother', but it now seems more likely that the term is derived from analogues in Hebrew and Aramaic, both of which refer to notions of community or social solidarity.

The *ummah* of Medina was originally a sort of 'defence pact' which united the city's clans in a collective pledge to protect Muhammad and his followers. This alliance system was codified in a treaty of sorts, usually referred to as the Constitution of Medina. In essence this document provided a sense of overarching political logic for the anarchic settlement – exactly what the oasis city had been lacking. Because it demanded complete loyalty to Muhammad from the various factions in Medina, it also effectively prevented the formation of unstable alliances between these clans. Just who was included within the *ummah*'s original jurisdiction is however not easy to determine. This is made all the more difficult by the fact that the documents we have from this period appear to contain several disparate usages of the term, reflecting various modifications and amendments during the Medinan years. Does the *ummah* refer to relations of kinship, religion or territory? It would appear that at the time of Muhammad's arrival it included elements of all three. Certainly the *ummah* was initially confined to the major clans of Medina and several local Jewish and Christian groups, in addition to the core group of Muslim emigrants. Once the Prophet had succeeded in consolidating his authority in Medina, however, the character of the *ummah* began to evolve. It is likely that Muhammad became increasingly capable of demanding a commitment to his religion (or at the very least a renunciation of idolatry) from those seeking to enter into confederacies with his community. Impressed by the success of his raids against Meccan caravans, it soon became obvious to neighbouring nomadic tribes that the inclement political winds in eastern Arabia were blowing Muhammad's way. Many were anxious to pledge their loyalty to him in return for the shelter of his rapidly expanding *dhimmah*, a term which we might understand as referring to a 'zone of peace or security'.

The *ummah* as it existed in Medina is perhaps best characterized as a conglomerate of various communities: tribal, confessional and confederal. Certainly a good deal of traditional practice with regard to the formation of alliances and kinship ties was preserved in Muhammad's new mini-state, with the overtly religious aspects of the community confined largely to Muhammad's closest followers. As far as Allah's Messenger was concerned, however, the main imperative at this point was to bolster his numbers and to widen the basis of his popular support. If this involved the occasional pact with a pagan clan, so be it. The wholesale adoption of the new universal religion would, it was believed, arrive in due course. In this the Prophet was correct. As the propagation of Islam began in earnest during the years following Muhammad's death, so did the notion of a wider *ummah*, now understood quite specifically as a form of religious community, become increasingly prominent.

Islam and globalization

Having examined some of the original connotations of the *ummah* concept, we can now place it in the context of contemporary Islamic politics. In Muslim discourse today, the *ummah* often appears as a central normative concept appealing for unity across the global Muslim community. As discussed above, the essence of the *ummah* lies in the idea of renouncing one's factional identities (today we might speak of ethnicity or national allegiance) in the name of a greater solidarity with God: a communion of all Muslims. Since some of the central themes of globalization involve the bridging of distances and the removal of geographic barriers (e.g. the rise of a 'global village'), we might legitimately ask to what extent this phenomenon can help to bridge the distances and differences which separate the vast number of Muslim communities found in the world today. Let us begin by looking at the nature of contemporary Islam, and also at some of the ways in which it has reacted to the onset of globalization.

It is by now a commonplace to assert that Islam means different things to different people at different times. Whether we choose to talk about various 'Islams' or being 'Muslims through discourse', the underlying point is the same: within the religious tradition we call Islam there exist any number of interpretations as to what Islam is, what it means, and who possesses the authority to speak on its behalf (al-Azmeh 1997; Bowen 1993; Roff 1987). This internal diversity is the result of the various cultural, ethnic and national factors which have mediated the religion as it spread across much of the Middle East, Africa, Asia and, more recently, Western Europe and North America. The resulting syncretisms and interminglings have bequeathed to Islam a rich body of cultural material replete with difference, hybridity and, at times, contradiction. Indeed, it was the increasingly 'global' nature of Islam from the ninth century onwards that put a strain on the original *ummah*. Cracks inevitably began to appear as the original Muslim community rapidly grew to encompass a diverse range of peoples, lands and histories.

What happens, then, when this complex world discourse comes into contact with another set of ideas which also, by its very nature, claims universal jurisdiction: the discourse of globalization? Islam, and political Islam in particular, has exhibited a wide variety of responses to globalization. Certain aspects of this phenomenon have been appropriated eagerly while others have been vociferously rejected. Indeed, aspects of globalization, such as the phenomenal rise of globalized information technologies, have been mobilized explicitly in response to other aspects, such as the perceived spread of American culture, which many Muslims find distasteful. First of all, though, what do we mean when we talk of globalization?

Even the most cursory reading of recent literature will reveal that globalization is currently one of the most ubiquitous buzzwords in social theory. The difficulty in theorizing the concept stems in part from the fact that the processes which it purports to describe often appear to contradict one other. For example, the term would seem to imply the global adoption of certain modes and norms of interaction with regard to international politics, finance and law. Increased economic interdependence, and the rise of a 'global culture' are also often included. Simultaneously, however, the same mechanisms which permit (or require) this homogeneity of practice also produce a curious inverse side-effect: localizing the global can also at times serve to *globalize the local*. The channels which open spaces of local political community to the global outside can also be appropriated by those 'receiving' communities in order to export their own notions of the particular. As Arjun Appadurai puts it:

> The globalization of culture is not the same as its homogenization, but globalization involves the use of a variety of instruments of homogenization (armaments, advertising techniques, language hegemonies, clothing styles and the like), which are absorbed into local political and cultural economies, only to be repatriated as heterogeneous dialogues of national sovereignty, free enterprise, fundamentalism, etc.

> (Appadurai 1990: 307)

This model questions the common idiom of globalization which tends to portray the wholesale bulldozing of 'traditional' local cultures by the rampaging juggernaut of late Western (usually American) capitalism. A claim is not being made here that the exchange of materials is equal in both (or all) directions, only that the popular monoflow paradigm of a globalizing Western modernity is a severe misrepresentation. The majority of academic treatments of this phenomenon have, fortunately, been far more nuanced in their analyses (Featherstone 1990; King 1991; Robertson 1992). Missing from the literature, however, is an extended study of those communities who seek to appropriate the mechanisms of globalization for their own ends, and in the process of doing so to articulate an authentic local response to 'other' value systems, of which the incoming cultural material is the embodiment. To be sure, a great deal of transnational traffic does flow from the West to the Rest, but this phenomenon is not altogether hegemonic. Significant exchange also occurs between the Rest and the West and, above all, important processes of globalization are certainly at work *within* the Rest. Indeed, the very categories 'West' and 'Rest' become analytically useless under the condition of globality because Rest is already in the West, and vice-versa.

Globalization refers to an ongoing *process* (or set of processes) in which economic, political, and cultural structures become increasingly transnational and interdependent (or integrated). Globalization also involves the geographic dispersal of systems, peoples, ideas, technologies, cultures, and information, all of which are defining characteristics of late modernity. Other key features of this phenomenon relate to the capacities engendered by the enabling technologies of globalization, of which the most salient for the present study are the rise of information technology and the growing influence of what we might term 'distanciated communities'. This latter designation alludes to those groups who make use of the infrastructural trappings of globalization (e.g. telecommunications, electronic information transfer and air travel) in order to bypass the geographical barriers to social interaction. Migrants, exiles, and diaspora groups are examples here. All are cases which involve the globalization of forces such as ethnicity and identity which, according to Appadurai, are:

> sentiments whose greatest force is in their ability to ignite intimacy into a political sentiment and turn locality into a staging ground for identity. [They] have become spread over vast and irregular spaces, as groups move, yet stay linked to one another through sophisticated media capabilities.
>
> (Appadurai 1990: 306)

In globalization, physical presence or proximity is no longer a prerequisite for the practice of community. 'Globalization concerns the intersection of presence and absence', writes Anthony Giddens, 'the interlacing of social events and social relations "at distance" with local contextualities' (Giddens 1991: 21). The concept of 'distancia-tion' is implicated in the ability of certain groups to engage in, sustain, or reproduce particular forms of community across great distances and in the face of competing traditions.[3]

Another key feature of this state of affairs is the way in which we are beginning to conceive of the world as an increasingly compressed space – a notion most popularly captured in Marshall McLuhan's metaphor of the 'global village', and theorized by Roland Robertson (1992) as a state of consciousness. Robertson's term 'globality' refers to a mindset, an awareness of the world as a single space. This apparent diminution of space and time is the result of several develop-ments in global infrastructure during the twentieth century: advances in transportation give the illusion of dramatically reduced distances, and the phenomenal rise of information technology has meant that the velocity of international communication has increased exponentially. But how is the condition of globality experienced by individuals and the societies within which they go about their daily lives? What impact has globalization had upon the ways in which people conceive and imagine their senses of community and culture?

In a recent piece on large-scale social organization and the creation of community, Craig Calhoun argues that:

> [a] world knit together by *indirect relationships* poses three chal-lenges in the realm of everyday personal existence: to make sense through abstract concepts of forms of social organization for which everyday experience gives us misleading preparation, to establish a sense of personal rootedness and continuity of existence where connections across time are mainly impersonal, and to establish a sense of place and social context when the coordination of action – and the action of our own lives – constantly transcends locality.
>
> (Calhoun 1991: 114)

The latter two (interrelated) issues have perhaps the most relevance in the context of this chapter, in that they relate to the tangible experi-ences of displacement, alienation and antagonism which often characterize the individual's experience of globality. In this sense, Calhoun's notion of 'indirect relationships' highlights an important aspect of the distanciated community.

The same forces which have brought about globalization have also brought about phenomenal increases in the extent to which people communicate and encounter each other across the boundaries of cultures, ethnicities, nations and other communities. Indeed, globality has been responsible for bringing about significant changes in the nature and locations of these very same boundaries. In addition, the processes of decolonization and a changing international labour environment have resulted in new dynamics of migration which have challenged (if not eradicated altogether) the very possibility of the homogeneous nation-state. Over the last fifty years or so, globalization has also given birth to transnational actors on a scale which is historically unprecedented: ethnic minorities, diaspora groups, and migrant workers are all examples of this phenomenon. When bodies travel, so do cultures. The aim is to examine the ways in which the traditions of our increasingly transnational cultures are reformulated and reimagined when forced to transcend locality.

It has emerged from this discussion that globalization is not simply about enabling community and communication. Although rapid developments in media and information technology have made communication across distances much easier, their cultural implications are actually far more complex. The rise of globalized IT should not be viewed simply as a tool for bringing different peoples together, but rather as a complex set of social processes which serves to highlight and radicalize the heterogeneity *within* any community or tradition it encounters. That is, globalization is about bridging distances, but it is also about *discovering difference*. The implications of this latter point in the context of Islam will be revealed in the sections to follow.

Islam and IT: some general issues

So how have the trappings of information technology shaped normative practice in the history of Islam, and in the lived experience of 'being Muslim'? The salience of technology in bringing about religious change has been well documented (Robinson 1993; Atiyeh 1995; Eickelman and Piscatori 1996). In early Islam, oral transmission was the preferred mode for disseminating religious knowledge, with each religious scholar (*'alim*, pl. *'ulama*) granting his student a licence (*ijaza*) which permitted him to pass on the texts of his teacher. Literacy among wider populations, even in urban centres, was very low. This state of affairs allowed the *'ulama* to maintain a virtual monopoly over the production of authoritative religious knowledge. We should note here that in a sense it is almost mistaken to speak of Islam as possessing 'holy scriptures'. The Quran is, quite literally, a recitation,[4] the literal word of God as revealed to Muhammad via the archangel Gabriel. It is a collection of words whose message resonates most strongly when read aloud – when given voice. Even to this day, the process of learning the Quran is first and foremost an exercise in memorization and oral repetition. This goes some way to explaining why the Muslim world hesitated to embrace the technologies of 'print-capitalism' even when they were readily available. It was the experience of European colonialism and the concomitant perceived decline in Muslim civilization which paved the way for the rise of print technology in the nineteenth century. The book, the pamphlet, and the newsletter were all taken up with urgency in order to counter the threat which Europe was posing to the Muslim world. The *'ulama* were initially at the forefront of this revolution, using a newly expanded and more widely distributed literature base to create a much broader constituency. An inevitable side-effect of this phenomenon, however, was that the religious scholars' stranglehold over religious knowledge was broken. The core texts were now available to anyone who could read them; and to read is, of course, to interpret. As Francis Robinson puts it:

> Books...could now be consulted by any Ahmad, Mahmud or Muhammad, who could make what they will of them. Increasingly from now on any Ahmad, Mahmud or Muhammad could claim to speak for Islam. No longer was a sheaf of impeccable *ijazas* the buttress of authority; strong Islamic commitment would be enough.
>
> (Robinson 1993: 245)

The new media opened up new spaces of religious contestation where traditional sources of authority could be challenged by the wider public. As literacy rates began to climb almost exponentially in the twentieth century, this effect was amplified even further. The fragmentation of traditional sources of authority is hence a key theme with regard to the nexus of Islam and globalization. The rise of what we might call 'media Islam' or 'soundbite Islam' has been a major by-product of globalized information technology. Ideas and messages now possess the capability to bridge time and space almost effortlessly, and the political implications of this new capacity are not easily over-estimated.

A brief survey of various information technologies will now be undertaken in order to assess the impact of this phenomenon on Islam. Both the relevant technical aspects and religious implications of each technology will be outlined, and the discussion will then go on to provide some examples of how each is being used by Muslims today. Let me begin with what are, in a sense, the basics: those technologies which allow texts to be converted and stored in an electronic form. Of course, when these new media begin to be distributed an entirely new political dimension enters the picture. Those technologies involved in the *communication* of Islam will hence be dealt with in a separate section. The internet, in particular, provides one of the most apt examples of what was termed above 'globalizing the local'.

Digitizing Islam

The Anglo-centric nature of electronic media was for a long time a barrier to working with anything but the most well known religious texts, such as the Quran and those *hadith* collections available in English. The rise of the graphic user interface (GUI) in the mid-1980s, typified by the Apple Macintosh operating system and (from the mid-1990s) Microsoft's Windows, served to rectify this problem to some extent. The graphical nature of the interface allowed computer operators to make ready use of non-Latin scripts which had previously been difficult to render in the old command-line format. Operating systems and word processors began to become available in various non-English languages and, most notably for our purposes, in Arabic. Another important development here was the exponential increase in the storage capacity of the various magnetic media used by computers. This situation was again transformed with the advent of optical media such as the compact disc in the late 1980s. Computers graduated from storing programs and data on regular audio cassettes (very low capacity) to floppy disks (between just over 100kB to 1.4MB), to hard drives (20MB to several gigabytes), to the phenomenal array-based servers which chain together several high-capacity hard drives and provide enough capacity to store the complete contents of a large university or national library.

It is the read-only compact disc (CD-ROM), however, which has transformed the scene in recent years with its ability to easily transport chunks of data as large as 650MB between many computers. This provides enough capacity to comfortably store several multi-volume encyclopaedias, hours of high-quality sound, or even a full-length video film.

What does this mean for Islam? Given the voluminous nature of most Islamic texts, the CD-ROM has provided a medium which can contain the full contents of several works. This means that the entire

Quran, several collections of Prophetical sayings (*hadith*), Quranic exegesis (*tafsir*), and other jurisprudential works (*fiqh*) can easily fit on a single disc. The availability of such collections, all hyper-linked and cross-referenced, has created a new constituency for religious texts. Where Muslims previously would have had to rely on the expertise of the *'ulama* when dealing with these books, they are now all available in a single medium which can easily be searched by any computer user. According to Ziauddin Sardar:

> Instead of ploughing through bulky texts, that require a certain expertise to read, a plethora of databases on the *Quran* and *hadith* now open up these texts and make them accessible to average, non-expert, users. Increasingly, the *'ulama* are being confronted by non-professional theologians who can cite chapter and verse from the fundamental sources, undermining not just their arguments but also the very basis of their authority.
>
> (Sardar 1993: 55–6)

Sardar then goes on to speculate about how all the core jurisprudential texts (the *usul al-fiqh*) might be placed on single compact disc, along with an expert-system[5] that would guide the user through the literature and, in effect, allow her to generate her own religious edicts (*fatwas*). This sort of *ijtihad* toolkit would amount to a 'virtual' *'alim*, and would pose a further challenge to the authority of the traditional religious scholars.[6] It is unlikely, however, that such a system will replace the *'ulama* any time soon. They still command enormous respect in many communities and would, in any case, surely challenge the claim that their methodologies – the product of centuries of study and exhaustive research – can be reduced to a set of coded computer instructions.

The existence of such collections on CD-ROM has nevertheless become a reality in the past few years. The Islamic Computing Centre in London has been at the forefront of producing and distributing Arabic and Islamic materials in electronic format, and one only needs to glance at their product catalogue to confirm the enthusiasm with which Muslims have taken up this technology. In addition to several electronic Qurans (with full Arabic text, several English translations, and complete oral recitation on a single disc) the Centre also sells titles such as *WinHadith*, *WinBukhari* and *WinSeera*. Also available are several products which begin to approach the system which Sardar (1993) has envisaged. The *Islamic Law Base*, *Islamic Scholar* and *'Alim Multimedia 4.5* are all vast collections of religious texts such as the Quran, *hadith*, several volumes of *fiqh* covering all fours Sunni schools of jurisprudence, biographies of the Prophet and his Companions, and more recent writing by figures such as Abu 'Ala Mawdudi. All of these databases can be kept open simultaneously, and material between them is cross-referenced and fully searchable. Utilities for calculating prayer times anywhere in the world and for converting between the *Hijri* and other calendar systems are also available. That is not to say that the *'ulama* have been marginalized entirely: the moon sliver must still be visible to the human eye for Ramadhan to begin, regardless of whether a computer astronomy program insists that it is there. Some religious scholars have also become quite enthusiastic about computer technology themselves. At the Center for Islamic Jurisprudence in Qom, for example, several thousand texts, both Sunni and Shi'ite, have been converted to electronic form (MacFarquhar 1996).

The rise of electronic or 'print Islam' (Eickelman 1989) has not eradicated the saliency of the oral tradition. Electronic media are as adept with sound as they are with the written word. Audio cassettes, widely available and portable, may well serve to give the oral tradition a 'new lease of life' (Robinson 1993: 250). Certainly we have heard much of the role of the audio cassette in Iran's Islamic revolution, where recordings of Khomeini's sermons were smuggled into Iran from his Neauphle-le-Chateau headquarters near Paris and widely distributed, much to the Shah's dismay. The Friday sermon, or *khutba*, is today recorded at many mosques throughout the Muslim world, and the distribution of these recordings along with addresses by prominent ideologues such as Sayyid Qutb, Ali Shariati, and Abu-l A'la al-Mawdudi, serves to politicize Islam before a vast audience. Recordings of sermons by dissident Saudi *'ulama* such as Safar al-Hawali and Salman al-'Awda also circulate widely both inside and outside the Kingdom, and this marks the first time that material openly critical of the Saudi regime has been heard by relatively large sections of that country's population. The website of a London-based Saudi opposition group has also made Salman al-'Awda's sermons available over the internet using the latest audio streaming technology (*http://www.miraserve.com*).

Communicating Islam: broadcast and network technology

'It is in their use as *distributive* and *decentralized* networks', writes Sardar (1993: 55), 'that [information technology's] greatest potential lies for Muslim societies and cultures'. Sardar is undoubtedly correct insofar as political impact is obviously strongest when these media are distributed, broadcast, or otherwise made available to a wider audience. This section will examine the implications of technologies such as telecommunications, television (both terrestrial and satellite) and, finally, the internet – all of which serve to politicize Islam through their 'global reach' capabilities.

Telecommunications are undergoing something of a mini-boom in the Middle East, and sophisticated systems are already in place or planned for the urban areas of many Asian countries such as Malaysia, Indonesia and Pakistan. The latest GSM mobile technology is also available in many countries of the Gulf – Jordan, Lebanon, Pakistan – and is planned for Syria (MEED 1996). It is in the West, however, that Muslims have made the most widespread use of telecommunications technology for religious purposes. The Islamic Assembly of North America (IANA), for example, operates a Fatwa Centre which can be reached via a toll-free telephone number. The *'ulama* of the centre will dispense edicts covering any subject to members of the Muslim community in North America (*http://www.IANAnet.org/fatwa/*). In the Middle East, activists in groups such as HAMAS have made use of Israeli cellular networks to stay in touch while moving around the West Bank and Gaza. Ironically, in one case this technology proved to be their downfall. The HAMAS bombmaker Yahya Ayash ('The Engineer') was assassinated by Israeli internal security agents using a booby-trapped cell phone packed with explosives.

An offshoot of telecommunications, the fax, has also been widely used by Muslims in the Middle East, and especially by Islamist groups seeking to question the legitimacy of various regimes. Organizations in Algeria and Egypt have made use of the fax machine in voicing protest to their respective governments, and the 'fax cascade' tactics of Saudi dissidents in London have become notorious. At the height of its activity, for example, the Committee for the Defence of Legitimate Rights (CDLR) was sending several thousand faxes per week to the Kingdom, where offices were forced to turn off fax machines at night in an effort to stem the flow. These faxes were reportedly photocopied and then distributed widely within the Kingdom (al-Mass'ari 1995; 1997). The organization's efforts have certainly caught the attention of the ruling regime and its 'official' clergy. The government was even forced to take the unprecedented step of urging Saudis (via a state-owned newspaper) to ignore the CDLR's faxes (*Saudi Gazette* 1994).

Television, which in the Middle East is often state-owned and censored, is not a forum which has been extensively co-opted by Muslims for political purposes. We do find references, however, to instances where there has been a coming together of politicized Islam and television. Abu-Lughod (1997) speculates about the impact of militant Islamist groups in Egypt on the standards of dress and appearance of television presenters, and Eickelman (1989) discusses officially sanctioned religious presentation on television as a form of national discourse. Television, and satellite television in particular, certainly have, however, been the objects of protests by both official religious voices and various Islamist movements. In Algeria, for example, soldiers of the Armed Islamic Group (GIA) have in the past threatened the owners of satellite dishes (Ruthven 1995). Several Arab Gulf states and Iran have official bans in effect on the private owner- ship of the dishes. In practice, however, these bans are very difficult to enforce, and the countries have in some cases been forced to provide rival satellite programming in an attempt to lure viewers away from 'sinful' and 'poisoning' Western programmes (Rathmell 1997). Saudi Arabia owns a vast media empire and controls much of the premier Arabic-language satellite programming via its Middle East Broadcasting (MBC) network. In 1996, an Italian-based satellite relay company with significant Saudi investment interests was forced to terminate its contract with the BBC after its Arabic-language televi- sion service gave air time to the Saudi dissident Muhammad al-Mass'ari and showed a programme critical of Saudi Arabia's human rights record (*Reuters*, 4 September 1996).

In at least one case Islamists have also turned to satellite television as a potential political tool. The Movement for Islamic Reform (MIRA), an offshoot of the CDLR in London, has rented a broad- casting slot on a satellite and is planning to begin transmitting propaganda programmes which question the legitimacy of the Saudi regime according to religious criteria. The group is hoping to take advantage of the several hundred thousand satellite dishes currently in use in the Kingdom (al-Faqih 1997).

The internet: globalizing local discourses?

What about the internet? It is perhaps here that some of the most interesting things are happening. It should be noted, however, that while many countries in the Middle East and Asia are starting to provide internet access to their populations, the vast majority of Muslim users of the internet are in Europe and North America. If the globalization of information technology is having a discernible effect on political community in Islam, then it is to the various Muslim dias- pora groups in the West, Arab, Iranian and South Asian, that we must turn to find it. Their activities can be seen as the appropriation of a global technology of Western origin which is then turned into a tool for the conduct and propagation of new hybridized practices. These are formed by inserting the normative discourse of Islam into the Western discourse of information technology. In this sense the use of the internet by Muslim diaspora groups provides one of the best examples of what was referred to above as 'globalizing the local'.

What, then, are the implications of this media revolution for those communities which inhabit global spaces? Whereas Anderson (1991) once pointed to the pioneering efforts of New World 'creoles' in the formation of imagined communities, he now speaks of the 'new creoles' of the information superhighway – political actors whose force lies in their adoption of the enabling technologies of electronic print and information transfer (Anderson 1995). However, we should not be too quick to declare that the internet is suddenly going to radically transform Muslim understandings of political community. We need to look realistically at the number of Muslims who actually have access to this forum, and to take careful note of each socio-political setting which receives information via this network:

> Transnational theories, fixated on media and forms of alienated consciousness distinctive of late modernity, tend to overlook the social organization into which new media are brought in a rush to the new in expression. Impressed by what Simmel much earlier called 'cosmopolitanism', we overlook measures of social organization in pursuit of media effects.
>
> (Anderson 1997)

In addition, we need to make sure that we have a more nuanced understanding of those Muslim identities which use the internet. We cannot start talking about new forms of diasporic Muslim community simply because many users of the internet happen to be Muslims. To comprehend the processes by which community is created, we need also to understand the circumstances under which these Muslim identities became diasporic. That is, how do other aspects of identity influence the terms of religious discourse on the internet? Issues such as culture and religion are often discussed on the internet using methods of reasoning and debate which derive from the natural and technical sciences, rather than in the 'traditional' idiom of religious discourse which might be found back home. This reflects the nature of the professional or student life of many diaspora Muslims who are often technicians, engineers or research scientists (Anderson 1997).

Another area to be examined is the internet's impact on centre/periphery relations in the Muslim world. A country such as Malaysia, usually considered to be on the margins of Islam both in terms of geography and religious influence, has invested heavily in information and networking technologies. As a result, when searching on the internet for descriptions of educational programmes which offer formal religious training, one is far more likely to encounter the comprehensive course outlines provided by the International Islamic University of Malaysia rather than the venerable institutions of Cairo, Medina or Mashhad. Government officials in Indonesia have also recently begun to explore the potential of the internet for raising the profile of Indonesian Islam (Cohen 1996). Even the ayatollahs of Iran have jumped on the information bandwagon. Eager to propagate Shi'ite teachings, the scholars of Qom have digitized thousands of religious texts which they plan to make available over the internet. An e-mail *fatwa* service is also planned (Evans 1996).

We have to keep reminding ourselves, however, that the vast majority of the world's Muslims cannot afford to pay for internet access. When available in the Middle East and Asia, internet accounts are usually prohibitively expensive, hence subscriptions tend to be limited to elite groups who are often more sympathetic to Western bourgeois values. As noted above, it is usually amongst the diaspora Muslims of the Western world that we find the internet being appropriated for political purposes. The American media, for example, has recently been full of scaremongering about 'radical fundamentalists' who use the United States as a fundraising base for their operations overseas. Reports often cite the internet as a primary tool for the dissemination of propaganda by Islamic militants. We are told, for example, that Islamist websites distribute the communiqués of Algerian militant groups and provide a forum for the teachings of Sheikh Omar Abdel-Rahman, the Egyptian cleric said to be behind the World Trade Center bombing (Cole 1997). In a recent piece, even Benedict Anderson seemed to sensationalize the advent of diaspora activists:

> [They] create a serious politics that is at the same time radically unaccountable. The participant rarely pays taxes in the country in which he does his politics; he is not answerable to its judicial system; he probably does not cast even an absentee ballot in its elections because he is a citizen in a different place; he need not fear prison, torture, or death, nor need his immediate family. But, well and safely positioned in the First World, he can send money and guns, circulate propaganda, and build intercontinental computer information circuits [*sic*], all of which can have incalculable consequences in the zones of their ultimate destinations.
>
> (Anderson 1994: 327)

A more sober examination of the situation, however, would most likely reveal that very few of the Muslim groups who have a presence on the internet are involved in this sort of activity. To be sure, there do exist several prominent sites which advertise information on 'digital jihad' and 'on-line activism', or which claim to provide resources for Islamist politicians, but it is unlikely that any of these – which are often run by students or part-time volunteers – actually have the capacity to engage in the sort of international intrigues alluded to above.[7] Recent events, such as the terrorist attacks of 9/11 do show that the Islamic diaspora poses some threat to the US. However, the subsequent anthrax scare and the earlier bombing of the federal building in Oklahoma City, also indicate that a country such as the United States probably has more to fear from disillusioned sections of its own population or from various cult and millenarian movements than it does from the Muslim diaspora.

For the overwhelming majority of Muslims in the West, the internet is mainly a forum for the conduct of politics *within* Islam. Because very few 'official' Muslim organs, such as the Organization of the Islamic Conference, the Muslim World League or the various eminent religious schools. actually have any presence on the internet, we can characterize many of the Muslim sites which do exist as 'alternatives' (Anderson 1996). That is, in the absence of sanctioned information from recognized institutions, Muslims are increasingly taking religion into their own hands. The internet provides them with an extremely useful medium for distributing information about Islam and about the behaviour required of a 'good Muslim'. Given that most of this discourse involves diaspora Muslims, much of the conversation on these information networks tends to be about how Muslims should deal with the various cultural phenomena which they encounter in, say, Los Angeles, Manchester or The Hague. There has also been a great effort to make the classic works of religious learning as widely available as possible. Numerous websites offer various translations of the Quran and the *hadith*, and also articles by prominent contemporary Muslim thinkers. Traditional spaces such as the mosque have also not gone untouched. In 1996, for example, the Muslim Parliament of Great Britain recommended that all mosques in the UK be wired up to the network in order to provide 'porn-free access to the internet and [to] establish places where Muslims can socialise in a *halal* [permissible] environment' ('British Mosques on the Superhighway' 1996).

The internet has also served to reinforce and reify the impact of print-capitalism on traditional structures and forms of authority.

Instead of having to go down to the mosque in order to elicit the advice of the local mullah, Muslims can now receive 'authoritative' religious pronouncements via the various e-mail *fatwa* services which have sprung up in recent months. The Sheikhs of al-Azhar are totally absent, but the enterprising young *'alim* who sets himself up with a colourful website in Alabama suddenly becomes a high-profile representative of Islam. Due to the largely anonymous nature of the internet, one can also never be sure whether the 'authoritative' advice received via these services is coming from a classically trained religious scholar or a hydraulic engineer moonlighting as an amateur *'alim*. As we noted above, however, the authority of the traditional scholars is not easily undermined. Many of them, especially in the Middle East, are highly charismatic and demand a loyal following which cannot easily be poached away by an unknown computer personality. And again, the impact of these services must be measured realistically, based on the number of Muslims who actually make use of them. However, it can perhaps be said that they are having a fairly significant effect with regard to those questions which concern the details of daily life for a Muslim in the West. Diaspora Muslims are likely to find it convenient to be able to turn to one of their own – someone who has also lived Western culture – so as to receive a hearing that is sympathetic and more in tune with local contexts.

More than anything else, the internet provides a space where Muslims, who often find themselves to be a marginalized or extreme minority group in many Western communities, can go in order to find others 'like them'. It is in this sense that we can speak of the internet as allowing Muslims to create a new form of imagined community, or a reimagined *ummah*: 'It is imagined because the members...will never know most of their fellow-members, meet them, or even hear of them, yet in the minds of each lies the image of their communion' (Anderson 1991: 6). Hence the various Islams of the internet offer a reassuring set of symbols and terminology which attempt to reproduce familiar settings and terms of discourse in locations far remote from those in which they were originally embedded. It is inevitable when such traditions travel that various processes of cultural translation are set in motion. The resulting syncretisms then give rise to new forms of Islam, each of which is redrawn to suit the unique set of socio-cultural contingencies into which it enters. This is what we mean when we speak of globalizing the local; or to be more precise, the globalization of cultural material which is then *re-localized* in new and distant contexts.

The internet in the Persian Gulf: localizing the global?

> This internet issue has made everything else pale into insignifi-
> cance. These networks are accessible to everyone; people can find
> political, security and pornographic materials, songs, films, and
> scenery there. Unfortunately, some of our officials do not pay
> attention to these things. I do not understand why they are so
> confused; why there is no logic to what they do; they are
> expanding these things. They should explain themselves.
>
> (Ayatollah Ahmad Jannati)

What happens, though, when the internet begins to spread into a region
of the world populated by societies whose normative orientation takes
strong issue with some of its content? The question of how globalization affects cultural dynamics in the Arab Gulf countries is extremely
salient here. We need first to note that the Gulf does not by any means
represent a parochial, primitive backwater. Rather it provides a fasci-
nating case for understanding how rapid influxes of technology and
industry impact upon traditional socio-cultural patterns and practices.
Gulf society is itself already something of a hybrid, a merger between
traditional norms and forms of social organization and the very latest
in modern technology. The region's affluence is the result of its crucial
role in world energy provision, and both of these factors have allowed
(if not forced) the Gulf to undergo rapid processes of industrialization
and modernization – processes which in other regions of the world
usually occur over the space of many generations rather than in just
over half a century. Given these circumstances it is inevitable that
tensions emerge between the traditional and the modern. For the most
part Gulf societies have demonstrated extreme flexibility and a willingness to exploit the latest trends in technology as well as the global
division of labour. The presence of an enormous Asian migrant labour
force is well known, and this phenomenon is prevalent at every level of
social structure in the Gulf. Among Bedouin tribes in Saudi Arabia, for
example, it is not uncommon to find camels being herded by a
Pakistani rather than by a local Arab – likewise the trappings of
modern technology. Bedouin in the UAE make extensive use of that
country's GSM mobile telephone network; globalization, it would
seem, has even found its way into the desert.

The arrival of the internet in the Gulf has been a complex affair.
There is a distinction to be drawn here between the availability of
internet access for a limited number of specialized research institutes,
and the availability of accounts to the wider public. Various universi-

ties and hospitals in the Gulf had internet gateways (often via Europe) during the early 1990s, but it is only since about 1995 that private accounts have started to appear in a few locations. The reasons for this are obvious. These countries are all ruled by conservative dynastic regimes which, to varying degrees, wield overwhelming editorial control over their respective media forums. This has meant that local political issues receive virtually no coverage except via the occasional heavily veiled wording in a newspaper. All magazines, television programmes, films and videos from abroad are censored, with any references to the Gulf and its various regimes removed unless unequivocally laudatory. Bare skin and alcohol advertising are also banned, as are sexually explicit or other religiously questionable materials. Several Gulf states, such as Kuwait and Qatar, have been experimenting with a certain modicum of free press and participatory politics. Even here, however, there are tacit parameters which are not to be transgressed. For the most part, Gulf Arab society remains closed.

What happens then with the advent of the internet, a medium which, by its very nature, is heavily resistant to any attempt at control, censorship, or regulation? Governments in the Gulf find themselves in something of a quandary. On the one hand they are as anxious to take advantage of the internet as they have been to make use of every other new form of technology; its scientific and educational potential have certainly not gone unnoticed in the Gulf. On the other hand they are worried about the perceived threat to their relatively closed societies. Pornography, sex, religious and political debate – all these things would suddenly be available to Gulf citizens. In addition, countries such as Saudi Arabia and Bahrain feel themselves under threat from exiled religious opposition groups who make use of the latest information technology to question the legitimacy of the regimes. The internet services offered by groups such as the Movement for Islamic Reform in Arabia (MIRA) and the Bahrain Freedom Movement (BFM) in London have in the past been aimed primarily at fellow countrymen abroad such as students and travelling businessmen. Internet access in the Gulf would provide these groups with a much-desired constituency which had previously been reachable only via the fax (al-Faqih 1997). The challenge, then, has been to reconcile these two concerns, that is, to get hooked up to the internet as everyone else seems to be doing, while at the same finding some sort of means to prevent citizens from accessing 'undesirable' information and images.

This latter problem has been circumvented by two main approaches. The first, as noted above, has been to severely limit internet access. Initially only specialized scientific and medical universities and research institutes were allowed onto the internet, and all material accessed was noted. This parallels the experience in Iran, where until early 1996 only higher education establishments could tap into the internet, and then only over a clogged, high-traffic route via Vienna. The second approach to internet control involves the installation of hardware and software safeguards which prevent users from accessing specific sites known to be 'bad'. The system operators keep a list of all banned locations on the central file server and any request for one of these sites by a user is refused. The websites of the various Gulf dissident organizations would, one might assume, be at the top of these lists. The enormous size of the internet tends to foil this method, however. Internet sites divide, multiply, and mirror themselves on a daily basis and it becomes impossible to keep track of where data is migrating on the internet. Hence also impossible to restrict access to all possible sites. Another method of censorship involves the computer actually searching all downloaded data, looking for references to banned keywords and scanning for graphic patterns that match those of naked bodies. This method, however, severely slows down one's connection to the internet and is likely to fail in its efforts as often as it is to succeed.

A combination of these methods has been used in those Gulf countries which do allow public access to the internet. The UAE's sole service provider Etisalat, for example, has installed a 'proxy-server system' which allows it to select the sites available to its users at any one time. The UAE is also negotiating with a British security company for the installation of an elaborate system which would allow police to monitor all requests for data sent by UAE internet accounts and would alert them whenever banned materials were requested by users (*IPS* 1997). Indeed, it is the availability of such systems which has convinced many Gulf countries to gradually phase in the availability of private internet access. Kuwait was first, followed by the UAE, Bahrain and Qatar. Oman went online in early 1997, but Saudi Arabia, the largest and most conservative of the Gulf states, continues to hesitate, with its advertised deadlines for the provision of private internet service constantly pushed back.

At this point it is too early to tell what the long-term impact of the internet will be on Gulf society. Its presence has, however, already provoked a number of telling incidents. Dubai's chief of police, Major General Dhahi Khalfan Tamim, has been vocal in emphasizing the need to control access to the internet, and has even found himself embroiled in a public feud with the service provider Etisalat, a rare occurrence in the Emirates. The conflict centred around the question of who possesses jurisdiction to issue licences for internet access. Dhahi claimed that the police and security forces were ultimately responsible for monitoring the flow of information in and out of the emirate, while the 60 per cent state-owned Etisalat insisted that its own expertise should have the deciding hand (*Reuters*, 18 June 1996). In other comments Dhahi has expressed fears about Israel trying to disrupt Arab countries using the internet, and has also recommended that the UAE follow the lead of Singapore in placing tight restrictions on internet access (*IPS* 1997). So it is difficult to read the politics behind an event such as the opening of the region's first internet café in Dubai. This enterprise, which brings the internet out into the open, can be understood in a number of ways. We might choose to see it as the popularization of the internet, as an indication that the internet has well and truly arrived in the Gulf. In this case its installation in a very public space, a shopping centre, represents a victory of consumer demand over state authority. Alternatively, however, we might just as easily read the situation as one of government intervention. This rendition would hold that state authorities sanctioned the establishment of an internet café precisely so that the network would be brought into the open. Instead of accessing the internet from the privacy of their own homes where government monitoring is more difficult, the café encourages potential users to go online in a very public setting. According to this logic people would be less likely to attempt to access questionable material in circumstances under which they are easily scrutinized.

The religious sector has also reacted to the arrival of the internet. Islamist deputies in Kuwait, for example, submitted a bill to that country's parliament which called on the government to be wary of 'sin-inducing' material on the internet which '[does] not suit our social values' (*Reuters*, 28 August 1996). The proposal also recommended that the government act swiftly to put control mechanisms in place. Two months later the Kuwaiti Ministry of Communications announced that it would regulate the country's main internet connection point. 'This operation', they announced, 'will give us full control of the internet in Kuwait, as well as full control of the necessary equipment. Anyone who wants to be an [internet service] provider will have to do so under certain conditions which we are currently drafting' (*Xinhua*, 4 November 1996). Although it is difficult to determine whether or not this new policy was prompted by the protests of the Islamist parliamentarians, their contemporaneous publicizing of the issue must certainly have been a factor.

In Iran users have been told that their e-mail has to comply with Islamic laws and traditions (Bogert 1995), and in the Arab Gulf countries the various regimes have worked to ensure that the internet feeds entering their societies are devoid of controversial and 'sinful' materials. By effectively reducing the content of the internet in this way and by heavily promoting their own Arabic-language sites, these countries manage to 'localize the global' to some degree. Recent plans to expand the region-specific GulfNet project is another pointer in this direction, an indication of how technologies from the 'outside' can be appropriated for purely local use. But this is only one side of the story. The arrival of networked forums such as the internet in the Gulf offers the possibility of something for which Arab Gulf society is becoming increasingly impatient: a modicum of civil society. 'We have agreed to ban sex, religion and politics on the internet to respect local laws', notes one user, 'but when someone downloads from North America and they discuss God, for example, the chatting continued and you learn something. The authorities can't do anything about this' (*Reuters*, 4 April 1996).

Spaces of public debate are few and far between in the region, with only a few of the countries only just cautiously easing back their tight controls over the media. The socio-economic situation in the Gulf, and especially in Saudi Arabia, is such that the citizens of these countries are increasingly coming to demand that they be treated *as* citizens; that is, that they be granted a certain degree of political rights. High levels of unemployment among recent graduates, for example, have spawned a generation which is largely disillusioned with the Sa'ud regime. Substantial numbers of young Saudis suddenly find themselves needing to criticize the government, but without any effective forum in which to do so. Inspired by exile groups such as the CDLR or MIRA, and by charismatic local *'ulama*, Islamist discourse is increasingly becoming their chosen language of protest. The regime is well aware of this potential instability, and hence it is very hesitant to give the Saudi population access to computer-mediated communication. Preventing users from downloading pornography and sinful texts from 'out there' is one thing; it will be far more difficult for governments to prevent their citizens from talking to each other. The vast majority of these populations have no interest in Western pornography. For them, problems closer to home are much more pressing. Open computer networks in the Gulf would provide a means by which local political issues could be discussed and debated, responses planned, and actions coordinated. For these people the internet offers a semblance of political civility, albeit somewhat different in form from the very specific model of 'civil society' which we derive from the Western tradition of political philosophy (Seligman 1992). If we contextualize the socio-political implications of Gulf internet use in this way, then the sense in which it represents a localization of the global starts to become clear.

It has become apparent that the encounter between Islam and the globalized technologies of communication is as multifaceted as the religion itself. The advent of globalization, it has been argued, must be understood as a culturally heterogenizing force just as much as it is seen as a source of homogeneity. In this regard we spoke of how globalization can lead to increased localization and vice-versa. In the case of Islam the nature of these processes depends upon where the Muslims concerned are situated. For diaspora Muslims, globalized communication means intermingling and dialogue between disparate local interpretations of what it means to be 'Islamic'. The politics of authenticity which inevitably ensue from this also serve to further fragment traditional sources of authority, such that the locus of 'real' Islam and the identity of those who are permitted to speak on its behalf becomes ambiguous. This is, in effect, the globalization of various local Islams. In the case of the Arab Gulf countries, however, a global force such as the internet is made local in two key ways. Official censorship tries to reduce its content such that it fits within the normative constraints of Gulf Muslim society; and at the same time various religio-political communities or movements in the Gulf may attempt to appropriate it as a form of 'digital civil society', perhaps explicitly in opposition to the various ruling regimes. In a sense, the dichotomy between these two identities, the global diaspora Muslim and the local Gulf Muslim, is false. Individuals can move fluidly between these roles, picking and choosing as convenient, emphasizing and de-emphasizing different identities as the situation demands. The globalization of information technology has undoubtedly had a strong impact on Muslim politics wherever they take place: It has provided Islamists with effective new tools with which to network, disseminate information and raise their profiles abroad. Increased interaction between various 'local' conceptions of Islam (as mediated by cultural, regional, and national traditions) also serves to emphasize the religion's inherent heterogeneity.

Conclusion

In order to come to a conclusion, we need to know to what extent the globalization of information technology provides a new framework within which Muslims can reimagine the *ummah*. First and foremost, it is important to recognize that with a medium such as the internet we are dealing with forms of 'virtual community' (Rheingold 1994). These are contexts in which indirect and distanciated relationships are sustained through computer-mediated communication. To invoke

Gibson's (1984) metaphor, participants in this kind of community are 'wrapped in media', such that one's corporeal existence becomes significantly de-emphasized. To what extent, though, is community created, or in this case re-created, within these contexts? On the nascent electronic frontier, it is perhaps most useful to understand community primarily as a *shared normative framework*. Community here is quite literally the product of communication; an active process. Contrast this with forms of community into which one is born or which can be 'made real' through the possession of a passport (e.g. ethnicity or nationality). Here, community is enacted through the creation of discourses based upon common modes of interpretation. This is illustrated by the fact that so many of today's virtual communities, MUDS, chat rooms, and Usenet, for example, tend to be organized according to specific themes or interests.[8] The 'order' of such worlds is often derived from the symbolic language of popular television shows, novels or films. There is no reason, therefore, why it would not be possible to develop forms of 'virtual *ummah*' whose discursive norms derive from an Islamic framework.[9]

Entry into the traditional *ummah* is, in theory, available to any individual willing to recognize the singularity of God and the prophethood of Muhammad. Historically, of course, this has not prevented the ruptures and schisms which characterize the history of any great world religion. What role could IT possibly play in unifying so polysemic a community?

Recalling our discussions above, we might envisage a virtual *ummah* playing several roles:

- Fostering social networks through which 'distanciated' Muslims can organize and communicate.
- Providing spaces for critical dialogue, debate about Islam and encounters with the Muslim 'other'. This function might be seen as comparable to that played by the diasporic mosque described by Fischer and Abedi (1992).
- Allowing Muslim political movements to locate and share resources.
- More generally, opening forums in which Muslims can find solidarity, support and like-minded people. Our discussion of Muslim diasporas on the internet above highlighted this aspect of the virtual *ummah*.

But to what extent would the original sense of the *ummah* as a new social paradigm be recreated; that is, as a form of community in which factional identities are subordinated to a greater religious whole? This aspect of the virtual *ummah* is the most problematic, but we might still want to speculate about computer-mediated communication permitting Muslims to transcend ethnic or national boundaries. If the 'common language' (or the most resonant discourse) found by a Muslim wandering through the internet is Islam rather than 'Malayness' or 'Iranianess', then to what extent might the religious aspects of her self-identity become reified?

What about politics within such a space? The internet began as a community with no centre and with no clear hegemony. As Lyon points out,

> Whatever the eventual trajectory of virtual communities, the extent to which they are able to be consequential will depend on how subjectivity and meaning are understood and mobilised within them. And if they are to be politically consequential, questions of access, participation and co-ordination would also have to be addressed.
>
> (Lyon 1997: 36)

Who would administrate the virtual *ummah*? Our earlier discussion has pointed to the fact that in the first few years of relatively widespread internet access it was the more peripheral countries of the Muslim world which hastened to create a virtual presence. As more and more 'official' organs of the Islamic world (e.g. the Organization of the Islamic Conference, the Muslim World League, etc.) come online, they may well seek to assert their hegemony in the virtual *ummah*. There has certainly been a temporary leavening effect, but for how long? Will the traditional centres and peripheries of the Muslim world simply reproduce themselves in cyberspace? The point must be made that virtual communities do not exist in a political or economic vacuum. Access to information technology requires resources in more than one sense. Prospective members of the virtual *ummah* would need both someone to pay for their internet access *and* someone to permit them the political liberty to actually make use of online resources. As we have seen in the case of the Gulf countries, this latter imperative is not always so easily secured.

Changes are undoubtedly taking place, however. Some writers, such as Dale Eickelman, speak of the onset of an Islamic Reformation. 'Increasingly in the Muslim world', he writes, 'religious beliefs are self-consciously held, explicitly expressed, and systematized. It is no longer sufficient simply to "be" Muslim and to follow Muslim practices. One must reflect upon Islam and defend one's views' (Eickelman 1998). Information technology and computer-mediated communication may serve to further radicalize this critical trend in that they allow greater numbers of people to take Islam into their own hands, opening new spaces for debate and critical dialogue. The complex nature of globalized information technology, however, ensures that there will always be extreme tensions within its effects on a given tradition. While information technology does in some senses offer the world's Muslims the capability to bridge the distances between them, it also furnishes Islam with a mirror to hold up to itself and an opportunity to gaze upon its many diverse faces.

Notes

1   Quran, Sura 2:43 – 'We have made you a community [*umma*] in the middle so that you may bear witness against mankind'. Ali and Arberry render 'in the middle' as, respectively, 'justly balanced' and 'just', a translation which I find dissatisfying since it ignores the spatial implications of the Arabic *wasat*, 'middle or centre'. Various interpretations regard this as implying that Islam is to be seen as a religion in between Christianity and Judaism (Montgomery Watt) or as the religion of Arabia which 'is in an intermediate position in the Old World' (Yusuf Ali). It may also refer to the mediatory position which Muhammad's community occupied in Medina.
2   See Quran, Sura 6:38.
3   There is an obvious link here to Benedict Anderson's concept of the 'imagined community' (Anderson 1991), and an even stronger echo can be found in some of his more recent writings (see Anderson 1994).
4   *Al-qur'an* means 'the recitation'.
5   This is a program which contains rules and guidelines which tell a computer how to process, 'think' and make decisions with particular sets of data. It is usually written in an artificial intelligence language such as PROLOG.
6   *Ijtihad* refers to independent judgements made through the interpretation and/or extrapolation of religious texts by scholars.
7   See, for example, *http://www.uoknor.edu/cybermuslims/cy_jihad.html*.
8   Multi-user Domains (MUDS) are virtual communities in which 'real' users assume the guise of a character or nickname. These communities often have elaborate infrastructures, sometimes emulating entire cities. Internet Relay Chat (IRC) allows users from all over the world to log into and 'chat' in real time on dozens of channels organized by topics of interest. Usenet is a complex electronic bulletin board on which users follow 'threads' of discussion in various newsgroups which are, again, organized according to different topics of interest.
9   In a Muslim MUD we might, for example, expect to see users adopting names which carry religious symbolism. Conversation and discussion would, presumably, take place according to Islamic discursive norms. The question of who gets to set those norms in any given context is, however, another set of issues altogether. One could easily imagine Shi'a-influenced MUDS competing with other, predominantly Sunni, domains.

References

Abu-Lughod, J. (1991) 'Going Beyond Global Babble', in Anthony D. King (ed.) *Culture, Globalization and the World-system*, London: Macmillan.

Abu-Lughod, L. (1997) 'Dramatic Reversals: Political Islam and Egyptian Television', in Joel Beinin and Joe Stark (eds) *Political Islam*, London: I. B. Tauris.

Anderson, B. (1991) *Imagined Communities*, revised edn, London: Verso.

——(1994) 'Exodus', *Critical Inquiry*, 20.

Anderson, J. (1995) ' "Cybarites", Knowledge Workers, and New Creoles on the Superhighway', *Anthropology Today*, 11.

——(1996) 'Islam and the Globalization of Politics', paper presented to the Council on Foreign Relations Muslim Politics Study Group, New York City: 25 June.

——(1997) 'Cybernauts of the Arab Diaspora: Electronic Mediation in Transnational Cultural Identities', paper presented at the Couch-Stone Symposium on 'Postmodern Culture, Global Capitalism and Democratic Action', University of Maryland, April.

Appadurai, A. (1990) 'Disjuncture and Difference in the Global Cultural Economy', in Mike Featherstone (ed.) *Global Culture: Nationalism, Globalization and Modernity*, London: Sage.

Atiyeh, G. N. (ed.) (1995) *The Book in the Islamic World: The Written Word and Communication in the Middle East*, Albany: SUNY Press.

al-Azmeh, A. (1997) *Islams and Modernities*, 2nd edn, London: Verso.

Bogert, C. (1995) 'Chat Rooms and Chadors', *Newsweek*, 21 August.

Bowen, J. R. (1993) *Muslims Through Discourse*, Princeton: Princeton University Press.

'British Mosques on the Superhighway', at *http://www.malaysia.net/muslimedia/*, 30 June 1996.

Calhoun, C. (1991) 'Indirect Relationships and Imagined Communities: Large-scale Social Integration and the Transformation of Everyday Life', in Pierre Bourdieu and James S. Coleman (eds) *Social Theory for a Changing World*, Boulder: Westview Press.

Cohen, M. (1996) 'Modern Times: Islam on the Information Highway', *Far Eastern Economic Review*, 29 August.

Cole, R. (1997) 'Islamic Terrorists Organize, Raise Funds in U.S. while Plotting Attacks', *Associated Press*, 24 May.

Eickelman, D. F. (1989) 'National Identity and Religious Discourse in Contemporary Islam', *International Journal of Islamic and Arabic Studies*, vol. 6, 1–20.

——(1998) 'Inside the Islamic Reformation', *Wilson Quarterly*, vol. 22, 80–9.

Eickelman, D. F. and Piscatori, J. (1996) *Muslim Politics*, Princeton: Princeton University Press.

Evans, K. (1996) 'Thoroughly Modern Mullahs', *Guardian*, 16 March.

al-Faqih, S. (1997) Personal interview. London: March.

Featherstone, M. (ed.) (1990) *Global Culture. Nationalism, Globalization and Modernity*, London: Sage.

Fischer, M. M. J. and Abedi, M. (1990) *Debating Muslims: Cultural Dialogues in Postmodernity and Tradition*, Madison: University of Wisconsin Press.

Gibson, William (1984) *Neuromancer*, New York: ACE.

Giddens, A. (1991) *Modernity and Self-identity*, Cambridge: Polity Press.

IPS (1997) Internet Provider Service.

Jones, S. G. (ed) (1995) *CyberSociety: Computer-Mediated Communication and Community*, London: Sage.

King, A. D. (ed.) (1991) *Culture, Globalization and the World-System*, London: Macmillan.

Lapidus, I. (1988) *A History of Islamic Societies*, Cambridge: Cambridge University Press.

Lyon, D. (1997) 'Cyberspace Sociality: Controversies over Computer-mediated Relationships', in Brian D. Loader (ed.) *The Governance of Cyberspace*, London: Routledge.

MacFarquhar, N. (1996) 'With Mixed Feelings, Iran Tiptoes to the Internet', *New York Times*, 8 October.

al-Mass'ari, M. (1995 and 1997) personal interviews, London, June 1995, March 1997.

MEED (1996) 'Region Joins the Global Revolution', *MEED Special Report*, 1 March.

Rathmell, A. (1997) 'Netwar in the Gulf', *Jane's Intelligence Review*, January, 29–32.

Rheingold, H. (1994) *The Virtual Community*, London: Minerva.

Robertson, R. (1992) *Globalization: Social Theory and Global Change*, London: Sage.

Robinson, F. (1993) 'Islam and the Impact of Print', *Modern Asian Studies*, vol. 27, 229–51.

Roff, W. R. (ed.) (1987) *Islam and the Political Economy of Meaning*, London: Croom Helm.

Ruthven, M. (1995) 'The West's Secret Weapon against Islam', *Sunday Times*, 1 January.

Sardar, Z. (1993) 'Paper, Printing and Compact Disks: The Making and Unmaking of Islamic Culture', *Media, Culture and Society*, VOL. 15, 43–59.

Saudi Gazette (1994) 'Bin Baz Calls on Muslims to Ignore Bulletins Seeking to Split Their Ranks', 12 November.

5 Islam and human rights in the age of globalization

Mahmood Monshipouri

In the last quarter of the twentieth century, human interactions have become deeply immersed in a global context brought about by sweeping technological, political, cultural and socioeconomic changes. Of the many factors that have contributed to these changes, the most eminently visible ones are: the liberalization of access to information and the transmission of ideas via electronic media; the interconnection of economies through international finance; the linking of social problems and ecological concerns made possible by improving information technology; and the growth of global normative standards and rules, particularly those concerned with international human rights. The result has been *globalization*, or the emergence of a 'fluid' international political order.

This new order has called for a drastic paradigm shift in thinking about the operative variables of contemporary international relations. Although it is hard to predict what the future holds, it is obvious that globalization has thus far met with cultural resistance in many parts of the world. In particular, globalization has posed myriad challenges to the Muslim world's ethical and cultural constructs, and resurrected, in the process, charges of Western cultural imperialism and rationalist hubris. In addition to resisting the cultural and normative hegemony of the West, some in the Muslim world question the wisdom of integration into a world market system with uncertain prospects.

Globalization can be described in several ways; the two most pervasive are, first, an evolutionary process of change driven by technological and scientific progress in the postmodern era; and second, a new hegemonic system upheld by the world's major capitalist economies of the post-Cold War world to promote their own political and economic interests. It is the latter that is widely regarded by Muslims as a menace to their cultural authenticity, solidarity, and even survival. Much of the backlash against globalization in the Muslim world assumes cultural forms, even though many criticisms are also being couched in economic and ecological terms.

Closely related to such cultural concerns is the notion of the internationalization of human rights. The specific issue addressed in this chapter is the impact on Islamic ethical perspectives of this growing worldwide concern over human rights. In order to analyse this issue, I shall begin by addressing the Muslim world's cultural concerns against the backdrop of globalization. I shall then turn to this chapter's central theme that Muslim scholars view Islamic normative perspectives as an alternative to a Eurocentric model of globalization. Finally, I shall explore the extent to which globalization supports the emergence of international moral standards that transcend the national boundaries of Muslim countries.

Globalization: an evolutionary process of change

As an all-inclusive process, globalization dictates a rethinking of politics, religion, economics, gender roles, and the relation of the human sociosphere to the ecological biosphere (Peterson *et al.* 1999). The globalization of recent years has encompassed conflicting forces, both neo-liberal (economic processes) and democratic (political and social processes) (Mittelman 1996). The neo-liberal economic process, as supported by the International Monetary Fund and the World Bank, has undermined governments' capacity to pursue certain social and economic policies, and has left citizens' socioeconomic demands unmet. The poor and other excluded classes have become the victims of the immediate costs of reform under the banner of structural adjustment (Monshipouri 1997). In some Muslim countries, such as Algeria and Turkey, the failure of neo-liberal policies, along with the inability of the state to uphold core religious values, has provoked an Islamic revivalist backlash.

Islamists' active involvement in development has filled a void in national development (Mittelman and Pasha 1997: 95). It has also given credence to the idea that the struggle for civil-political rights and democracy cannot be disconnected from the quest for socioeconomic rights. Some market economies protect civil-political rights but abuse social, economic and cultural rights (Falk 1995: 131). The market logic of globalization-from-above shows minimal attentiveness to its adverse human and environmental side effects (Falk 1995: 199). Market economies are not concerned with combating the evils of child malnutrition, epidemic diseases and widespread illiteracy in the Third World.

Free markets are designed to respond not to basic needs but to the interests and demands of those with 'market power', namely those with income, wealth and information. Hence market economies have the capacity to generate gross socioeconomic inequalities (Donnelly 1995: 249). Heavily dependent on market expansion, globalization deepens existing socioeconomic divisions and stratification, and promotes those market freedoms that are not necessarily 'geared toward social justice or wide political participation' (Ghai 1999: 247). Given that civil and political rights alone do not guarantee the fulfilment of economic, social and cultural rights, the economic freedom of the marketplace can be as much a threat to human rights as is political repression (Ghai 1999).

Furthermore, neo-liberal globalization creates enormous personal insecurity and a moral vacuum. Although the Muslim world has resisted unfettered neo-liberal globalization, it has embraced certain aspects of it for fear of becoming marginalized. Integration into the global economy has in turn resurrected the old fear of the Muslim world, namely that in such a globalized economy, key decisions affecting the vast majority of people throughout the world would be made by the 'core' Western countries, multinational corporations, the International Monetary Fund, the World Bank, big power summits and international business bodies (Icbiyo 1993).

These fears are exacerbated by the perception that state autonomy *vis-à-vis* the global economy would recede to insignificance. Some of these fears are exaggerated. Others are not. David Potter makes a poignant observation concerning such overstated fears: 'as markets and economic relations are becoming increasingly globalized, all states are not becoming correspondingly less important in terms of their autonomy' (Potter 1992: 232). Even where state autonomy is minimal in relation to the international flow of capital, he adds, 'state power has been and remains absolutely essential in that global context' (Potter 1992: 232). This is because, as Potter reminds us, states monitor territories, build infrastructure, and educate and control the labour force. Additionally, states continue to perform such political functions as security and stability for those who largely benefit from the global economy (Potter 1992). Whether or not the fears of individual states are justified, the gap between broadly based social movements and political leadership has widened, and too often internal opposition to states has intensified in the wake of the latter's inability to deal with national problems. The rise of Islamic groups to social and political prominence has been partially attributed to globalization.

Reinforcing Islamic revivalism

Broadly speaking, Islamic revivalism is a response to the failure of secular nationalists and the modern state to protect their people, both culturally and materially. More specifically, the socioeconomic failures of Muslim countries have led the marginalized segments of civil society to rebel against the state, using religion as a catalyst for mobilization and resistance (Ayubi 1999: 91). A broad consensus holds that this resistance is not about political economy alone; rather, social, cultural and religious factors have figured prominently in the rise of Islamism.[1] The high profile of Islam since the 1970s, it is argued, is not only about winning political power, but it is also widely concerned with the survival and durability of Islamic beliefs and moral codes in alien or modernizing societies (Haynes 1999: 254).

The revivalist Islamic trend in North Africa and the Middle East has symbolized Muslim leaders' search for the cultural legitimization of their political and economic goals and strategies (Deng 1993: 108). Multiple political, economic and social crises have collectively provided the necessary milieu for the growth of political religion (Haynes 1999: 242). The resurgence of Islamism has provided a cultural sustenance to Muslims who have suffered from the negative effects of economic liberalization. Put differently, resistance to neo-liberal globalization has assumed a cultural form (Pasha and Samatar 1996: 187–201).

Cultural resistance to neo-liberal globalization has become drastically visible throughout the world, and is likely to stand as a symbol of protest in years ahead. Decades of modernization and social change in the Muslim world, principally along the Western model, have simultaneously created economic integration into the global economy and cultural fragmentation from the West. Annabelle Sreberny-Mohammadi puts the problematic nature of the global diffusion of modernity this way:

> modernity has created a paradoxical global unity which remains deeply problematic in its patterns of inequality and domination. Yet it may also hold some opportunity. A recognition of the many inextricable linkages that bind us is part of an emergent global consciousness that might just do some good.
>
> (Sreberny-Mohammadi 1997: 68)

The acknowledgement of a common humanity manifests itself in many ways. In the Muslim world, for instance, it has appeared in the form of conflicting demands for autonomy, equity, justice and unity by various groups (Deng 1993: 109).

The future of globalization is controversial and inconclusive. Many questions regarding the nature, effects and implications of globalization remain unresolved. Reflecting on uncertainties surrounding the globalization process, Michael Smith writes, 'the global system is changing, but there is no certainty about the direction of change or the kind of world it will produce' (Smith 1992: 267). A characteristic feature of the twenty-first century, Smith adds, is the uneasy coexistence of centralization and fragmentation, of nationalism and transnationalism, and of the traditional and the modern.

One observer views globalization as the present-day 'dominant cultural ecology', whose international communication networks and intellectual-cultural power will keep the centrality of the United States and a few European powers at the top in political, military and economic affairs (Mowlana 1993: 414). This globalizing process inevitably promotes inequality within such cultural systems as Islam and others in the Third World. Linking the rise of Islamic revivalism to such a global dominance, Mowlana argues that as the dominant Western powers control

> the ability to create the norms and institutions of the international economic and political systems, the so-called *retribalized* and *nomadic* politics of other cultures in the form of states, institutions, and groups will be released in response to submerged cultural tendencies in changing societies.
>
> (Mowlana 1993: 414)

Globalization: a democratic or hegemonic system?

Democratic globalization is likely to pressurize Muslim states into initiating political reforms. In the 1980s and 1990s, Muslim countries have officially recognized certain international human rights conventions. More than half of the Middle Eastern and North African countries have ratified the International Covenant on Civil and Political Rights and the International Covenant on Economic, Social and Cultural Rights. Only one country in the Muslim world (Saudi Arabia) has neither ratified nor signed a single international human rights convention.

As for democratization measures, the Muslim world has uniformly lagged behind. The fact remains that seeking a democratic alternative to authoritarian regimes is bound to complicate the tasks of ruling regimes in the Muslim world. As the challenge to maintain and institutionalize democracy intensifies, the Muslim world will not be immune to such democratizing pressures. Those Muslim leaders who fear the globalization of democracy and its consequences view such pressures as a new attempt by the West to meddle in their internal affairs.

Evidence suggests that the West often uses the human rights argument to justify hostile policies toward governments with which it fundamentally differs. Similarly, a country's poor human rights record may scarcely present a problem for the establishment of close relations. Turkey's dismal treatment of its Kurdish citizens has not threatened military, economic, or political support to that country (Hunter 1998: 25). Nor has Saudi Arabia's closed society been much of a hurdle to close relations with the West, 'provided that the external behaviour of that country does not threaten Western interests or have the potential to become a competition on a regional or an international level' (Hunter 1998: 26).

Nevertheless, the global resurgence of democracy has posed a powerful challenge to Muslim countries, especially those with a multi-ethnic fabric, such as Indonesia, Iran, Iraq, Lebanon, Malaysia, Nigeria, Pakistan, Sudan and Turkey. Furthermore, the spread of information and education about universal human rights, coupled with the global democratic revolution, has placed immense external pressures on states to adjust to emerging normative standards. It is in this area that Muslim countries feel under siege by the West. The post-Cold War imposition by Western countries of the new cultural values and norms, often couched in human rights terms or free-market parlance, has further intensified the cultural debate between the Muslim and Western worlds.

Although the number of economic transactions with the secular West is very likely to increase indefinitely, cultural divisions and tensions between the two worlds point to a variety of seemingly problematic situations. The emergence of Islamic political movements as a challenge to Western cultural influence has been accompanied by an Islamic ideological framework, one that is potentially capable of providing a competing alternative to Western values and institutional forces.

In the Third World, says Robert W. Cox , there is evidence that 'people are turning their backs on the state and international organizations, which they see as their enemies rather than as possible supports' (Cox 1996: 27). Cox has argued that this tendency is 'accompanied by a resurgent affirmation of identity (defined by, for instance, religion, ethnicity, or gender) and an emphasis on locality rather than wider political authorities' (Cox 1996: 27). Viewed from this perspective, globalization has redrawn new road maps in the minds of identity-conscious individuals, raising a whole set of new human rights issues in the postmodern era.

An intensification of the debate on human rights

Before analysing the various impacts that globalization has on the state of human rights in the Muslim world, a brief description of Islamic ethical views is essential. The normative and theological bases underpinning Islamic perspectives emphasize human duties and moral obligations. According to Islam, rights are entirely owned by God. Moral obligations to other persons and peoples take precedence over individual human rights. This ethical construct is built around a *collective* ideology or social ethics of protecting the underprivileged in the Muslim community. For Muslims, *sharia* (Islamic law) is the source of human rights. It emanates from the pure law of God and differs fundamentally from Roman law. The divine origin of *sharia*, which is based on revelation not manmade law, makes it virtually immutable.

Since the mid-twentieth century, the differences between classical Islamic law and the modern interpretations of *sharia* have deepened. The modern Islamic scholars see a clear association between universal human rights standards and Islamic ethical constructs. They argue that Muslims should distinguish between Western hegemonic rule and the universality of human rights. While embracing social change and 'cultural modernity', they defend a legitimate form of cultural relativity.

Modern and reformist Islamic groups concede to several claims made by the advocates of international human rights. They agree, for example, that there is a widespread consensus, in both theoretical and practical terms, on certain fundamental standards of humanity and human dignity. This consensus has made it implausible to place the blame on a Western hegemonic agenda or the globalization process. No longer can *Western* roots or origins of those norms forfeit their legitimacy.

The globalizing pressures have refocused the world's attention on such marginalized groups as women, minorities and the poor. Hence the increasing worldwide attention to gender rights, the rights of minorities and indigenous people, and the right to development. The issue of the persecution of religious minorities, such as Ahmediyas (Pakistan), Baha'is (Iran and Tunisia), Coptic Christians (Egypt and Sudan), Jews (Syria and Yemen), and the Al-Arqam group (Malaysia), has received substantial international exposure by mass media. A systematic campaign by the Malaysian government to eliminate the Al-Arqam group and ban its publications since August 1994 has precluded engaging this group in the processes of the 'cultural mediation' of human rights. The government essentially has denied them the reality of the cultural diversity of an increasingly globalized world (An-Na'im 1999).

Perhaps the most daunting challenge facing Islamic law is the international outcry against its treatment of apostasy (repudiating one's faith) and heresy (dissenting from or denial of an established religious belief or doctrine). The sentence of the death penalty for apostasy or blasphemous speech is contrary to internationally recognized standards of international human rights laws that give individuals the right to free exercise of religion. The legality of the death edict (*fatwa*) against Salman Rushdie remains highly problematic. Although international law is less clear on the specific subject of internal religious pluralism, it emphatically denies the purported right of religious orthodoxy to punish heresy and dissension by criminal sanction or any form of physical or psychological intimidation.[2]

The debate regarding 'gender relations' has also assumed a renewed importance in the wake of the global spread of information and education about human rights. If anything, the emancipatory force of globalization has resulted in changing attitudes about gender roles, expectations and possibilities, with profound implications for gender empowerment and the reduction of domestic violence.[3] The Muslim world is, now more than ever, under burgeoning pressure to come to grips with such external standards as women's human rights. Consider, for example, the growing debate in the Muslim world over the *diyeh* or blood money: the amount payable for injuries inflicted to a woman is half that for injuring a male. Increasingly, the traditional rationale behind such gender distinctions is called into question by reformist movements and the media in Muslim countries (*Iran Times*, 4 June 1999: 4).

With regard to the right to development, the prevailing view among Muslims is that such a right is reassuring and, indeed, indispensable for the enjoyment of other rights. The realization of the right to development, it is widely believed, hinges on necessary structural transformations. The willingness of the rich countries of the North to support such transformations is doubtful, at best (Eide 1992: 26). The UN Declaration on the Right to Development (1986) links the right to development to a broad implementation of human rights and fundamental freedoms, reaffirming that respect and protection of individual rights is essential in order to achieve development (Eide 1992: 26). In the 1990s, the right to development has been increasingly linked to the ability of indigenous peoples to improve their standard of living. Development, some analysts observe, ought to take the form of *ethnodevelopment* (Stavenhagen (1992: 148). The recognition of such a right in the wake of an upsurge in ethnonationalistic sentiment among minority groups such as the Kurds will have profound implications for some Middle Eastern countries.

Competing tendencies: the politics of culture

The present-day Muslim world is organized around a nation-state system characterized by wide ranging political, historical and local circumstances. These states differ not only in their political and economic orientations but also in their ideological commitment to Islam. Paradoxically, but understandably, a new element in the religion/state debate is the growing salience of the state in processes of globalization and modernization at the turn of the century (Beeley (1992: 310). The fact remains, Brian Beeley notes, that 'Islam *can* replace nationalism as a basis for legitimacy and allegiance *if* it is permitted to do so by individuals, groups and states, but it shows no sign of replacing the state' (Beeley (1992: 310).

There are also splits among Muslims over the question of whether or not to adjust to the transitional state of global politics. While some accept a compromise with non-Islamic Western values, institutions and practices, others seek to reaffirm the traditional pattern of Islam. These differences separate individuals (or groups) as much as states (Beeley (1992: 300). They also reflect the struggle in the Muslim world over authoritative definitions of cultural meaning and symbols. This struggle has been called a 'politics of culture' in an arena where power interests assert competing claims to cultural constructs such as labels, ideals and symbols that are highly valued in Muslim communities (Anderson *et al.* 1998: 145). It is within this context that I shall identify varying reactions to globalization in the Muslim world.

Conservatives: the localizers

Islamic conservatives (whether orthodox or extremist) look to both classical and medieval periods of Islam for their worldview. They oppose the influence of Western ideas, practices and institutions. They view Islam as an immutable and perfect religion that transcends time and space (Husain 1995). Conservatives are opposed to modern secular – Western or socialist – ideas, practices and values. They are keen on the creation of the Islamic state ruled by the *sharia*, and support the execution of a constitution that is compatible with Islam (Husain 1995: 156).

Both orthodox and extremists have objected to at least two Articles of the Universal Declaration of Human Rights (UDHR): Articles 16 and 18. Article 16-1 states that

> Men and women of full age, without any limitation due to race, nationality or religion, have the right to marry and to found a

family. They are entitled to equal rights as to marriage, during marriage and at its dissolution.[4]

Conservatives object to the provisions on women's rights, questioning the equality of gender roles, obligations and judgements. In short, equality of marriage rights is negated. Islam, they argue, prohibits the marriage of a Muslim woman to a non-Muslim man.

Conservatives also question the universality of Article 18:

Every one has the right to freedom of thought, conscience and religion; this right includes freedom to change his (or her) religion or belief, and freedom, either alone or in community with others and in public or private, to manifest his religion or belief in teaching, practice, worship and observance.[5]

The freedom of religion and the right to change one's religion, according to conservatives, are against Islamic traditions. Apostasy (*ridda*), they stress, clearly presents a danger of falling away from Islamic guidance. Proselytizing among Muslims is forbidden and apostasy is a capital offence. In most parts of the Muslim world, including Iran, Egypt, Pakistan and Sudan, amendments have been introduced into constitutions that make apostasy punishable by death (Esposito and Voll 1996: 72–3, 188). This treatment of individuals falls foul of modern-day human rights standards.

Conservatives advocate a strong version of cultural relativism, one that is closer to a dogmatic view of the established truth. They accept an unmitigated Islamic vision in which political and socioeconomic equality of the sexes is unnatural. They emphasize equivalency – not equality – of the particular functions and duties that male and female members perform. Such fixed interpretations of gender relationships from the language of the Quran have invited controversies and debates from some quarters in the Muslim world. In recent years, the status of women in matters relating to marriage, divorce and child support has improved largely because of the modernization of the Islamic law.

Secular and modernizing pressures continue to pose powerful challenges to conservatives. Conservatives are especially wary of globalization, which they view in much the same manner as modernization, that is, as a ploy projected by the West upon the rest of the world. They contend that globalization is bent on homogenizing indigenous cultures, and that it is a form of cultural invasion by images, consumerism, television and video (Hetata 1998: 289). This view is shared by many Muslims who argue that the North, under the cloak of globalization, intends to appropriate the culture of the South, instead of letting the people in the South speak for themselves (Hetata 1998: 289).

Conservatives assert that the Islamic community paradigm, based on *tawhid* (the unity of God, human beings and universe), provides meaning and spirit to life and action, and cannot be subordinated to the notion of the information society paradigm and the emerging global information community.[6] The Islamic notion of community, or *ummah*, is a universal society with inclusive membership but binding commitment to Islam. The *ummah*, Mowlana writes, 'acknowledges and respects diversity but it emphasizes unity' (Mowlana 1993: 405). Explaining Muslims' apprehension about the forces of globalization, Mowlana notes that the Muslim world today is incorporated into a global order that enhances its fragmentation, but not its integration into a unified community (Mowlana 1993: 407).

Globalization is regarded as closely tied to broader Western political, ideological and commercial interests. In short, it is synonymous with Western global hegemony in the post-Cold War world. Thus understood, globalization is construed as another form of 'Westoxification' aimed at provoking religio-political conflicts in the Muslim world (Ayubi 1999: 71–3). Because globalization promotes an international capital system with an impoverished, marginalized and fragmented periphery, the marginalized masses are likely to seek solutions in the new religiously based appeals (Randall 1999: 50).

Conservatives flatly deny the universal validity of a global moral vision or a global culture based on Western values and ideals. In this sense, they can be truly called 'localizers', that is to say, those who foster the application of authentic Islamic beliefs, values and traditions. Conservatives generally consist of Islamic scholars, learned theologians, ideologues and leaders. Hassan al-Banna (1906–49), Ayatollah Ruhollah Khomeini (1902–89), Muhammad Zia-ul-Haq (1924–88), and some factions within the Iranian clerical establishment represent this tendency within the Muslim world.

Modernists: the semi-integrationists

Islamic modernists call for the *Islamization* of discourse, while seeking a fit between modern and traditional Islamic constitutions. They hold the view that Islamic civilization can at all times be reconstructed, reinvented and renewed. Revivalism, they insist, is an integral part of the Islamic tradition (Eickelman and Piscatori 1996). It follows then that not only can modernization be Islamic, but that it must be distinguished from a type of modernization that excludes Islam, or components of it, in favour of Western alternatives like secularism (Beeley 1992: 310). Clearly, the modernization experience in non-Western societies has generated contradictory results. For one thing, it has revived traditional loyalties and affiliations to ethnic and religious groups. For another, as Jeff Haynes points out, it has demonstrated that 'popular faith in progress, via secular modernization, has widely collapsed' (Haynes 1999: 247).

Islamic modernists do not adhere to cultural relativism as closely as do Islamic conservatives. They seem reluctant to question its validity altogether, however. They invoke democratic concepts and ethical constructs within the Islamic tradition, including *ijtihad* (independent reasoning), *shura* (consultation), *ijma* (consensus of the *'ulama*, the religious scholars), and *baya* (holding the leaders to certain standards of accountability). These social and ethical constructs demand democratic accountability and respect for social justice on the part of the authorities.

Islamic modernists view religious resistance to secularization as *legitimate*, calling into question the rationalist arrogance and moral superiority associated with Western experiences. They tend to rely largely on Islamic ethical and cultural constructs to challenge the Western understanding of secular modernization. Taking a critical view of the individualistic ethos of Western moral philosophy, modernists advocate an Islamic model of the good society that is based on collective and communitarian norms and structures. Modernists, who share some of the conservatives' sceptical views regarding globalization, display considerable flexibility towards globalization, but raise legitimate questions about what drives it. They suggest that if what lies behind globalization is an attempt to construct a moral discourse to justify foreign intervention and domination, then the human rights discourse is bound to be seen 'as yet another implement for the Americanization of world culture' (Saif 1994: 61).

Aware of the hegemonic undercurrents of globalization, Muslim modernists seek a renegotiation of the new global order. They reserve the right to participate in the globalization process, leaving open the possibility of retrenchment, especially when globalization is seen as a menace to their cultural survival. To the extent that they attempt to strike a balance between nationalist and integrationist goals, Islamic modernists are referred to as 'semi-integrationist'. Contemporary examples of modernists include Muhammad Abduh (1849–1905), Muhammad Iqbal (1873–1938), Ali Shariati (1933–77), Ayatollah Hussein-Ali Montazeri, Hassan Turabi, and the current Iranian President Mohammad Khatami.

Liberals: the globalizers

Islamic liberals (or revisionists) are mainly concerned with altering the link between culture and human rights. They consider a 'weak' form of cultural relativism acceptable, one that tolerates cultural diversity but not at the expense of universal human rights. Liberals insist on modifying or rejecting those cultural traditions that, in their view, are contradictory to modern international human rights standards. Cultural traditions are seen as socially constructed and thus subject to change. Some Islamic liberals espouse the idea of joining the global civilization, arguing that Islamic civilization *cannot* be reconstructed. To achieve objectives such as sustainable development and democratic governance requires, Muslim liberals insist, that we seek a global civil society based on shared assumptions, norms and social interactions.

Also known as Muslim universalists, liberals have noted that the values associated with Western civilization, not Westernization or modernization, merit global attention. Today, they add, the Western world's values such as liberty, equality and fraternity, are easily *universalizable* (Mozaffari 1998). Far from challenging Western civilization, Muslim liberals call for submission to it (Mozaffari 1998: 44). Liberals assert that Muslim thinkers and intellectuals must embrace this universal civilization, while seeking ways to improve it with their contribution and participation (Mozafffari 1998: 45). It is in this sense that liberals have come to be known as the so-called 'globalizers' in the Muslim world.

Islamic liberals argue that concepts such as *shura*, *ijma*, *ijtihad* and *baya* do not collectively amount to a viable theory of government, and that there appears to be no alternative to reconciling Islamic moral constructs with international human rights norms (An-Na'im 1998). Some liberals, such as Iranian philosopher Abdu-Karim Soroush, have called for the separation of religion and politics. Advocating a vibrant civil society and a pluralistic political rule, Soroush calls into question the clerics' monopoly over the interpretation of what constitutes the truth (Soroush 1993). Others, like Sudanese-born American professor of law Abdullahi Ahmed An-Na'im, have maintained that *sharia* must be reconciled with the realities of modern multi-religious nation-states, and that since *sharia* is a 'historically-conditioned *human* interpretation of the fundamental sources of Islam, alternative, modern interpretations are possible' (An-Na'im 1995: 59).

Islamic liberals advocate a paradigm shift in Islamic thinking, calling for Islam to adapt its norms and moral principles to those of international human rights standards. They call for the renegotiation of gender relations, contending that the combination of the new international division of labour and the global telecommunications revolution demands new social norms, such as gender equality within the Muslim world. Women's access to resources of participation in the larger society has been assisted by several factors, including, but not limited to, the growing necessity for more women to earn a cash income, the market expansion in women-oriented and women-run social and political movements, the rise in demand for female literacy levels, and the concern with population planning and its effects on national economic goals (Weiss 1994: 128–31). In short, Muslim liberals see globalization as a liberalizing process with palpable consequences for gender relations. While seeking its emancipatory features, liberals warn about its economic and political implications, such as an uneven distribution of wealth and benefits, as well as the reign of multinational corporations.

The expanding global ethical space

Modern technological and communication revolutions have created a new global awareness by enabling individuals to leapfrog time and space. This, along with a growing respect for human rights, has given credence to universal standards transcending national boundaries and interests (Peterson *et al.* 1999: 38–9). There is an unprecedented consensus around the notion that international human rights represent, in the most basic sense, ethical dimensions of an evolving global culture. There are, however, some disagreements over, first, whether politics remain primary to the future normative synthesis of such a global culture; and second, whether religion is relevant to the emerging global culture.

The common good of both humanity as a whole and of the planet itself requires the renegotiation of principles and procedures between and among groups, cultures, nations, religions and civilizations that constitute the global civil society. This renegotiation, some experts observe, is premised on the idea that 'new inclusiveness recognizes universal principles while allowing for cultural distinctiveness' (Peterson *et al.* 1999: 67). In such circumstances, the considerations of local cultures must be adjusted to the realities of an emerging global civil society.

It is important to recall that attempts to define proper human rights standards have been stimulated by both the Muslim diaspora and local elements (Ahmed and Donnan 1994: 7). Human rights are not only entitlements emanating from the principles of justice, but are also integral parts of the construction of indigenous identities and claims for self-determination (Wilson 1997: 23). The globalization process has forced some dramatic changes upon traditional cultures, raising issues for Muslims that can no longer be ignored. Muslims are compelled to engage with and respond to these issues (Ahmed and Donnan 1994: 17). Muslim responses to the Rushdie Affair and the Gulf War have been reactions based more on anger and passion than on reflection and pragmatism. The result, as Akbar Ahmed and Hastings Donnan remind us, has been a 'more pronounced polarization in the Muslim world, one which creates a disjunction between radical Islam and the West' (Ahmed and Donnan 1994: 17).

Some human rights scholars note that although a global communication space already exists, and that this has direct and definitive normative implications, a global ethical space is still evolving. The trend towards this shared global ethical space is irreversible (Meyer 1998: 215). This trajectory, as William H. Meyer so aptly reminds us, should not obscure the fact that 'defining and applying global standards of human rights are ultimately political acts. Politics is the primary sphere for future normative synthesis at the global level' (Meyer 1998: 215). The question of which values are to be included in or excluded from this emerging global culture is a political question rather than a matter of philosophical debate over the definition of rights (Meyer 1998: 216).

Regarding the role of religion in this emerging culture, it is important to note that the intensification of religious faith, largely a response to secularization in the Muslim world, has generated distinctly Islamic responses to the new forces of change and modernity (Esposito 1988). As noted earlier, modernization has *not* led to a decline of religion; rather, it has spawned powerful movements of counter-secularization. Alternatively, secularists and Islamists have come under pressure to find a way to coexist. This need for pragmatism is especially felt in the realm of human rights. Human rights, by virtue of their *humanness*, cannot and should not be separated from the secular sphere. Islamists' choice need not be relegated to either the rejection or toleration of secularists; rather, their task must be to create a workable balance between cultural integrity and universal civility.[7]

Such a middle ground will also do much to narrow the gap between the Muslim world's ethics and those of the West, minimizing the likelihood of cultural tensions between the two. Cultural differences, even if irreconcilable at points, do not necessarily translate into a conflict of civilization. The dialogue between and among civilizations is desirable and, indeed, imperative. In fact, globalization has increasingly become a symbol of bridge-building civilizational dialogue. The rhetoric that perpetuates the reductionism of the 'Islamic threat' myth or the 'clash of civilizations' paranoia will only inhibit progress that would be beneficial for all (Esposito and Voll 1996: 32). As is becoming strikingly clear at the beginning of a new millennium, the Muslim world and the West live in an interconnected world; they both have the necessary moral resources and the means to contribute to the construction of a new international moral order.[8]

Conclusion

The challenges posed by globalization are varied and many. So too are the opportunities and paradoxes that it creates. Globalization entails many contradictory trends and implications. This chapter has been primarily concerned with the cultural dimension of such consequences, arguing that globalization tends to both revitalize certain aspects of indigenous cultures and traditions, and to raise problems for other aspects. The ramifications of the globalization process as such are worth exploring.

In some cases, globalization has given a renewed vitality to the meaning of group and ethnic identity, broadening the appeal of Islamic revivalism. To the extent that globalization is equated with Western cultural domination, its underlying rationale is certain to come under attack in the Muslim world. It is true that 'religion has certainly not been shrinking in sociopolitical significance in the Third World' (Haynes 1999: 242). But it is also true that globalization has diffused certain effects and values. The increasing acknowledgement of democratic norms and the calls for the protection and promotion of international human rights attest to the budding of a common language of humanity.

In other cases, globalization has problematized local cultures and traditions. There is growing support in the Muslim world for challenging traditionally dominant cultural interpretations. Increasingly, Muslims have nodded to the assertion that a cultural renovation, along with an enlightened interpretation of the *sharia*, is the best safeguard for the realization of human rights. Such a forward-looking approach has made it both desirable and necessary for Muslim leaders to adopt a new pragmatism. In reality, however, much depends on the internal political dynamics of the power struggle between the localizers, the semi-integrationists and the globalizers in the Muslim world.

Modern Islamic thought and some parts of the *sharia* are incompatible. The mandatory punishment for apostasy as prescribed in classical Islam runs counter to modern norms and laws of human rights. The number of Muslims calling for the reform and reinterpretation of orthodox Islamic laws and traditions is on the rise, as the Muslim world finds it imperative to adjust to the extraordinary pace of the global democratic revolution. Respect for gender equality, for the fair treatment of minorities, for the freedoms associated with the minimal conditions of civil society, and for the right to vote have gained universal recognition. In this most fundamental sense, the Western universalist discourse of human rights, insofar as the origin of such rights are concerned, is immaterial to the universal validity of certain 'core' rights (Forsythe 1991). But if the *raison d'être* of human rights is to be grounded in an inter-civilizational perspective, West-centric biases must be overcome (Yasuaki 1999: 112).

The era of globalization, regardless of what drives it, has energized the moral force of human rights as a powerful tool to counter oppression and to assure equality. The Muslim world has no alternative but to carve out its own space in this globalized world by renegotiating the basis for global civil society. While embracing its challenges and opportunities, Muslims must ward off those hegemonic Western ideas and institutions that have disruptive effects on their society. This may require a paradigm shift in contemporary Islamic thinking regarding the post-Cold War world in which human rights will play a larger role in human life. Such a shift, if and when it occurs, will result in balance and control without necessarily sacrificing the Muslim world's values and ethical perspectives.

Notes

1 See, for example, Pelletreau *et al.* (1994: 12–13); Pasha and Samatar (1996).
2 For an interesting discussion on legal aspects of the death bounty put on Salman Rushdie's head, see Arzt (1996: 441–2).
3 For an illuminating discussion on the implications of globalization, see Weiss (1994).
4 *Twenty-four Human Rights Documents*, New York: Center for the Study of Human Rights, Columbia University, 1992, 7–8.
5 *Twenty-four Human Rights Documents*, New York: Center for the Study of Human Rights, Columbia University, 1992, 8.
6 This argument is offered in Mowlana's essay (1993: 398–407). Here, I extrapolate that this view is regularly invoked by orthodox Islamic groups as a backlash to globalization.
7 For further discussion on this, see Monshipouri (1998b: 26).
8 For a critique of the Samuel Huntington's *The Clash of Civilizations and the Remaking of World Order*, New York: Simon and Schuster, 1996, see Monshipouri (1998a).

References

Ahmed. A. S. and Donnan, H. (1994) 'Islam in the Age of Postmodernity', in Akbar S. Ahmed and Hastings Donnan (eds) *Islam, Globalization, and Postmodernity* New York: Routledge, 1–20.

Andersen, R. R., Seibert, R. F. and Wagner, J. G. (1998) *Politics and Change in the Middle East: Sources of Conflict and Accommodation*, 5th edn, New Jersey: Prentice-Hall.

An-Na'im, A. A. (1995) 'Islamic Foundations of Religious and Secular Discourse in Islamic Societies', in Mahnaz Afkhami (ed.) *Faith and Freedom: Women's Human Rights in the Muslim World*, Syracuse NY: Syracuse University Press, 51–60.

——(1998) 'Does Culture Matter?', *Human Rights Dialogue*, vol. 11, June, 22–3.

——(1999) 'The Cultural Mediation of Human Rights: The Al-Arqam Case in Malaysia', in Joanne R. Bauer and Daniel A. Bell (eds) *The East Asian Challenge for Human Rights*, New York: Cambridge University Press, 147–68.

Arzt, D. E. (1996) 'The Treatment of Religious Dissidents Under Classical and Contemporary Islamic Law', in John Witte Jr and Johan D. van der Vyver (eds) *Religious Human Rights in Global Perspective: Religious Perspectives*, The Hague: Martinus Nijhoff, 387–453.

Ayubi, N. (1999) 'The Politics of Islam in the Middle East With Special Reference to Egypt, Iran, and Saudi Arabia', in Jeff Haynes (ed.) *Religion, Globalization, and Political Culture*, New York: St Martin's Press, 71–92.

Beeley, B. (1992) 'Islam as a Global Political Force', in Anthony G. McGrew and Paul G. Lewis (eds) *Global Politics: Globalization and the Nation-State*, London: Polity Press, 293–311.

Cox, R. W. (1996) 'A Perspective on Globalization', in James H. Mittelman (ed.) *Globalization: Critical Reflections*, Boulder: Lynne Rienner, 21–30.

Deng, F. M. (1993) 'Africa and the New World Dis-Order', in Jeremy Brecher, John Brown Childs and Jill Cutler (eds) *Global Visions: Beyond the New World Order*, Boston MA: South End Press, 103–11.

Donnelly, J. (1995) 'Post-Cold War Reflections on the Study of International Human Rights', in Joel H. Rosenthal (ed.) *Ethics and International Affairs: A Reader*, Washington DC: Georgetown University Press, 236–56.

Eickelman, D. F. and Piscatori, J. (1996) *Muslim Politics*, Princeton: Princeton University Press.

Eide, A. (1992) 'National Sovereignty and International Efforts to Realize Human Rights', in Asbjorn Eide and Brent Hagtvet (eds) *Human Rights in Perspective: A Global Assessment*, Oxford: Blackwell, 3–30.

Esposito, J. L. (1988) *Islam: The Straight Path*, New York: Oxford University Press, 116–61.

Esposito, J. L. and Voll, J. O. (1996) *Islam and Democracy*, New York: Oxford University Press.

Falk, R. (1995) *On Humane Governance: Toward a New Global Politics*, University Park: Pennsylvania State University Press.

Forsythe, D. P. (1991) *The Internationalization of Human Rights*, Lexington: Lexington Books.

Ghai, Y. (1999) 'Rights, Social Justice, and Globalization in East Asia', in Joanne R. Bauer and Daniel A. Bell (eds) *The East Asian Challenge for Human Rights*, Cambridge: Cambridge University Press, 241–63.

Haynes, J. (ed.) (1999) *Religion, Globalization, and Political Culture*, New York: St Martin's Press.

Hetata, S. (1998) 'Dollarization, Fragmentation, and God', in Fredric Jameson and Masao Miyoshi (eds) *The Cultures of Globalization*, Durham NC: Duke University Press, 273–90.

Hunter, S. T. (1998) *The Future of Islam and the West: Clash of Civilizations or Peaceful Coexistence?* Westport: Praeger.

Husain, M. R. (1995) *Global Islamic Politics*, New York: Harper Collins.

Icbiyo, M. (1993) 'For an Alliance of Hope', in Jeremy Brecher, John Brown Childs and Jill Cutler (eds) *Global Visions: Beyond the New World Order*, Boston MA: South End Press, 147–62.

Meyer, W. H. (1998) *Human Rights and International Political Economy in Third World Nations: Multinational Corporations, Foreign Aid, and Repression*, Westport: Praeger.

Mittelman, J. H. (ed.) (1996) *Globalization: Critical Reflections*, Boulder: Lynne Rienner.

Mittelman, J. H. and Pasha, M. K. (1997) *Out from Underdevelopment Revisited: Changing Global Structures and the Remaking of the Third World*, New York: St Martin's Press.

Monshipouri, M. (1997) 'State Prerogative, Civil Society, and Liberalization: The Paradoxes of the Late Twentieth Century in the Third World', *Ethics and International Affairs*, vol. 11, 233–51.

——(1998a) 'The West's Modern Encounter with Islam: From Discourse to Reality', *Journal of Church and State*, vol. 40, no. 1, winter, 25–56.

——(1998b) *Islamism, Secularism, and Human Rights in the Middle East*, Boulder: Lynne Rienner.

Mowlana, H. (1993) 'New Global Order and Cultural Ecology', in Kaarle Nordenstreng and Herbert I. Schiller (eds) *Beyond National Sovereignty: International Communication in the 1990s*, Norwood NJ: Alex Publishing, 397–417.

Mozaffari, M. (1998) 'Can a Declined Civilization be Reconstructed: Islamic Civilization or Civilized Islam?', *International Relations*, vol. XIV, no. 3, 31–50.

Pasha, M. K. and Samatar, A. I. (1996) 'The Resurgence of Islam', in James H. Mittelman *Globalization: Critical Reflections*, Boulder: Lynne Rienner, 187–201.

Pelletreau Jr, R. H., Pipes, D. and Esposito, J. L. (1994) 'Symposium: Resurgent Islam in the Middle East', *Middle East Policy*, vol. 3, no. 2, 1–21.

Peterson, R. D., Wunder, D. F. and Mueller, H. L. (1999) *Social Problems: Globalization in the Twenty-First Century*, New Jersey: Prentice-Hall.

Potter, D. (1992) 'The Autonomy of Third World States Within the Global Economy', in Anthony G. McGrew and Paul G. Lewis (eds) *Global Politics: Globalization and the Nation-State*, London: Polity Press, 216–32.

Randall, V. (1999) 'The Media and Religion in Third World Politics', in Jeff Haynes (ed.) *Religion, Globalization, and Political Culture*, New York: St Martin's Press, 45–68.

Saif, W. (1994) 'Human Rights and Islamic Revivalism', *Islam and Christian-Muslim Relations*, vol. 5, no. 1, 57–65.

Smith, M. (1992) 'Modernization, Globalization and the Nation-State', in in Anthony G. McGrew and Paul G. Lewis (eds) *Global Politics: Globalization and the Nation-state*, London: Polity Press, 253–68.

Soroush, A. K. (1993) 'The Democratic Religious Rule', *Kiyan*, vol. 3, no. 11, March-April, 12–15.

Sreberny-Mohammadi, A. (1997) 'The Many Cultural Faces of Imperialism', in Peter Golding and Phil Harris (eds) *Beyond Cultural Imperialism: Globalization, Commuincation, and the New International Order*, London: Sage, 49–68.

Stavenhagen, R. (1992) 'Universal Human Rights and the Cultures of Indigenous Peoples and Other Ethnic Groups: The Critical Frontier of the 1990s', in in Asbjorn Eide and Brent Hagtvet (eds) *Human Rights in Perspective: A Global Assessment*, Oxford: Blackwell, 135–51.

Weiss, A. M. (1994) 'Challenges for Muslim Women in a Postmodern World', in Akbar S. Ahmed and Hastings Donnan (eds) *Islam, Globalization and Postmodernity*, New York: Routledge, 127–40.

Wilson, R. A. (ed.) (1997) *Human Rights, Culture, and Context: Anthropological Perspectives*, London: Pluto Press.

Yasuaki, O. (1999) 'Toward an Intercivilizational Approach to Human Rights', in Joanne R. Bauer and Daniel A. Bell (eds) *The East Asian Challenge for Human Rights*, Cambridge: Cambridge University Press, 103–23.

6 The culture and politics of human rights in the context of Islam

Ali Mohammadi

The purpose of this chapter is to identify the major differences between Islamic and Western approaches to the concept of human rights and to explore ways of minimizing the differences between the two views. In order to disseminate the notion of a universal concept of human rights, we need to find a way of educating people in the Islamic states about the importance of human rights and the changes which are emerging as a consequence of globalization. In order to evaluate the differences between Islamic and Western views on human rights, it is crucial to look at the case of the Islamic Republic of Iran and the pertinence of reports by the United Nations' Commission on Human Rights. The reaction of Western governments to violations of human rights by the Islamic states must also be examined if a way of implementing human rights in Islamic nations is to be found.

Introduction

The pursuit of human rights is a universal concept, but its form is shaped by the culture of a people. Politics is also a cultural activity, reflecting tradition and environment. In the modern global system, Muslims have an interest in human rights. They have always claimed that the original concept of human rights comes from the Quran:

> Islam gave humanity an ideal code of human rights 1400 years ago. The purpose of these rights is to confer honour and dignity on humanity and to eliminate exploitation, oppression, and injustice. Human rights in Islam are deeply rooted in the conviction that God, and God alone, is the author of Law and the source of all human rights. Given this divine origin, no leader, no government, no assembly or any other authority can restrict, abrogate or violate in any manner the rights conferred by God.
> (Arkoun 1994: 106)[1]

This Islamic code of human rights is conceptually very different to secular human rights declarations. In order to identify the differences between the two approaches, we will look briefly at the premise of the concept of human rights in the West.

In the twentieth century serious discussion about human rights was initiated with the United Nations Declaration of Human Rights in 1948. This was followed by the Convention for the Protection of Human Rights and Fundamental Freedoms in 1950. In 1966, The International Covenant on Civil and Political Rights was approved by the United Nations Security Council. In these discussions, Western powers concentrated on discovering common denominators, rooted in the Judaeo-Christian traditions of human rights. Islamic traditions were not considered, even to the extent of ignoring Muslim representations from Islamic countries. Politically, it was quite obvious that the views of Islamic governments were not important in the establishment of a human rights commission during 1950s. The debate on human rights assumed that, despite the differences which characterize the diversity of cultures, political conduct can be conceptualized within certain common circumstances and values (Said and Mohammadi 1978).[2]

Human rights in the West

The idea of human rights in Western civilization has its roots in the philosophical traditions of the Greek and Roman civilizations. In recent centuries, Western political traditions have accommodated various theories of political behaviour and reshaped them into certain rights. These rights have been endorsed in various treaties among the European nations.

Prior to the First World War, there were efforts to promote individual rights at the national level. These efforts took as a reference point important historical documents, such as the French Declaration of the Rights of Man and the Citizens in 1789, and the Brussels 16 Nations Convention about the total cessation of the slave trade and the recognition of various rights for human beings in 1890 (Fareed 1977; Renteln 1990).[3] The politics behind these discussions proceeded from the assumption that all states share a common agenda of goals. This assumption carried with it a reinforcement of the perception of the universality of Western values.

By maintaining a focus on various historical documents in the West, human rights were expressed in terms of demands for the redress of grievances and for the satisfaction of new needs. In Graeco-Roman and Judaeo-Christian traditions, both rights and duties were asserted as part of the 'natural law' arguments. We also see, in the West, a movement away from the individual's obligations to the state, and towards an approach that demands that the state perform more duties. As each stage gradually developed, the number of individual rights expanded at the same time as the scope of individual obligations was reduced. The demand for the expansion of the duties of the state could only be satisfied through the enlargement of state powers. These contradictory aspects run deep in the present human rights debate in the West, and place the state in the cross-fire between individuals and groups demanding equal rights. The essential contradiction is that government intervention to meet the demands of an individual or a group decreases the rights of other individuals or groups in exact proportion to the success of the intervention. This trend will persist until such time when there occurs a change in the allocation of power (Said and Mohammadi 1978).[4]

We must recognize the connection between the type and number of rights and the nature of the environment. In the West there has been a definite shift from an abstract concept of universal rights towards a concrete concept of essential rights. Some of these changes can be found in the debate on the 'new global order' where corporate rights may increase against the reduction of nation-state rights. This shift is indicative of societal conditions, particularly in the context of the dialogue on human rights.

Honouring Islamic experience

The historical development of socio-politics in the West was very different to that of the Islamic states. The particular problems associated with Islamic development have not been experienced in the recent history of the West. The differences in development between the West and the Islamic world have a continuing influence on the position of human rights in Islamic states. The increased institutionalization of the Western nation-state has accentuated the confrontation between the individual and the state. In the West, human rights tensions derive from frustrated efforts to fit the contemporary environment into the nation-state; tensions in the Islamic world represent equally frustrated efforts to fit the nation-state into traditional institutions. The emphasis on Western common denominators represents a parochial view of human rights which is exclusive of the cultural realities and present existential conditions of developing countries in general, and of Islamic governments in particular. This approach continues to cause tremendous anxiety, resentment and cultural paranoia among Islamic nations around the world.

Setting an agenda for Islamic human rights

In September 1981, at a UNESCO meeting called on the initiative of the Islamic Council and its secretary, Salem Azzam, a Universal Islamic Declaration of Human Rights was presented for the first time (Arkoun 1994).[5] This was a reaction to the Western dictation of human rights laws. The Muslim scholars and jurists, who prepared the text of the twenty-three articles of the Universal Islamic Declaration of Human Rights, were representatives of current Islamic thinking, mainly from the official Sunni compilations of *hadith* (sayings of the prophet). There was no Shi'ite scholar among this group, and no reference to various Shi'ite *hadith*; but the gists of all the principles were from the Quran. The discussion about secular aspects within a religious approach to the universal concept of human rights did not bring the Islamic countries to a compromise position (Arkoun 1994).[6]

In order to minimize the differences within an Islamic text of human rights, foreign ministers of the Muslim countries gathered in Cairo in August 1990 and unanimously approved an Islamic human rights declaration, with twenty-five articles. This bill had two more articles than the previous one. It was also less biased against the Shi'ite branch of Islam. The text of the Cairo Islamic Human Rights Declaration is closer to certain articles of the UNDHR, demonstrating progress towards further cooperation with the general theme of human rights (Mehrpour 1996).[7]

In order to clarify the conceptual differences between Western and Islamic texts of human rights, it is vital to review the context of the Islamic discussion of human rights. The major emphasis of the UNESCO and the Cairo meetings on universal Islamic human rights was on the fact that human beings are created in the image of God. They are also God's representatives on earth and are empowered by the divine being to govern themselves because God has created human beings who seek perfection. Human beings have certain God-granted rights, and a right, by definition, is the exercise of power. In this way, personal freedom lies in surrender to the divine will and in purifying oneself inwards to become liberated from all external conditions which limit one's freedom. The freedom of the individual is the supreme end; it is not only a means to an end.

As previously mentioned, the Cairo human rights declaration opened a new window of hope for bridging the gap between the secular notion of human rights and the religious notion. The human rights declaration by the Islamic states focuses on a role for the state and on the essentials of life. One can say, therefore, that the Islamic countries have taken a progressive step through the portrayal of the Islamic notion of human rights. This step is based on the six fundamental concepts of human rights in Islam:

1 Islam and individual freedom
2 Islam and intellectual freedom
3 Islam and the foundation of liberty
4 Islam and access to the court of law
5 Islam and equality
6 Islam and the question of race and colour

Islam and individual freedom

There are three aspects of Islamic thought on the concept of individual freedom that we need to consider: jurisprudence, theology and philosophy within the Islamic tradition. Jurisprudence sees human freedom as a result of personal surrender to the divine will, rather than as an innate personal right. In law, human beings are created by God and have no personal power to create. They are dependent on God and therefore can only receive what is given to them by the source of their own being. Human rights are a consequence of human obligations and not their antecedent. Individuals possess certain obligations towards God, nature and other human beings, all of which are defined by *shariah* (religious law). Within the theological perspective, the Ash'arites school negates human freedom completely in favour of a deterministic view, but other schools, such as the Mutazilite and the Shi'ite, believe in human freedom and reject the total determinism of the Ash'arites. In general, philosophers react strongly against the theologians on this question and firmly assert the reality of human freedom (Al-Alili 1974).[8] The early Muslim philosophers, such as Farabi and Avicena, were interested in political philosophy and were well acquainted with Plato, Aristotle and the Stoics. On the question of freedom, philosophers approach the issue from the point of view of the Islamicized political philosophy of Farabi rather than in purely Greek terms. The *shariah*, the Islamic community and the legitimacy of political rule derived from the source of revelation, was a reality for all philosophers. Today this interpretation has been accepted by the two principal Islamic sects, the Sunnis and the Shi'ites. The reality of human freedom is asserted by them, but only in the context of the community of Islam, and not from the point of view of a universal secular humanism.

Islam and intellectual freedom

The verse in the Quran that God first revealed to His Prophet is the one that says, 'Proclaim in the name of thy Lord who created, created man from a dot of blood. Convey and the Lord is most Generous. Who taught [man] by the pen, taught [man] what he knew not'

(96:1–5). Learning is to be pursued in the name of God and not to be in the name of passions, resentments or partisan feelings. For Islam, knowledge possesses a certain sanctity. No man should use it for his own interest which is incompatible with justice, since justice is one of the attributes of God. Honouring knowledge, the God of Islam has also honoured its instruments. God swore first by the pen in the Quran. In His words, 'By the pen and by that which they write' (96:1), and so the second thing sworn by was writing itself.

The Quran mentions the term 'knowledge' and its derivatives about 850 times in connection with God, His messengers and mankind (Kamil 1967).[9] God instructs the Prophet to invoke Him, and says: 'Say, O Lord, increase me in knowledge', and God commanded His Prophet to ask Him for it when He directed him to call upon Him (4:41). For this reason, the Prophet puts the ink of learned men on the same plane as the blood of the martyrs, and calls upon man to discover the secrets of the universe: 'in the Creation of heavens and the earth...there are indeed signs for men to understand' (3:190–1) (Said and Mohammadi 1978).[10]

This attitude of Islam, to encourage learning and the study of natural and social phenomena, paved the way for scientific research and development which in turn established one of the most developed and sophisticated world civilizations. It was such an attitude that helped Muslim scholars to create extremely valuable works in nearly all aspects of human life, to translate the works of scientists and philosophers of other nations, such as the ancient Greek philosophers, and to improve scientific methods at a time when Europe was still in the dark ages. Scientific method, usually attributed to Francis Bacon (1561–1626), had already been applied several centuries earlier by Ibnal Haitham and other Muslim scholars, whose rigorous and systematic approach to the collection and investigation of data demonstrated their determination to ensure logical and empirically sound conclusions (Kamil 1967: 14).[11] Hayyan, in the ninth century, advised his students to experiment, and stressed the necessity of accurate observation. He warned against jumping to conclusions: 'Your first duty is to carry out tests...follow the steps of nature, for the quality which you seek in every object is inherent in its nature' (Kamil 1952: 146).[12] Thus it is clearly evident that Islam has recognized and acquired the freedom of learning, the freedom of speech and writing, and the freedom of undertaking scientific research in all fields of study.

Islam and the foundation of liberty

Having a state based on justice is essential in order to safeguard and to advance human values in all directions, and to guarantee the welfare of individuals. Some Islamic scholars argue that Islam has broken all the chains and removed all the barriers surrounding human beings, in order to provide the individual with the highest degree of liberty necessary to approach his God freely and directly with the dignity of a free person. Islam has guaranteed individual liberty in order to enable people to search freely for the truth and to progress towards the highest degree of self-consciousness and spiritual and intellectual achievements. Therefore, Islam views its people as the highest on the earth in terms of their status to represent and reflect the Lord of creation. By declaring that 'I am going to place one who shall rule in it' (ii.30), God has viewed man as His reflection on the earth, with all the rights and liberties which are necessary to function in that position. Again, 'Islam wants to grant you liberty so that it enables you to create a paradise by your acts of fraternity, love and justice and take others to abide in good company and in an atmosphere of peace and harmony' (Kamil 1952: 20).[13]

The foundation of liberty along with freedom of worship has also been recognized and guaranteed for non-Muslims living in an Islamic state. God has declared: 'Lord, those who are Jews and Christians and whoever believe in God and the Last Day, do the right things, surely their reward is with their Lord, and there shall no fear come upon them, neither shall they grieve' (v.69). Also in respect of the beliefs of non-Muslims God commands:

> say Ye: 'We believe in God and what has been revealed to us, and what was revealed to Abraham and Ishmael, and Isaac and Jacob and [his] children, and what was given to Moses and Jesus, and what was given to [all other] Prophets from their Lord. We make no differences between any of them; and to him we submit ourselves'.
>
> (2:136)

These two quotations clearly indicate that, in spite of religious conflicts throughout history, the sanctity of all religions and respect for their followers has continued to be proclaimed and respected in the land of Islam.

Islam and access to the court of law

Islam established equality before the law and practised it to an extent never practised before or since: 'Accordingly, all people regardless of their race, sex or positions, are equal before courts with absolute right to access to courts' (Kamil 1952: 136, 152).[14] The prophet never considered himself to be above the law and offered himself to others for retaliations even when he had hit them unwittingly (Kamil 1952: 23–4).[15] Islam also granted the right to communities of different cultures that their cases may be decided among themselves according to their own personal laws. By doing this, Islam has safeguarded the rights of non-Muslims living in a Muslim state. This policy, which has been called the 'Millat System', has been practised for many centuries in the land of Islam. Moreover, in addition to their own laws and courts, non-Muslims living in the Muslim state have the right of access to the Islamic courts. As for the judge himself, he is merely required to be learned, competent and of high morality; his race and colour are immaterial and he judges all men impartially (Kamil 1952[16]; Alghazali 1962[17]).

Islam and the concept of equality

Many theologians and Islamic scholars regard the concept of equality as the greatest gift granted to man by Islam. According to the Quran, 'God created you from a single being' (iv.I). Humanity is fundamentally one because man was created from one single origin. Also, as the Prophet has noted, all people should be treated as the children of God and 'as such they have an equal right to nourishment and upbringing to develop to the full their special endowments' (Kamil 1952: 22).[18] It should be noted that in all its teachings Islam strongly emphasizes the doctrine of oneness or unity, for God has said: 'O ye people, fear your Lord, who created you from a single soul and created therefore its mate, and from them twain scattered abroad many men and women' (4:1). Thus Islam views humankind as one family created from a single soul. In this way, Islam has clearly indicated that human beings become high or low only by character, and all other criteria are false. It follows from this that all inequalities based on race or gender have been strongly condemned by Islam. Through the abolition of hereditary monarchies, privileged ranks of priesthood and all other types of classes and castes, Islam acknowledged an equality of opportunity for all.

Islam and the question of race and colour

Islam, with its eternal and universal laws applicable to all Muslims, regardless of their race or gender, does not approach the problem of human equality from the viewpoint of a person's race or colour of skin. However, Islam's task was to establish stronger, more stable nations. In the first place this would be done through intellectual development in the hope that a new social structure would be established, broadly based on faith, human brotherhood and righteous works. The story of creation as told by Islam clearly indicates that all people, whatever their race or colour or gender, were born from two parents, namely Adam and Eve. As previously mentioned, the Quran emphasizes this on many occasions: 'O ye people, Fear your Lord, who created you from a single soul and created therefore its mate, and from them twain scatter abroad many men and women; and fear of Allah, in whose name you appeal to one another' (4:1). There is also to be human brotherhood; Islam has been fortunate in discarding, from the very first, differences of race and colour, country and language, in favour of the universal brotherhood of the faithful.

From the Quran:

> O, mankind, be careful of your duty to your Lord, who created you from a single male and female, and we have made you nations and tribes that ye may distinguish one another. Lo, the noblest of you in the right of God, is the one who feareth [Him] most. Lo, God is knower, Aware.
>
> (xI ix.13, other verses to the same effect, cf. vi.99, vii is9, xxxix.6)

Or, on the subject of Brotherhood: 'The believers are not else than brothers. Therefore make peace between two brothers of yours (if they happen to oppose each other), and observe your duty to God that ye may obtain mercy' (xl ix.10). All these sections of the Quran indicate that in Islam the differences between men, in terms of colour and language, are but phenomena testifying to the great mastery of the creator; and that not only are all human beings descended from the same couple, but also that even their religions have the same source. The Quran, as the main source of Islamic laws and Muslims' rights, and the practice of the Prophet, as the second source of Islamic laws, provide more evidence that in Islam no one race is superior to any other: 'Islam sees mankind as a large garden, in which there are flowers of many colours, but no one colour is superior to any other' (Kamil 1952: 29).[19]

Islamic human rights in historical context

Through a critical examination of all the major concepts of the Universal Islamic Declaration of Human Rights, it is can be seen that Islam, as a religion, is open to the proclamation and the defence of human rights. All these rights were defined by the words of God in the beginning of the seventh century, almost 1,000 years before the American Declaration of Independence in 1776 and the exposition of human rights by Thomas Jefferson and the French Revolution in 1789 (Arkoun 1994).[20]

In one of the major texts on this issue, *Fundamental Human Rights*,

Abdul Hakim Kamil has made a great effort to give a clear perception of Islam's approach to human rights. In an intriguing way he argues that, because of the suppression of man by feudalism, by absolute monarchy, and, in the latter phase, by the propertied bourgeoisie and the fact that 'Islam is buried under heaps of retrograde legalism and life-thwarting practices, and centuries of despotism and clericalism have smothered the spirit of Islam' (Kamil 1952: 3).[21] It is now time to define and to safeguard the rights of individuals, not only in the Muslim world but in the non-Muslim world too. Kamil suggests that: 'in a truly Islamic Welfare State', referring to the prophet's words, 'There shall be no Caesar and "Clossoes"', Islam is definitely against hereditary monarchy. This is why the Persian and the Roman Empires were conquered and the first four caliphs were elected by Muslims. This was actually the outcome of true teaching of the Quran (Kamil 1952: 4).[22]

In Islam, sovereignty always belongs to God and traditional thought calls upon believers to perform the five canonical obligations:

1   To express the faith, *shahada* in Islam
2   Prayer, five times a day
3   Almsgiving
4   Fasting in Ramazan
5   Pilgrimage to Mecca (Al-Ghazali 1962).

Through absolute obedience, individuals gradually internalize the notion of the right of God. Respect for human rights is the basic condition of the right of God. The state surrenders its sovereignty to God, and accepts the position of vice-regent under God's suzerainty. Since the purpose of the individual is the service of God, the existence of an organized community of believers requires the establishment of government. The legitimacy of government lies in its ability to ensure the service of God through counsel among Muslims.

The Islamic state is a blend of theocracy and some kind of collectivism. It is theocratic as it is predicated upon the doctrine of sovereignty of God. However, it does not delegate the vice-regency of God to a priesthood. The caliphate is vested in the believers who are virtuous. The state is collective, since the right to govern derives from counsel among the believers; a form of general will. However, the rights of the people to change the law of the state are limited. The *shariah*, the *hadith* and the *fiqh* provide a check which ensures that the life of the community remains consistent with the law of God and is protected from executive, legislative and judicial revisionism.

If we accept that the *shariah* is derived from the Quran, then we are obliged to accept the argument that it is the state's duty to enhance human dignity and alleviate conditions that hinder individuals in their efforts to achieve happiness. However, in practice, the Islamic legal system provides no adequate mechanism to protect and defend individual rights against the state (Said and Mohammadi 1978).[23]

Islam and modernity

It is very important to remember that between the seventh century and the present day something significantly interrupted the continuity of life and space in Islam. That interruption was 'modernity'. The process of modernization emerged alongside colonial forces. In the nineteenth century, Europe justified its colonial expansionist policy as a civilizing mission. Colonies were necessary, it was argued, in order to raise backward people to the level of understanding of Western civilization and culture. Muslim countries, in the struggle against colonialist powers, gradually became familiar, in a fragmented way, with the concepts of the eighteenth-century Enlightenment, which were the foundation of secular society in the Western world (Said & Mohammadi 1994).[24]

In the course of the twentieth century, a very small number of students from upper-middle-class Muslim families in colonized countries were able to gain access to the universities and the literature of the West. These liberal and intellectually minded students were from India, Indonesia, Turkey, Persia, Iran and Arab countries. They were all very excited about the modernity that had brought such change to Europe. Some of this elite group made every attempt to enlighten traditional thought in their own countries. Jamal-aldin Assadabadi (from Iran) and Muhammad Abduh (from Egypt) both showed an interest in the concept of human rights and freedom, as did Ataturk in Turkey, Gamal Abdel Nasser in Egypt, Dr Mossadeq in Iran, Sukarno in Indonesia, Farahat Abbas in Algeria, Habib Bourguiba in Tunisia, Allal al Fassi in Morocco and Michel Aflaq in Syria. All these leaders believed in national liberation, human rights and the secular revolution of their countries which had long-established Islamic traditions (Arkoun 1994).[25]

But there were difficulties; the intellectual and political elites in these Islamic countries could not find support from an enlightened, progressive and dynamic social class who were able to comprehend the importance of the secular institutions and state apparatus necessary for the implementation of an enlightenment project. In Iran, for instance, a Tehran University professor, seeking protection against the traditional Islamist clergy, cried out for freedom of speech, ideas and cultural awareness in a letter to the President (*Guardian*, 7 June 1996).[26]

It is now quite clear that the traditional Islam of the seventh to fourteenth centuries lost its dynamism for self-renewal long before the intrusion of colonialism. With the triumph of the ideology of national liberation during the 1950s, came a crisis in traditional Islamic identity. Arkoun suggests that: 'the discourse of the so called Islamic revolution in Iran took up the great themes of the ideology of national liberation, which retained a socialist, secular coloration, and reworked them to include Islamic sources and to encompass struggle against Westernization' (Arkoun 1994: 110).[27]

The traditional Islamist, instead of allowing space for rational, civil discourse, blocks the process by using the persuasive rhetoric of cultural imperialism and by employing a conspiracy theory to freeze the dynamism of modern thought. This halts the progress of a nation towards a rational discourse for a civil society. Sorush, who is a progressive Islamist and a well known author, attempts to open the debate on human rights in Islam by suggesting that 'In the Muslim world, we have talked only of duties, not of rights. In modern civilisations, however, believing in God is not a duty, but a right' (*Guardian*, 6 June 1996).[28]

Looking through the records of violations of human rights in Islamic countries, as reported by Human Rights Watch, reveals evidence which is embarrassing and deplorable. The conditions of human rights in Saudi Arabia, Turkey, Algeria, Egypt and Sudan are the worst but, through the claims of Western media, conditions in Iran are made to look even more extreme.

The Islamic Republic of Iran as a case study

Since Human Rights Watch began in 1978, with funding from Helsinki, Human Rights Watch divisions have been established around the world. Their major function is to cover five collaborative projects: arms transfers, free expression, prison conditions, children's rights and women's rights. Human Rights Watch groups have offices in New York, London, Rio de Janeiro, Hong Kong, Brussels, Dushanbeh, Los Angeles, Washington and Moscow. All these offices are funded privately. The major decision makers and top personnel are US citizens because most of the private funding comes from the United States.

Human Rights Watch Middle East, founded in 1989, covers Algeria, Egypt, Iran, Iraq and Iraqi Kurdistan, the Israeli-occupied West Bank and Gaza strip, Kuwait, Morocco and the Western Sahara, Saudi Arabia and Syria. In the Human Rights Watch Report (1996),[29] Iran, like many other Middle Eastern countries, is under scrutiny for grotesque human rights violations.

It is crucial to look at some important cases in order to underline the difficulties of implementing basic human rights in Iran. The following is a summary of violations of human rights in Iran between 1993 and 1996, according to the report by Human Rights Watch Middle East. Included in the summary are some observations about the violations and the resistance to censorship.

A sixty-five year-old government critic, who was not associated with any opposition organization, was arrested at his home in Tehran and held at Ewin prison, where he was denied access to a lawyer or to his family.

A cartoonist who depicted a handicapped football player who, a critic believed, resembled Khomeini, was jailed for ten years. The cartoon was used to illustrate an article on the poor state of football in Iran in the science magazine *Farad*. The magazine was banned and the editor-in-chief imprisoned for six months.

Article 19 of the International Covenant on Civil and Political Rights, to which Iran is a party, guarantees that:

> Everyone shall have the right to freedom of expression; this right shall have freedom to seek, receive and impart information and ideas of all kinds regardless of frontiers either orally, in writing or in print, in the form of art, or through any other media of his choice.
>
> (Human Rights Watch 1996: 127)[30]

On 26 August 1993, the editor in chief of the daily *Salam* was arrested by order of the Islamic Revolutionary Courts.

On 4 September 1993, a publisher and member of the radical Tehran Clergy Association was summoned to appear before a special court for the clergy to answer charges of slander filed by the Education Minister and the Friday prayers leader of Ahwaz.

In November 1994, Saidi-Sirjani, a writer and critic of censorship died in detention.

In December 1994, 500 journalists joined the writers' protest against censorship and government control of the press and publishing houses.

In February 1995, the *Jahan-e-Islam* newspaper was banned because of a serialized interview with the former interior minister,who was very critical of the policy of President Rafsanjani.

In March 1995, the literary journal *Takapou* was closed on the grounds of allegations that it was not Islamic enough.

In August 1995, *Paym-e-Daneshjou*, a weekly news magazine,was banned because of its criticism of government policies.

In October 1995, the provincial daily *Tous* was closed for criticizing the government. Also at this time, the government changed the press law and gave more power to the Ministry of Islamic Guidance to close newspapers and publishing houses prior to court approval.

In violation of the constitutional prohibitions on government ownership of newspapers, government officials commenced the publication of two newspapers, *Iran* and *Akhbar*.

In addition to the obvious violation of the Islamic Republic's Constitution, the restrictions of freedom of expression are not limited to the press, but also include film and television. In June 1995, 214 filmmakers signed an open letter to the government calling for the lifting of direct government controls on film and television.

In July 1995, approximately 107 professors sent an open letter to President Rafsanjani urging him to uphold the Constitution for the protection of people's rights.

Despite the publication of documents and newspapers reports about grotesque violations of basic rights in Iran, intrusive restrictions on everyday life are rising.

According to a recently imposed rule by the Islamic National Assembly, any interview about the Islamic Republic with foreign broadcasters or newspapers is regarded as an act of treason and the penalty is death. The Human Rights Watch Middle East Report indicates that

> The Iranian Government's conduct in different arena of expression betrays an underlying belief that, through the close monitoring and restriction of information, it can control the thought of its citizens and secure the dominance of a prescribed set of values.
> (Human Rights Watch 1996: 128)[31]

Human rights in crisis

Documented above is an extensive and deplorable human record. Both non-government organizations and Western media have focused on these violations. One might ask why all the activities of human rights organizations have so far not had the slightest impact on the interactions and the behaviour of the Islamic justice system in Iran. There are, of course, a number of reasons why the Islamic government in Iran refuses to cooperate with the UN Commission on Human Rights. The major reason, as the Islamic government argues, is that the human rights records of Egypt, Turkey and Saudi Arabia are no better than that of Iran, so why should the Western media be so biased towards the Islamic Republic? And, in the light of this, why should Iran cooperate with the UN? (Human Rights Watch 1996).[32]

The establishment of a nation-state in the contemporary Islamic world is accompanied by intellectual and political institutional discontinuity with the old Islamic world. The nation-state model requires Islamic governments to enter into competition and to challenge traditional authority. While the old has been destroyed, the new has not yet appeared. Where is the Islamic government today that has firmly institutionalized a secular system in order to enter into a civil, rational discourse for the implementation of modernity? Turkey and Egypt are suffering very badly through not having engaged sufficiently in this rational discourse of modernity and through failing to establish liberal and popular institutions.

The backbone of government may be modern in form but unfortunately it is empty in substance. However, environmental and technological changes in the Islamic world are gradually outstripping traditional structures. The promise of higher levels of material growth, the rapid development of consumer markets, and the expansion of international television and communications networks compete with the negative conditions of underdeveloped existence to push down human rights priorities. The collision of old values, new concepts and foreign exploitation underlies the problem of development. This is a period of maximum transition in the Islamic world because of the powerful forces of globalization. While receptiveness to new ideas and visions is strong, it is very hard to convince people to accept traditions which are fourteen centuries old, or expect them not to think about the reality of life for today or tomorrow. As Abdolkarim Sorush, acting as a Shi'ite reformist since the revolution, argues, there are certain principles in Islam that are impossible to change. He suggests that there are some accidents in history which stem from the socio-psycho politics and geographical location of a period of history. Most of the laws and traditions of such a period can be subjects for discussion and interpretation in Islam. It is time to take human rights seriously, and it is very hard to refer to the socio-politics of fourteen centuries ago and to ignore the need of human beings today.

As far as human rights are concerned, the Islamic government in Iran has brought about an ideological hardening that rejects modernity. The present approach of the Human Rights Commission towards the Islamic government has been counter-productive. Traditionalists persist in continually reinforcing the Shari'ite, while the entire infrastructure of the government is Western and very secularly based. Thus, as Arkoun rightly suggests: ' "religion" is very much like language, it is a "collective force" that governs the life of societies' (Arkoun 1994: 113)[33] But today secularism has softened the dogma of traditional religion, and as Arkoun says, 'it is illusory and dangerous to ask of religion more than it can give'

(Arkoun 1994: 113). He also supports Sorush's argument that the implementation of Islamic traditions would not be an adequate response to modernity. Consequently, at the dawn of the twenty-first century, only human beings with extraordinary ability and enthusiasm are able to progress and to challenge the obstacles to their own freedom.

The major obstacles to the implementation of human rights in the Islamic world today

In order to discover how we can ensure the implementation of human rights in the Islamic countries, it is first of all essential to survey the basic obstacles:

(a) One can start by looking at the constitutions of each Islamic country. A detailed study of each Islamic government's constitutional laws reveals that, with the exception of Turkey, they have all been made through a reconciliation between Islam and modern legislation. As a consequence of this mixed adoption, constitutional laws are not secular in a Western sense and they are not purely Islamic. The question of human rights within a secular legal system is problematic within Islamic countries. In addition, there are problems relating to the legal status of women in Islam, as this is totally contradictory to the secular laws. A set of provisions called the 'personal statute' (*Al-ahwal al-shakhsiyya*) covers the conditions for women in Islamic countries (Arkoun 1994).[34] It is extremely difficult to change the status of women in Islam as this gives rise to a very serious theological problem. Much remains to be done in Islamic societies before liberty, justice, dignity and equality can be implemented. Religions have provided significant educative and therapeutic functions over many centuries, but their effectiveness has always been limited or abused by the clergy. Current Islamic thought believes that it can confront and defy the thought and the historical experience of the West. Although it is fair to note that the eighteenth-century Enlightenment in Europe did not necessarily enfranchise women, many legal battles have been won in this area in the last sixty years.

(b) Education and the dissemination of the concept of human rights across and within the Islamic countries, targeted on government policy makers and the clergy, is vital. In the 1990s, Germany, one of the close trade partners of the Islamic government in Europe, organized a series of educational seminars and discussion groups about human rights which took place in Hamburg and Tehran alternatively. The aim of these seminars was to educate Iranian officials about the importance of human rights in Islamic due process, and to clear the cloud of mistrust and suspicion that existed between the Islamic government of Iran and Germany. An immediate consequence of the annual meetings of the two groups was the establishment of parliamentary groups in Tehran which promote a better understanding of secular and religious concepts of human rights. A follow-up project, under the direct supervision of the attorney-general, was also established, but the overall outcome of the discussion groups was disappointing, and did not move the Islamic government towards even a consideration of cooperating with the human rights monitoring system (*Human Rights Journal*, no. 2, summer 1995).[35] However, the meetings did spread the modern conception of human rights throughout the Islamic Council Assembly. One of the active participants in the joint meetings revealed in an interview that the poor perception of Islamic authority, particularly in the justice department, is not the only stumbling block. A lack of understanding of the impact of the human rights issue on the international image of Islamic governments is also an obstacle which blocks progress towards a greater understanding of the concept of human rights in Iran.

(c) The Islamic government in Iran experiences the action and resolutions of the UN Security Council as biased, and it is also highly suspicious of Western governments' or NGOs' attempts to persuade Iran to cooperate with the UN Commission on Human Rights. Such active persuasion is seen as a threat and as direct interference in the internal affairs of Iran. Distrust and misjudgement on the one hand, and a misunderstanding of the importance of UNCHR as a moral obligation for the improvement the image of Islamic governments on the other, are serious problems for the process of implementing human rights in the Islamic World.

Major considerations for the implementation of human rights in the Islamic world today

In Islamic countries, the modernization process and the adoption of new technologies for increased productivity are in progress. Societal values are not in harmony with the pace of development; however, because the vision of the development derives from the cultural reality only, and not from Western liberalism, human rights in Islamic countries are sacrificed for modernization. Regardless of time and place, individuals must employ all of their own development for the greater expansion of their dignity.

There are many views of human rights, but little clear focus. Human rights in the West are now expressed in terms of demands for the redress of grievances and for the satisfaction of new needs, while in the past they represented a desire to be left alone. The Graeco-Roman and Judaeo-Christian traditions asserted both rights and duties, as expounded in the 'natural law' arguments. In the West, we see a movement away from the individual's obligations to the state in favour of demands that the state perform more duties. As each stage develops, the number of individual rights expands while the province of individual obligations narrows. On the other hand, the demand for the expansion of the duties of the state is satisfied only through the enlargement of state powers. These contradictory aspects run deep in the present human rights debate in the West. This contradiction has placed the state in the cross-fire between individuals and groups demanding equal rights. The essential contradiction is that government intervention to meet the demands of an individual or a group decreases the rights of other individuals or groups in exact proportion to its success. The trend will persist until such time when there occurs a change in the allocation of power.

We must recognize the connection between the type and number of thoughts and the nature of the environment. In the West there has been a definite shift from the abstract concept of universal rights towards a concrete concept of essential rights. The shift is indicative of societal conditions that must be taken into consideration in the dialogue of human rights. The West was in a stage of development substantially different from many Islamic states. The differences in developmental conditions between the West and the Islamic world has an influence on the position of human rights in Islamic states. In the West, human rights tensions derive from frustrated efforts to fit the contemporary environment into the nation-state; tension in the Islamic world derive from its equally frustrating effort to fit the nation-state into its traditional institutions (Said and Mohammadi 1978).[36]

Human rights concerns in Islamic states focus on the nature of the social structure, on a role for the state and on the essentials of life, rather than on liberation movements and lifestyles. In the mean time, protagonists of change in Islamic countries suffer various indignities and their demands for human rights continue to expand. Eventually, the Islamic world will be drawn into a cycle of evolution of human rights similar to that of the West, but in a more variable order than that of concrete essential rights – abstract universal rights – concrete essential rights again. In the process of human rights, conflict in specific circumstances and the reasons for differences in particular lists of rights, are both historical and functional. The need for a trade-off between the ideal and the possible forces the Islamic world to assign priorities. However, it is not too early for the powerful Islamic elites to account for themselves.

So far the development of a global conception of human rights suffers from lack of agreement about the sources of human rights, including the very foundation of international law. Uncertainty about the content of the doctrine of human rights, including the lack of a common philosophical core, poses additional obstacles. Indeed, the very conception of the organization of society differs from one culture to another. The West places more emphasis on rights, while Islam values obligations. The West focuses on freedom in order to avoid the outcome of a despotic system, while Islam emphasizes virtue as a goal to perpetuate the traditions of a society that often supports a coercive system. The West emphasizes individual interests while Islam values the collective good.

In areas where natural rights transcend cultural values, as in the right to survival, the vested interests of foreign policy elites have so far served as a basis for disagreement in the exercise of global human rights. However, it is interesting to note that in the last months of the twentieth century, the arrest in England of Augusto Pinochet, the former military dictator and a present senator of Chile, was an important step towards resolving the debate on international law. If we consider human rights to be a global issue, then we need genuinely global cooperation in order to resolve the issue of human rights violations around the world once and for all. By endorsing ethical practice in foreign policy, the British Labour government provides hope that other European governments will follow. Such cooperation and support could mean that it will be possible to persuade the US government to withdraw its opposition to the establishment of a permanent international court for the punishment of human rights violators around the world.

Notes

1 For further discussion see Arkoun (1994: ch. 22).
2 Said and Mohammadi (1978).
3 Fareed (1977).
4 Said & Mohammadi (1978).
5 Arkoun (1994).
6 *ibid.*
7 See Mehrpour, (1996) *Human Rights as International Instruments and the Position of the Islamic Republic of Iran*, Ettla, t, Tehran.
8 Al-Alili (1974) *Public Liberties in Thought and Political Systems in Islam*, Cairo.
9 Kamil (1967)
10 Said and Mohammadi (1978).
11 Kamil (1967: 14)
12 Kamil (1952: 146).
13 Kamil (1952: 20).

14 Kamil (1952: 135 and 152)..
15 Kamil, Kamil (1952: 23–4).
16 Kamil, (1952).
17 See Alghazali (1962).
18 Kamil. (1952: 22).
19 Kamil. (1952: 29).
20 Arkoun (1994).
21 Kamil (1952: 3).
22 Kamil (1952: 4).
23 Said and Mohammadi (1978).
24 *ibid.*
25 Arkoun (1994).
26 *Guardian*, 7th June, 1996.
27 Arkoun (1994: 110).
28 *Guardian*, 7th June, 1996.
29 See *Human Rights Watch Report* (1996).
30 See *Human Rights Watch Report* (1996: 127).
31 See *Human Rights Watch Report* (1996: 128).
32 See *Human Rights Watch Report* (1996).
33 Arkoun (1994: 113)
34 Arkoun (1994).
35 *Human Rights Journal* n.2, Summer, 1995.
36 Said and Mohammadi, 1978.

References

Al-Alili, A. A. H. (1974) *Al-Huriyyat al-ommah filfikr-wal Nidham al-Siyasi Fil Islam* (Public Liberties in Thought and Political Systems in Islam) Cairo.

Al-Ghazali, M. (1962) *Huquq al-Insan Bayn Ta'alim al-Islam* (Human Rights in the Teaching of Islam) Arabic, Cairo: Al-Matbah al-Tijariyah.

Amnesty International (1987) *Iran Violations of Human Rights*, London: AIP.

Arkoun, Mohammed (1994) *Rethinking Islam: Common Questions, Uncommon Answers*, Boulder: Westview Press.

Fareed, N. J. (1977) 'The United Nations Commission on Human Rights and its Work for Human Rights and Fundamental Freedoms', Ph.D. dissertation, Washington State University.

Human Rights Watch (1996) *World Report: Events of 1995*, New York: Human Rights Watch.

Kamil, A. H. (1952) *Fundamental Human Rights*, Lahore (n.p.).

Mehrpour, Hossein (1996) *Human Rights as International Instrument and the position of the Islamic Republic of Iran*, Tehran: Ettela't.

Renteln, A. D. (1990) *International Human Rights: Universalism versus Relativism*, London: Sage.

Said, A. A. and Mohammadi, A. (1978) 'Human Rights: An Islamic Context', International Studies Association Annual Meeting.

7 The globalization of rights in Islamic discourse[1]

Charles Kurzman

In the past twenty-five years, influential voices have emerged with a common refrain throughout the Islamic world. They offer an Islamic defence of rights through the sociology of religion, primarily the rights of Islamic interpretation but, by extension, all sorts of other rights. The basic point, as expressed by the Iranian scholar Soroush, in *Liberal Islam: A Source-Book* (1998: 245),[2] is that 'Religion is divine, but its interpretation is thoroughly human and this-worldly'. Soroush explains:

> The text does not stand alone, it does not carry its own meaning on its shoulders, it needs to be situated in a context, it is theory-laden, its interpretation is in flux, and presuppositions are as actively at work here as elsewhere in the field of understanding. Religious texts are no exception. Therefore their interpretation is subject to expansion and contraction according to the assumptions preceding them and/or the questions enquiring them. We look at revelation in the mirror of interpretation, much as a devout scientist looks at creation in the mirror of nature...[so that] the way for religious democracy and the transcendental unity of religions, which are predicated on religious pluralism, will have been paved.
>
> (*Liberal Islam*: 245, 251)

Similarly, the South African scholar Esack (1997) cites the words of 'Ali ibn Abi Talib, the son-in-law and second successor to the Messenger Muhammad: 'this is the Qur'an, written in straight lines, between two boards [of its binding]; it does not speak with a tongue; it needs interpreters and interpreters are people'. Esack translates this into contemporary terms: 'Every interpreter enters the process of interpretation with some preunderstanding of the questions addressed by the text – even of its silences – and brings with him or her certain conceptions as presuppositions of his or her exegesis' (Esack 1997: 50). Esack's preunderstandings emerge from the multi-religious struggle against apartheid in South Africa, and he argues that this commitment resonates with the spirit of early Islam, when an 'emerging theology of religious pluralism was intrinsically wedded to one of liberation' (Esack 1997: 179).

Likewise, around the Islamic world:

Hassan Hanafi (Egypt):

> There is no one interpretation of a text, but there are many inter-pretations given the difference in understanding between various interpreters. An interpretation of a text is essentially pluralistic. The text is only a vehicle for human interests and even passions....The conflict of interpretation is essentially a socio-political conflict, not a theoretical one. Theory indeed is only an epistemological cover-up. Each interpretation expresses the socio-political commitment of the interpreter.
>
> (*Liberal Islam* [Kurzman 1998]: 26)

Amina Wadud-Muhsin (USA):

> when one individual reader with a particular world-view and specific prior text [the language and cultural context in which the text is read] asserts that his or her reading is the only possible or permissible one, it prevents readers in different contexts from coming to terms with their own relationship to the text.
>
> (*Liberal Islam*: 130)

Abdullahi An-Na'im (Sudan):

> there is no such thing as the only possible or valid understanding of the Qur'an, or conception of Islam, since each is informed by the individual and collective orientation of Muslims.
>
> (An-Na'im 1995: 233)

Rusmir Mahmutehaji (Yugoslavia-Bosnia):

> No institution or group of believers has the exclusive right to 'understand' and 'interpret' a faith and its origins.
>
> (Mahmutehaji 1995: 148)

Nurcholish Madjid (Indonesia):

> Among the freedoms of the individual, the freedom to think and to express opinions are the most valuable. We must have a firm conviction that all ideas and forms of thought, however strange they may sound, should be accorded means of expression. It is by no means rare that such ideas and thoughts, initially regarded as generally wrong, are [later] found to be right....Furthermore, in the confrontation of ideas and thoughts, even error can be of considerable benefit, because it will induce truth to express itself and grow as a strong force. Perhaps it was not entirely small talk when our Prophet said that differences of opinion among his *umma* [community] were a mercy [from God].
>
> (*Liberal Islam*: 287)

Ali Asghar Engineer (India):

> It is very difficult to establish what the real intention of God is. Everyone tries to approach His intention according to one's own *a priori* position. It was not for nothing that the classical commentators, after giving their opinion on the verses, used to say *Allaho a'alam bis sawab*, that is, truth is known to Allah.
>
> (Engineer 1990: 130)

None of these scholars, to my knowledge, is familiar with the work of the others. Yet all of them have independently come up with the same sort of position. I call the position the 'interpreted *sharia*': the position that all interpretation of Islamic sources is humanly interpreted, and therefore fallible, and therefore unworthy of imposing upon others.[3]

What accounts for the simultaneous emergence of this Islamic defence of human rights around the Islamic world in the past quarter century? I make the case for four sources:

1   The rise of the global discourse of rights
2   Increasing secular education, breaking the monopoly of the seminaries over theological research
3   Increasing international communication, granting educated Muslims access to global cultural trends
4   The failure of Islamic regimes to provide an attractive alternative to the dominant global institutions

Islam and the global rights discourse

At the dawn of the 'rights era', as we might label the period since World War II, the global rights discourse had not entirely permeated the Islamic world. It was still possible, at that time, for Muslim leaders to deny that individuals have rights. Two sorts of objections were raised, one traditionalist and based on the duties of monarchical subjects, the second revivalist and based on the duties of submission to God.

The traditional objection was stated most clearly by representatives of Saudi Arabia, whose polity was based on a concept of legitimate kingship. King 'Abdul 'Aziz, founder of the modern dynasty, created no constitution, no laws (he ruled by decree), and no parliament (though he briefly had a council of advisers). His advice to his chosen successor in 1933, for example, echoed 'mirrors for princes' of the pre-modern era, and displayed no hint of 'rights' discourse:

> You should be diligent in looking after the affairs of those who will be under your control and advise them openly and secretly. Be just towards your friend and enemy. Observe this rule in large and small matters. Do not be afraid of others blaming you when you are directing yourself according to the laws of Islam.
>
> You should mind the affairs of Muslims generally and the affairs of your family especially. Consider the aged as your father, the middle as your brother and the young as your son. Also be humble and forgive their faults. Always advise them and comply with their wants as far as you can. If you now follow this advice of mine and be faithful and truthful, you will secure success in everything.
>
> I recommend you to indulge in the company of the righteous and learned people. Sit with them and respect them. Take their counsel and be strict in teaching them the doctrines of the religion and literature, for people are nowhere if God and knowledge do not help them.
>
> (al-Rashid 1976: 178)

'Abdul 'Aziz nonetheless conceived of his kingship as equivalent in certain respects to modern states, and participated in the founding of the United Nations. During the discussions at the United Nations over the Universal Declaration of Human Rights in 1948, the Saudi representative rejected the guarantee of rights that are 'at variance with the patterns of culture of Eastern States', and argued that 'the words 'dignity and rights' used in the first sentence were ambiguous and had different meanings in different countries'. He castigated delegates from other Islamic countries for approving of 'universal rights' at variance with their religion, and abstained from the final vote on the declaration (Kelsay 1988: 35–6).

The revivalist objection to rights was exemplified by *Mawlana* Abu'l-A'la Mawdudi (India-Pakistan, 1903–79), the foremost representative of Islamist revivalism in South Asia. Mawdudi began his political career in British India with a rejection both of Western concepts such as rights, and of Muslims who sought to align Islam with modern values:

> Whenever such enlightened and modernized people discuss any issue, their ultimate argument is, perhaps the strongest argument in their view, that it is the general trend and a universal practice, how can we dare to go against it, and how can we survive with such opposition....Thus, be it culture, social life, ethics, education, economy, law, politics or any other field of life, they want to follow the west instead of the principles of Islam, on the ground that the changing trends of the world cannot be ignored and that we must keep pace with the fast moving world in culture and fashions. They try to logically justify adoption of western way of life, ignoring the fact that it amounts to revolt against Islamic concept of life and, in a way, it leads to apostasy.
>
> (Mawdudi 1991 [1936]: 254–5)

> There are others who, in their misguided zeal to serve what they hold to be the cause of Islam, are always at great pains to prove that Islam contains within itself all the social and political trends which influenced contemporary thought and action, especially if such trends happen to have received the approval of their rulers. Such people perhaps look upon Islam as an orphan whose sole hope of survival lies in securing the patronage of some influential person. Or, perhaps, they believe that our position as mere Muslims can bring us no honour unless we are able to show that our religious system agrees mostly with current modern ideologies.
>
> (Mawdudi 1939: 3–4)

Mawdudi may not have been consistent in this condemnation. He could also argue that Islam accorded with modern values, for example, that an Islamic state would guarantee freedom of thought and speech, maximize individual development with no regard to inequalities of birth and status, and allow political participation for Muslims, at least within the boundaries set by the sacred sources (Mawdudi 1939: 49–55). But these considerations did not prevent him from rejecting rights discourse as a Western innovation adopted only by insecure Muslims.

In the decades since World War II, however, global rights discourse has become so dominant that Islamic counter-discourses, traditionalist and revivalist, have largely disappeared. Traditionalists and revivalists still object to certain rights stipulated in the UN Universal Declaration of Human Rights, and prefer to couch rights talk in terms of sacred sources rather than secular humanism (Mayer 1999). But these distinctions mask a historic shift: the opponents of rights talk are now engaged in rights talk themselves. According to one study of the world's constitutions, by 1970 Islamic countries were just as likely as non-Islamic countries to grant rights to their citizens: 86 per cent include a constitutional right to freedom of expression, compared with 76 per cent of non-Islamic countries; 17 per cent included women's right to equality, compared with 24 per cent of non-Islamic countries; and so on (Boli 1998: table 1). Let us consider the two examples already introduced.

Mawlana Mawdudi, upon his move to Pakistan during the partition of British India in the late 1940s, began to define the Islamic state 'in increasingly Western terms' (Nasr 1996: 88). He helped to draft an Islamist 'Objectives Resolution' in 1949, for example, that framed the desired Islamic state in near conformity to global rights discourse:

> Wherein the principles of democracy, freedom, equality, tolerance and social justice, as enunciated by Islam shall be fully observed...
>
> Wherein shall be guaranteed fundamental rights including equality of status, or opportunity and before law, social, economic and political justice, and freedom of thought, expression, belief, faith, worship and association, subject to law and public morality...
>
> Wherein adequate provision shall be made to safeguard the legitimate interests of minorities and backward and depressed classes...
>
> So that the people of Pakistan may prosper and attain their rightful and honoured place amongst the nations of the World and make their full contribution towards international peace and progress and happiness of humanity.
>
> (Binder 1961: 142–3)

The final reference to the world community signals a striking reversal of Mawdudi's rejection of world culture in the 1930s. Mawdudi later helped to draft the 1956 Constitution of the Islamic Republic of Pakistan (Nasr 1994: 142–3; 1996: 44), which included the earlier 'Objectives Resolution' as its preamble. This document listed a series of 'fundamental rights' that essentially reproduced the list proposed in 1950 by the secularists whom Mawdudi opposed: equality before the law, freedom of speech and assembly, freedom of religion, the right not to pay taxes supporting another's religion, the right to appointment to public service, and so on. The constitution went on to stipulate a series of Islamist 'Directive Principles of State Policy', but none of these were understood to undermine the designated fundamental rights. Indeed, the principles added further modern rights, including the right to education, 'just and humane conditions of work', distribution of wealth, and pensions (Choudhury 1967: 274–6, 397–401). In the last years of his life, Mawdudi embraced rights discourse so completely that he published a book entitled *Human Rights in Islam* (Mawdudi 1975).

Saudi Arabia, for its part, resisted rights discourse for decades longer, becoming publicly engaged in rights talk only in the 1980s. In 1981, the Saudi regime funded, and Saudi representatives helped draw up, the 'Universal Islamic Declaration of Human Rights' (UIDHR). In 1990, a Saudi representative joined in the 'Cairo Declaration of Human Rights' passed by the nineteenth Islamic Conference of Foreign Ministers, and a Saudi representative presented the declaration to the 1993 World Conference on Human Rights in Vienna. In 1992, the Saudi monarchy promulgated a Basic Law modelled on Western constitutions (Mayer 1999: 21–3). In the late 1990s, Saudi diplomats in Washington distributed brochures on 'Human Rights in Islam', correcting those who accuse Islam of ignoring or abusing such rights:

> In Islam, human rights are granted by God (Allah), not by kings or legislative assemblies, and therefore they can never be taken away or changed, even temporarily, for any reason. They are meant to be put into practice and lived, not to stay on paper or in the realm of unenforceable philosophical concepts or United Nations declarations.
>
> (Human Rights in Islam [n.d.])

In all of these documents, the justification for rights is distinctively Islamic, but the rights themselves are familiar throughout the world, including the following from the 1992 Basic Law:

Article 26 [human rights] The state protects human rights in accordance with the Islamic *shariah*.

Article 27 [welfare rights] The state guarantees the rights of the citizen and his family in cases of emergency, illness and disability, and in old age; it supports the system of social security and encourages institutions and individuals to contribute in acts of charity.

Article 28 [work] The state provides job opportunities for whoever is capable of working; it enacts laws that protect the employee and employer.

Article 29 [science, culture] The state safeguards science, literature and culture; it encourages scientific research; it protects the Islamic and Arab heritage and contributes toward the Arab, Islamic and human civilization.

Article 30 [education] The state provides public education and pledges to combat illiteracy.

Article 31 [health care] The state takes care of health issues and provides health care for each citizen.

Article 32 [environment, nature] The state works for the preservation, protection, and improvement of the environment, and for the prevention of pollution.

(Saudia-Arabia, Constitution, March 1992)

My point in briefly rehearsing this history is to suggest that global rights discourse has converted even its most hostile Islamist opponents. They do not speak precisely the same rights talk as the United Nations, and they may not honour in practice the rights they acknowledge in principle, but the very mouthing of such principles has opened up rhetorical space for other Muslims. The fact that the Saudi regime and Islamist hardliners are speaking of rights allows Muslim thinkers to do so too. They may be criticized for their positions, even arrested or killed, but the topic of rights is no longer out of bounds in and of itself.

Islamist rights talk has opened up institutional space as well. Repressive governments in the Islamic world have devoted funds to support the study of rights, have offered governmental and government-controlled university and parastatal positions to rights specialists, and have even hosted international conferences on rights, among which may be counted the International Conference on Human Rights (Tehran, 1968); the Seminar on Human Rights in Islam (Kuwait, 1980); and in Tunisia alone: the United Nations Seminar on the Human Rights of Migrant Workers (Tunis, 1975); the

International Colloquium of the Friedrich Naumann Foundation on the Media in the Service of Human Rights and Development (Tunis, 1981); the Governmental Conference on Human Rights in Tunis (Tunis, 1990); and the Regional Meeting of the World Conference on Human Rights (Tunis, 1992).[4]

In addition, official rights talk has opened up a gap between the ideal and the real that critics may exploit. Regimes in the Islamic world that do not live up to their stated ideals are inviting measurement by these standards. And few such regimes are living up to rights ideals. Figure 7.1 presents one rough-cut demonstration: the X-axis arrays the countries of the world by the percentage of the population that is (nominally) Muslim, as estimated by a Christian evangelical encyclopaedia (see sources on the figure); the Y-axis indicates the level of political rights and civil liberties in each country, as estimated by the Freedom House organization in New York (higher numbers mean more rights and liberties, with a minimum of 2 and a maximum of 14). The indicators might be replaced, but the general point would probably remain the same. Notice the bunching in the lower right-hand quadrant: few countries with large Muslim majorities are anywhere near the top of the rights scale. The two outliers are Gambia (85 per cent Muslim, 10.7 on the Freedom House rights scale) and Turkey (99 per cent Muslim, 9.1 on the rights scale) – neither of which regime particularly emphasizes Islamic justifications for its (limited) observance of rights. This bivariate chart expresses visually what multivariate regressions have shown for years: Islamic countries are less democratic and rights-respecting than other countries, even when controlling for level of economic development, level of education and other factors.[5] Even if we do not wish to ascribe this statistical regularity to some essentialized feature of the religion, the lag is too clear to dismiss as Orientalist propaganda.

Increasing secular education

The gap between rights talk and rights reality does not announce itself. It takes observant individuals to notice it and make a fuss. The authoritarian regimes of the Islamic world have busied themselves for the past half-century or more producing just such a class of observant individuals. Beginning in the colonial era, and continuing since as part of the ongoing power struggle with religious leaders, state elites have built vast systems of secular schools to compete with the religious leaders' madrasa and seminary systems. This battle is largely over, and religious education has been effectively marginalized. A century ago,

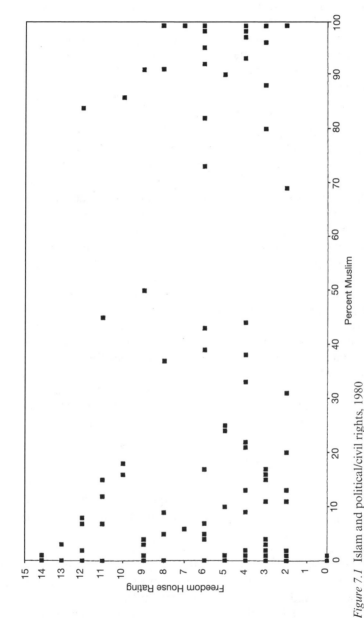

Figure 7.1 Islam and political/civil rights, 1980

Source: Percentage Muslim: Farzana Shaikh, editor, *Islam and Islamic Groups: A Worldwide Reference Guide* (Harlow: Longman, 1992); supplemented by David B. Barrett (ed.) *Worldwide Christian Encyclopaedia* (Nairobi: Oxford University Press, 1982). Political rights and civil liberties: Freedom House, *Freedom in the World*, annual edns (New York: Freedom House, 1987–95) (inverted so that higher numbers indicate more rights).

virtually all literate Muslims had been trained by religious scholars, who themselves had been trained, and permitted to teach, by other religious scholars. Today, the proportion is tiny. But in breaking the religious scholars' grip on education, the state has generated a potentially more dangerous enemy: a cohort of secularly educated intellectuals who believed their classroom textbooks' assurances that states ought to be well intentioned, democratic, respectful of rights, and violent only in the last resort. Insofar as secular education has succeeded in inculcating the state's modern values, including rights, it has trained the population to notice, and resent, the state's failure to live up to such values.

Secular education has not, however, removed all traces of religiosity. It is a common observation, though still not fully documented, that students and graduates of secular universities in the Islamic world are among the most ardent supporters of Islamist movements (Kurzman, in preparation). Liberal Islamic movements also find their greatest, perhaps their only, base of support on secular campuses. Both of these heterodox religious movements – heterodox in the sense that they challenge the teachings and religious leadership of the traditional seminaries – draw on the growing pool of the university-trained. As shown in Figure 7.2, only three of nineteen Islamic countries (defined as majority Muslim) in the Barro-Lee education dataset had more than 1 per cent of the adult population with university-level education in 1960; by 1990, only three of these countries had 1 per cent or *less* trained at this level.

Autodidacts are, in a literal sense, practising theology without a licence. When secularly educated elites engage in religious discourses, they do so as competitors, as often as allies, with seminary graduates. The Muslim thinkers quoted at the start of this chapter, for example, took their graduate degrees in philosophy (Hanafi, Soroush), engineering (Engineer, Mahmutfnof;cehaji), law (An-Na'im) or religious studies at secular universities (Esack, Madjid, Wadud-Muhsin). One way to read the theological work of such figures is as an attempt to reconcile the modern values they learned in secular schools with the religious values they assimilated outside of school. Indeed, more than one critic has assailed these authors on such grounds. Hanafi, for example, was accused of apostasy by a leader of a seminary scholars' organization in 1997 (Egyptian Organization for Human Rights and International Freedom of Expression Exchange Clearing House 1997). Esack's work was savaged in a book review both for poaching on the ground of seminary-trained professional theologians, and for doing so in the service of modern values:

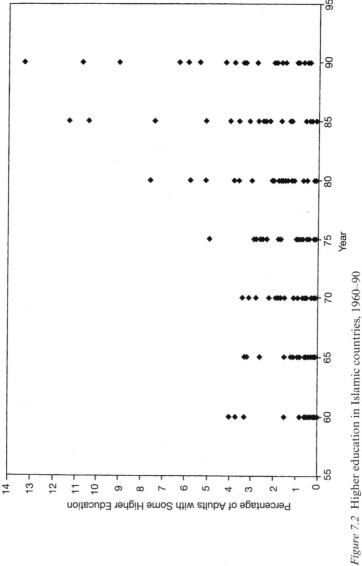

Figure 7.2 Higher education in Islamic countries, 1960–90

Source: Robert J. Barro and Jong-Wha Lee, *Data Set for a Panel of 138 Countries*, revised version, Cambridge MA: National Bureau for Economic Research [distributor] 1994.

Esack is here proposing an iconoclastic revolution in Islamic methodology, the result being a set of Islamic ethics which dovetail precisely with liberal values. No unsightly survivals from the past are to be permitted: the Qur'anic ethic is, despite all appearances, a miraculous prefiguration of late twentieth-century Western ideals.

(Murad 1997)

A first order of business, then, for many secularly trained theologians is to defend their right to trespass. Some do this with reference to their scientific background. Muhammad Shahrour (Syria, born 1938) for instance, appeals to methods he learned in engineering; Mehdi Bazargan (Iran, 1907–95) uses thermodynamics as an orienting device for Quranic analysis; Mohamed Arkoun (Algeria-France, born 1928) urges the application of linguistics and semiotics (*Liberal Islam*: 23, 82, 207). Others open up space for their own interventions by critiquing seminarians: gently, as in S. M. Zafar's (Pakistan, born 1930) suggestion that nobody today could possibly know all the seminary disciplines *and* all the secular disciplines necessary for applying theological knowledge to contemporary social problems; categorically, as in Mamadou Dia's (Senegal, born 1911) blanket comment that religious scholars are 'shackled' by the past; or aggressively, as in 'Ali Shar'ati's (Iran, 1933–77) condemnation of religious scholars as reactionary (*Liberal Islam*: 70, 279; Shar'ati 1971).

Others simply offer the analysis as its own justification. For example, Fatima Mernissi (Morocco, born 1940), trained in sociology rather than theology, examines the *hadith* (tradition of the Messenger, Muhammad):

'Those who entrust their affairs to a woman will never know prosperity!' This examination involves a study of the religious texts that everybody knows but no one really probes, with the exception of the authorities on the subject: the *mullas* [religious scholars] and *imam*s [prayer leaders].

(*Liberal Islam*: 113–20)

Mernissi looks up the *hadith* in Ibn Hajar al-'Asqalani's (1372–1449) *Fath al-bari* (The Creator's Conquest), a commentary on Muhammad ibn Isma'il al-Bukhari's (810–70) collection of epistemologically sound traditions, *Al-Sahih* (The Authentic). Mernissi finds that the *hadith* was attributed to Abu Bakra (died circa 671) – born a slave, liberated by the Prophet Muhammad, who rose to high social position in the city of Basra. He is the only source for this *hadith*, and he reported it twenty-five years after the death of the Messenger. Mernissi suggests that this *hadith*, though included in Al-Bukhari's collection and widely cited in the Islamic world, is suspect for two reasons. First, when placed in context, Abu Bakra's revelation of the *hadith* seems self-serving. He was trying to save his life after the Battle of the Camel (December 656), when, to quote Mernissi:

> all those who had not chosen to join 'Ali's clan had to justify their action. This can explain why a man like Abu Bakra needed to recall opportune traditions, his record being far from satisfactory, as he had refused to take part in the civil war. ... [Although] many of the Companions and inhabitants of Basra chose neutrality in the conflict, only Abu Bakra justified it by the fact that one of the parties was a woman.
>
> (*Liberal Islam*: 113–20)

Second, Abu Bakra had once been flogged for giving false testimony in an early court case. According to the rules of *hadith* scholarship laid out by Imam Malik ibn Anas (710–96), one of the founders of the science of *hadith* studies, lying disqualifies a source from being counted as a reliable transmitter of *hadith*. 'If one follows the principles of Malik for *fiqh* [Islamic jurisprudence], Abu Bakra must be rejected as a source of *hadith* by every good, well-informed Malikite Muslim' (*Liberal Islam*: 113–20). Mernissi's point is that seminary-trained theologians can be inconsistent when their methods contradict their gender bias; Mernissi's meta-point is that she, no less than seminary-trained theologians, is capable of reading and analysing the sacred sources according to the accepted standards of such research – indeed, that she is better at it because she is not limited by traditional blinkers.

Think of the implications of searchable CD-ROM or internet versions of al-Bukhari, al-'Asqalani, and other *hadith* collections: anyone literate in Arabic with a personal computer can investigate the sources of Islamic law and question the reigning interpretations.

Increasing international communications

International technologies of communication – newspapers, telegraph lines and international trade, as well as high-tech technologies such as radio, television, telephones, and the internet – are bringing educated people from around in the world into ever-closer contact. The ideals of

Western liberalism – like other Western ideals such as nationalism, authenticity and economic development – have entered people's homes around the world. For example, people in Gabon, West Africa, watched the fall of Communism in Eastern Europe in the news and started demanding democracy themselves. The dictator in Gabon commented derisively on the 'wind from the east [that is, the Communist Eastern bloc] that is shaking the coconut trees' (Decalo 1992: 7).

Some countries have tried to block foreign ideas from entering their countries precisely because they fear these sorts of inter-cultural interactions. But blocking foreign ideas, to quote US President Woodrow Wilson out of context, 'is like using a broom to stop a vast flood' (Mayer 1967: 602). Few countries are able to keep up this level of sweeping for long. Over the past century, advances in communications technology have made sweeping that much harder – older technologies do not disappear, but are joined by new avenues for the exchange of ideas. In Iran, for example, the Qajar dynasty struggled to block the importation of oppositional newspapers and books published abroad, which helped inspire the 1906 Constitutional Revolution – among them Mirza Malkum Khan's broadsheet *Qanun* (The Law), published in London; the newspaper *Habl al-Matin* (The Firm Clarion), published in Calcutta; and Haji Zayn al-'Abidin's novel *Siahat-namah-yi Ibrahim Bey* (The Travelogue of Ibrahim Bey), published in Istanbul, which pro-democracy activists passed around secretively and read aloud at oppositional political meetings (Kirmani 1968: 5, 8, 9, 20). The Pahlavi dynasty struggled to block not only books and periodicals, but also electronic communications from abroad during the 1979 Islamic Revolution, such as the telephone calls from France that delivered Imam Ruhullah Khomeini's pronouncements, and shortwave radio reports from the BBC Persian Service. Today the Islamic Republic – like other regimes in the Islamic world – is debating how to deal, in addition, with satellite television and internet access.

The scope of this international communication can be estimated, in a rough way, by the number of households having access to global television and the internet (see Table 7.1). The source of the television households come from advertising figures, and may be inflated, but the fact remains that hundreds of thousands of people in the Islamic world have access to global media: more than 10,000,000 households getting MTV in Indonesia, 200,000 getting the Discovery Channel in Malaysia, an estimated 1,000,000 getting CNN in Iran, and almost 100,000 households in Bahrain getting BBC television. Apparently, the pioneering Qatari television station Al-Jazeera is so popular that videocassettes of taboo-breaking programmes are circulated in large

Table 7.1 Cable/satellite television households and internet usage in selected Islamic countries, 1999

Country	BBC World	CNN International	CNBC	Discovery Channel	MTV Asia	Star TV	Internet usage
Afghanistan							
Algeria	95,000						750
Bahrain	1,500,000	19,100					32,500
Bangladesh	18,000					205,000	5,000
Brunei			1,000	36,431	36,431	35,400	
Chad							300
Comoros							200
Djibouti							300
Egypt	100,000	358,800					207,200
Gambia							150
Indonesia	40,000		2,411,946	21,411	16,000,000	22,500,000	80,000
Iran		1,000,000					
Jordan	90,000	56,000					50,300
Kuwait	50,000	178,000					62,800
Lebanon	210,000	467,090					132,200
Malaysia	2,000		181,418	214,387	182,737		600,000
Mali							500
Mauritania							100
Morocco		215,000					32,500

Table 7.1 cont

Country	BBC World	CNN International	CNBC	Discovery Channel	MTV Asia	Star TV	Internet usage
Morocco–Tunisia–Turkey (plus Cyprus)	1,565,000						
Nigeria		88,000					3,000
Oman	20,000	121,000					40,000
Pakistan	900,000					10,000	
Qatar	28,000	34,700					27,500
Saudi Arabia	1,350,000	1,416,000					112,500
Syria		100,000					
Tunisia		2,000					15,000
Turkey		1,139,100					600,000
United Arab Emirates	105,000	187,200					204,300
Yemen		208,000					6,300

Sources: Cable and satellite television: Multichannel Advertising Bureau International, http://www.cabletvadbureau.com/MAB/MABhome.htm. Internet usage: Arab countries (April 1999) from Fawaz Jarrah, 'Internet Users in Arab World Close to One Million' (Dubai, 30 May 1999) http://www.dit.net/itnews/newsmay99/newsmay77_table.html; other African countries (May 1999) from African Internet Connectivity, http://www3.wn.apc.org/africa/users.htm; remaining countries (Bangladesh, September 1997; Indonesia, May 1998; Malaysia, January 1998; Turkey, May 1997) from Nua Ltd (Dublin, Ireland) http://www.nua.ie/surveys/how_many_online. All websites consulted 9 September 1999.

numbers (Eickelman 1999). I don't need to suggest that television is brainwashing its viewers, or even affecting them particularly; one can as easily cast these numbers as indicative of consumers' desire to gain access to the outside world. Satellite dishes and cable hook-ups may be seen as expressing a pre-existing sympathy for the norms that global television represents. Internet access is an even clearer instance of active appreciation of global culture, in the broadest sense; and note the numbers in Malaysia (600,000), Turkey (600,000), Egypt (200,000), and the UAE (200,000) – these numbers are too large to be limited to a handful of elites, suggesting that significant portions of the educated middle classes are getting online.

Even the countries with tiny numbers of global media subscribers are worth noting. One wonders how many of the estimated 200 internet users in the Comoros, for example, are reading human rights reports online. What sites are the 300 internet users in Chad surfing? Access is presumably limited in such countries to trustworthy elites, but one can imagine the exposure to global rights discourse having an effect similar to smuggled broadsheets in an earlier era.

To give one example of the use of international media in the context of Islamic rights discourse, one may note the tremendous internet activity surrounding the trial of Anwar Ibrahim (Malaysia, born 1947). Anwar's trajectory from youthful Islamist militant to liberal reformist is itself a case study in the internalization of global rights themes, coinciding with his increasing use of quotations from William Shakespeare and other cross-cultural sources. When Anwar was arrested in autumn 1998, supporters of his reform movement turned to international communication through websites such as

Anwar Online (*http://members.tripod.com/~Anwar_Ibrahim*)
Anwar Ibrahim One (*http://www.anwaribrahim1.com*)
Gerakan Reformasi (*http://members.xoom.com/Gerakan*)
ADIL (*http://members.easyspace.com/reformasi*)
Reformasi Dot Com (*http://www.reformasi.com*, quoting poetry by
    Rabindranath Tagore)
Anwar's wife's official website, *http://www.anwaribrahim.org.*

Some of these sites registered hundreds of thousands of visitors in two or three months, if the hit counters are to be believed (with 600,000 internet users in Malaysia, these figures are not unreasonable). The link between domestic rights and international communication runs throughout these sites, as expressed in halting English on one flashing pro-Anwar banner:

Welcome to J's Reformasi Online, the site of the oppressed and depressed!! In the name of Allah, most gracious, most merciful....If you denied our freedom of speech [and] access to truth, [you have] sodomized our rights! As a pro-Anwar politician noted, 'With the Internet, people know there are much better alternatives to what you are fed in *Utusan Malaysia* [a leading pro-government newspaper]!'

(Sabri Zain's Reformasi Diary 1999)

Muslims around the world have responded with support for Anwar. Yusuf al-Qaradawi (Egypt, born 1926), a religious scholar in Qatar, issued a pro-Anwar *fatwa* condemning false accusations (Al-Qaradawi 1998). Abdurrahman Wahid (Indonesia, born 1940), leader of the world's largest Islamic organization, Nahdatul Ulama, wrote an article calling Anwar 'the hero of humanity', which Indonesian students in Cairo posted on the world wide web (Wahid 1998). Liberty for the Muslim World, a rights organization in London, issued a press release protesting de-democratisation in Malaysia ('Liberty Warns Against Repercussions of De-Democratisation in Maylaysia', 1998). Muslimedia, the online edition of Crescent International in England, ran a series of increasingly positive stories on Anwar.[6] In the US, the 'Minaret of Freedom Institute' in Maryland linked its website to several pro-Anwar sites.[7] Such communication was possible before the internet; transnational religious pronouncements, periodicals and travel have been a staple of the Islamic world since the beginning. But the new electronic media add an instantaneity and a common ground – the same web exists everywhere – in which transnational communications take on an increased importance. These communications are not used solely for rights discourse, but rights discourse has benefited greatly from their presence.

The failure of Islamic regimes

A fourth factor in the rise of Islamic rights discourse is the failure of alternative ideologies. In particular, there appears to be a growing sense that Islamic regimes have not lived up to their promise. Sudan and Pakistan, for example, have proved to be no less corrupt after the Islamization of the government than before. The recently departed Taliban regime in Afghanistan appeared to many Muslims as a true horror. One devout Muslim in Los Angeles even shaved off his beard in protest against the Taliban's enforcement of a mandatory beard policy (Abdullah 1997).

The disappointment for 'fundamentalist' Muslims, however, has got to be Iran. The Iranian Revolution of 1979 raised tremendous hopes among Islamists in Malaysia, in Africa, and throughout the Islamic world. This was going to be the showpiece of the Islamist movement. This was going to be the first place on earth since the seventh century where a truly Islamic society was going to be constructed, and it has been painful for these people to find that dream unfulfilled. Even revivalists who still cheer the goals of the Revolution are defensive about the reality, as in this recent editorial by a British-based Islamist periodical:

> The expectations which people had for an Islamic state which was bound to be embryonic and experimental, as well as being subjected to the most venomous hatred and enmity by the west, were not reasonable. Not all officials of the state can be expected to share the qualities of the Imam [Khomeini] himself. Having said that, in terms of nationalism and sectarianism in particular, too many have failed to maintain even minimum standards.
>
> (Muslimedia 1999)

Yet for others, disillusionment has led to a repudiation of hardline Islamist ideals in favour of rights. One example of this process is 'Abdul-Karim Soroush. Soroush, a wholehearted supporter of the Islamic Republic in the early years, participated actively in the revolutionary reorganization of the universities in Iran, which involved getting rid of otherwise qualified professors in the name of ideological purity. Yet even this staunch supporter of the Islamic Republic began to have doubts. By the mid-1980s he had started to distance himself from the official committees he had served on. By the late 1980s he began to criticize the government, to call for a reinterpretation of Islamic law, and to call for the academic and intellectual rights that his university reorganization had disregarded in the early 1980s. These themes, along with his impressive erudition and his talent for public speaking, made Soroush one of the most popular public speakers in Iran in the early 1990s. He spoke at mosques, at universities and on the radio, always with big audiences. Naturally the Iranian government found his words threatening, and Soroush has now been barred from speaking publicly in Iran. Instead Soroush now speaks outside of Iran, when he is allowed to travel, addressing international audiences, mainly in Europe and North America, stressing the commonality of his views with Western interpretations of religion. But the painfulness of Soroush's break with the Islamic Republic, his disillusionment, is apparently so great that he literally cannot deal with his own former hopes and aspirations. In interviews, Soroush denies that he was a supporter of the Cultural Revolution in Iran and denies that he was active in the reorganization of the universities.[8]

Conclusion

The permeation of rights discourse in the Islamic world is no different, I would suggest, from the permeation of automobiles or population control. All of these were invented in the West, packaged as universally applicable, and exported to the rest of the world, where consumers of various sorts (states, businesses, social groups) snapped them up more or less eagerly, with greater or lesser adaptation to local circumstances. This perspective, associated with the institutional theory of John Meyer and his colleagues,[9] moves the question of rights discourse away from normative debates as to whether 'Islam' is compatible with 'rights' – as though either term could be defined with any closure – and towards a sociological understanding of the social situations in which 'Islam' and 'rights' are understood to be compatible. I have tried to identify four global processes that have encouraged such an understanding:

1   the adoption of rights talk by previously hostile traditionalists and revivalists, even as they abuse rights in practice;
2   the growth of a class of secularly educated theological autodidacts;
3   the acceleration of international communication through electronic media; and
4   the disillusionment associated with alternative Islamist projects.

These global processes account for the pattern of rights discourse in the Islamic world: the simultaneous and independent emergence of parallel arguments in Egypt, Iran, India, Indonesia and elsewhere.

These arguments emerge from a common point in the social space: leading professionals who broke with a family background steeped in traditional Islamic learning to obtain a foreign education, and who maintain friendly and collegial relations with professionals in the West. Such individuals have an ongoing interest in reconciling their Islamic faith and their modern values, including global rights values. To do so, they must first defend their own status as interpreters of Islam, and this defence draws their arguments towards a particular rights discourse – basically a sociology of religion – in which no interpretation is recognized as definitive, and all interpretations are linked to the social milieux in which they are generated. This position, which I call the 'interpreted *sharia*', has a long history in Islamic discourse, beginning with the live-and-let-live routinization of the four Sunni schools (*madhabs*) a millenium ago. But the 'interpreted *sharia*' takes on a different, more challenging form when it is wielded by theologians outside of the recognized seminary institutions, against these institutions, in the service of rights talk that these institutions have historically not recognized as legitimate. Add to this the inherent hostility of repressive states to rights activism, indeed to any form of social mobilization not controlled by the state, and the rights campaigners face serious challenges in the Islamic world. I have tried to argue, though, that the globalization of rights talk in the Islamic world, as elsewhere in the world, is the product of social trends that show no sign of abating – and therefore that rights activism is only going to diffuse further, despite the challenges.

Notes

1   Earlier versions of portions of this paper were published in *MERIA Journal* (Middle East Review of International Affairs) vol. 3, no. 3, September 1999; and *Forum Bosnae* (Sarajevo) no. 2, March-April 1999. I thank Deborah Barrett, John Boli, Rusmir Mahmuthaji, Barry Rubin and Suzanne Shanahan for their assistance in preparing this paper.

2   In Charles Kurzman (ed.) (1998) *Liberal Islam: A Source-Book*, New York: Oxford University Press. This paper draws upon and develops the works contained in this anthology.

3   Other 'liberal' tropes are the 'liberal *sharia*', which holds that liberal positions are mandated by sacred sources; and the 'silent *sharia*', which holds that sacred sources leave certain fields to human invention, thus permitting liberal positions. See *Liberal Islam*: 14–18.

4   *International Conference on Human Rights at Teheran*, New York: United Nations, 1968; *Human rights in Islam: Report of a Seminar Held in Kuwait, December 1980*, Geneva: International Commission of Jurists, 1982; *Seminar on the Human Rights of Migrant Workers, Tunis, 12–24 November 1975*, New York: United Nations, 1976; *The Media in the Service of Human Rights and Development: Proceedings of the Fourteenth International Colloquium of the Friedrich Naumann Foundation, Tunis, 20–22 September, 1981*, Bonn: Liberal-Verlag, 1982; *al-Nadwah al-Dawliyah hawla Huquq al-Insan fi Tunis amama Mutaghayyirat al-'Alam al-Yawm, Tunis 10 Disimbir 1990*, Tunis: al-Tajammu' al-Dusturi al-Dimuqrati, 1990; *Actes de la Réunion Régionale pour l'Afrique de la Conference Mondiale sur les Droits de l'Homme*, Tunis: Tunisian External Communication Agency, 1992.

5   Recent statistical analyses of this subject include Midlarsky (1998: 485–511) and Abootalebi (1995: 507–29).

6   Compare the 1999 stories in *http://www.muslimedia.com/my-crisis/index.html* with the 1998 stories in *http://www.muslimedia.com/archives/sea.htm.*
7   'New Link to Anwar Ibrahim Website', 11 April 1999, *http://www.minaret.org.*
8   See the website devoted to Soroush's thought (*http://www.seraj.org*), and 'Intellectual Autobiography: An Interview', in Sadri and Sadri (forthcoming).
9   See the paradigm-building collections: Thomas *et al.* (1987) and Boli and Thomas (1999).

References

Aslam Abdullah (1997) 'Shaving Is His Protest Against Coercion', *Los Angeles Times*, 10 May.

Abootalebi, A. R. (1995) 'Democratization in Developing Countries, 1980–1989', *Journal of Developing Areas*, vol. 29, no. 4, 507–29.

An-Na'im, A. A. (1995) 'Toward an Islamic Hermeneutics for Human Rights', in Abdullahi A. An-Na'im, Jerald D. Gort, Henry Jansen and Hendrik M. Vroom (eds) *Human Rights and Religious Values: An Uneasy Relationship?*, Michigan: William B. Eerdmans Publishing.

Binder, L. (1961) *Religion and Politics in Pakistan*, Berkeley: University of California Press.

Boli, J. (1998) 'World Culture, World Cultures, and Human Rights Ideology: An Islamic Alternative?', unpublished paper, table 1.

Boli, J. and Thomas, G. M. (eds) (1999) *Constructing World Culture*, Stanford: Stanford University Press.

Choudhury, G. W. (1967) *Documents and Speeches on the Constitution of Pakistan*, Dacca: Green Book House.

Decalo, S. (1992) 'The Process, Prospects, and Constraints of Democratization in Africa', *African Affairs*, vol. 91.

Egyptian Organization for Human Rights and International Freedom of Expression Exchange Clearing House (1997) 'University Professor Branded an Apostate', *http://www.ifex.org/alert/00001971.html.*

Eickelman, D. F. (1999) 'The Coming Transformation of the Muslim World', *MERIA Journal* (Middle East Review of International Affairs) vol. 3, no. 3, September (*http://www.biu.ac.il/SOC/besa/meria/journal/1999/issue3/jv3n3a8.html*).

Engineer, A. A. (1990) *Islam and Liberation Theology*, New Delhi: Sterling Publishers.

Esack, F. (1997) *Qur'an, Liberation, and Pluralism*, Oxford: Oneworld.

'Human Rights in Islam' (n.d.) Washington DC: IFTA Office, Islamic Series no. 5.

Kelsay, J. (1988) 'Saudi Arabia, Pakistan, and the Universal Declaration of Human Rights', in David Little, John Kelsay and Abdulaziz A. Sachedina, *Human Rights and the Conflict of Cultures*, South Carolina: University of South Carolina Press.

Kirmani, M. N. I. (1968) *Tarikh-i Bidari-i Iranian* (History of the Awakening of the Iranians) Tehran: Intisharat-i Bunyad-i Farhang-i Iran.

Kurzman, C. (ed.) (1998) *Liberal Islam: A Source-book*, New York: Oxford University Press.

Kurzman, C. (in preparation) 'Who Are the Islamists? A Literature Review', paper in preparation.

Liberal Islam: A Source-book (1998) ed. Charles Kurzman, New York: Oxford University Press.

'Liberty Warns Against Repercussions of De-Democratisation in Malaysia', 24 September, *http://www.lmw.org.*

Mahmutehaji, R. (1995) *Living Bosnia*, 2nd edn, trans. Spomenka Beus and Francis R. Jones, Ljubljana: Oslobopenja International.

Mawdudi, S. A. A (1939) *The Political Theory of Islam*, Lahore: Markazi Maktaba Jamaat-i-Islami, Pakistan.

——(1975) *Human Rights in Islam*, trans. Kurshid Ahmad and Ahmed Said Khan (1976) Leicester: Islamic Foundation.

——(1991) [1936] 'Courage and Conviction: The Secret of Progress and Prosperity', in S. A. A. Mawdudi, *West versus Islam*, New Delhi: International Islamic Publishers.

Mayer, A. E. (1999) *Islam and Human Rights*, 3rd edn, Boulder: Westview Press.

Mayer, A. J. (1967) *Politics and Diplomacy of Peacemaking: Containment and Counterrevolution at Versailles, 1918–1919*, New York: Alfred A. Knopf.

Midlarsky, M. J. (1998) 'Democracy and Islam: Implications for Civilizational Conflict and the Democratic Peace', *International Studies Quarterly*, vol. 42, no. 3, September, 485–511.

Murad, A. H. (1997) 'Dancing with Liberalism', *Q-News International* (Great Britain) nos. 264–5, May, *http://muslimsonline.com/bicnews/BICNews/Qnew/qnews2.htm.*

Muslimedia (1999) 16–30 June, 1http://www.muslimedia.com/archives/editorial99/editor64.htm.

Nasr, S. V. R. (1994) *The Vanguard of the Islamic Revolution: The Jama'at-i Islami of Pakistan*, Berkeley: University of California Press.

——(1996) *Mawdudi and the Making of Islamic Revivalism*, New York: Oxford University Press.

al-Qaradawi, Y. (1998) 'Mr Anwar Ibrahim Fatwa', 10 September, *http://www.qaradawi.netenglish/fatwa/Mr-anwar-fatwa.htm.*

al-Rashid, I. (ed.) (1976) *Documents on the History of Saudi Arabia*, vol. 3, Salisbury NC: Documentary Publications.

Sabri Zain's Reformasi Diary (1999) 'Changing Times', 2 February, *http://www.geocities.com/CapitolHill/Congress/5868/change.htm.*

Sadri, M. and Sadri, A. (forthcoming) *Reason, Freedom, and Democracy in Islam: Essential Writings of Abdolkarim Soroush*, trans. Mahmoud Sadri and Ahmad Sadri, New York: Oxford University Press.

Saudi Arabia – Constitution (March 1992) International Constitutional Law website (ICL Document Status, October 1993) *http://www.uni-wuerzburg.de/law/sa00000.html.*

Shari'ati, A. (1971) *Tashayyu'-i 'Alavi va Tashayyu'-i Safavi*, Tehran: Intisharat-i Husayniyah Irshad.

Soroush, A.-K. (1998) in Charles Kurzman (ed.) *Liberal Islam: A Source-book*, New York: Oxford University Press.

Thomas, G. M., Meyer, J. W., Ramirez, F. O. and Boli, J. (1987) *Institutional Structure: Constituting State, Society, and the Individual*, Newbury Park CA: Sage.

Wahid, A. (1998) 'Anwar, Mahathir, dan Kita di Indonesia', 3 October, *http://www.muslims.net/KMNU/nu/1998/981003b.htm*.

8   The World Cup and Iranians' 'home-coming'

A global game in a local Islamicized context[1]

Manuchehr Sanadjian

This chapter focuses on the popular response in Iran to the World Cup tournament in order to examine the interplay between football as a globally defined *game* and its local reception in a *play*. Thus, from a paradigm of competition (a set of rules that determines what is a win and what is not), football is transformed into a 'deep' play in a local context where the relationship between football (signifier) and its audience (signified) assumes an indeterminate, ambiguous character. Against this ambiguity and the alternative interpretations for action to which it gives birth, this chapter argues that celebrating Iranians redefined their relationship with the Islamic state. Within the ambiguity-ridden, carnivalesque space of play, Iranians subverted the Islamic juridical rule which is geared to tight control over space and the body. The juridical rule, through the textual construction of the Muslim community (*ummat*) is the outcome of the state's negation of civil society which sustains the notion of legality. This chapter seeks to tease out the implications of their play in terms of a re-investment by Iranians in the territory they inhabit, with a specifically cultural import which maintains their position as a unique people-nation interacting with other equally unique people-nations. The Islamic state, although relying on territory as its power base, has refused to recognize the culturally specific terms in which Iranians define their relationship with this territory as a place, home. Unlike the modern state which, irrespective of its representative character, seeks to forge, through recourse to the notion of culture, an identity with the nation over which it presides, the Islamic state's juridical rule which is based on an universal religious allegiance, abolishes the mediation of culture. As with society, culture interrupts the Islamic state's textual construction of the Muslim community in which the body and space are tightly controlled. The global game of football offered Iranians the opportunity to slacken this control by rallying behind the iconic football players who represented them, through the global media, as a distinct people-nation. The massive World Cup celebration by Iranians is seen, therefore, as a temporary re-occupation of the space in which they, by and large, construct their national identity through 'secular pilgrimages'. As Gramsci put it:

> This contrast between thought and action, i.e. the co-existence of two conceptions of the world, one affirmed in words and the other displayed in effective action, is not simply a product of self-deception. Self-deception can be an adequate explanation for a few individuals taken separately, or even for groups of a certain size, but it is not adequate when the contrast occurs in the life of great masses. In these cases the contrast between thought and action cannot but be the expression of profounder contrasts of a social historical order. It signifies that the social group in question may indeed have its own conception of the world, even if only embryonic; a conception which manifests itself in action, but occasionally and in flashes – when, that is, the group is acting as an organic totality.
>
> (Gramsci 1971: 326–7)

Discussing 'organic totality' as a consequence of group action, exactly as Gramsci suggests, an Iranian football spectator argued that the Iranian Government was totally opposed to this:

> You see, football was susceptible to the expression of solidarity especially after the election which brought Khatami to power; when people, if not free, could at least express themselves a bit more freely. Government was quite happy to see the back of all this and an early exit by the country from the World Cup qualification race.
>
> (Iranian football spectator 1999)[2]

The young Iranian described this during his detailed, eye-witness account of the popular reaction in Iran to the unexpected result of the football match between Australia and Iran in Melbourne in November 1997.[3] In this match Iran qualified to join thirty-one other nations in the World Cup tournament in France in 1998. The young man echoed the sense of frustration of so many Iranians for whom the result in Australia came, in the wake of all the setbacks and difficulties in Iranian football, as a big surprise: 'The day the people set themselves free from the [Islamic] state was the day on which Iran played against Australia' (Iranian football spectator 1999).

It was only very recently that a Brazilian was appointed to the post of coach of the national team, as a result of growing public pressure to replace an officially favoured Iranian coach, a *hezbulahi*,[4] who had an avowed moral position and was widely blamed for the team's poor performances in qualifying matches. The Iranian coach, occupying a high moral ground, had publicly humiliated his players by commenting on their conduct outside the pitch. There were widely circulated rumours of schisms and unrest in the team which, in the absence of a reliable means of verification, eroded public confidence even further. The football spectator quoted above said

> Myself for one did not even think that our chance of qualifying was one percent...the problem was by no means merely to qualify for the World Cup but to achieve a self belief; the ability to feel this passionate and something.

Here the young man interrupted his recounting of the event to draw my attention to the two late goals scored by the two Iranian players, whose names were mentioned frequently in his account:

> 'When Iran scored the two goals. What happened then?'
> 'I do not know if you did watch the match? If you had you would have really found it absolutely impossible! After the match Terry Venables only said these words, "I do not believe it!". Their goalkeeper, who was also the goalkeeper of Aston Villa, said "This is absolutely impossible! Football is a bastard [*namard*]!". They could not believe it. Really they couldn't believe the result when we, imagine, how should I say this, were totally at loss in the match. The Iranian players were crying and shedding tears in joy at the end of the match. I saw myself, in all conscience, hundreds of people who were crying. What were they crying for? Was football that important? The fact of matter was that the ordinary man had grown a feeling inside which he wanted to get rid of. There was no question that something was happening. You see some people may say this is after all only a game of football and it does not matter much who wins. But there is a time when you have to look at football not for its winners and losers but for the sentiment it generates. For us it provided a means to express our sentiment....When the referee blew the whistle we who were hugging and kissing each other in the house said let's go outside. That was the time to go out....Once we came out in several cars we found ourselves in the Apocalypse! It was impossible to pass

through....It was unprecedented. Girls and boys were really dancing together'.

Noticeable in this account is the progressive move towards dramatization, together with the use of facial and bodily expressions as opposed to the use of words, in order to present directly the actions around which the narrative is organized. This dramatization reduces the role of the narrator as the interpreter by calling on his interlocutor to act as his witness. As such, the witness becomes someone who can turn, with his own presence, the match into an *event*, that is to confer authority on the players' actions as something significant – a heroic act to re-establish Iranian identity in a global contest against adverse local circumstances. The dramatization and the recourse to witness enables the narrator to bridge the gap between words and actions, thus increasing the contextual – as opposed to textual – aspect of the narrative performance. The Iranian players, whose two late goals secured Iran's entry into the World Cup tournament, needed the direct testimony of witnesses in sufficient number to have the goals they had scored transformed into the narrated *actions* as Iranian. That the young man and his friends still continued to watch the recorded match on video, and always found it enjoyable, particularly the goals scored by the Iranian players, reflected a recognition of the need for a continuous testimony without which the goals scored ceased to be acts of *representation*. Without a sufficient number of participants – as spectators – the play was ineffective as an alternative representation (construction) of Iranian identity. It was not the satisfaction derived from the skill demonstrated by the footballers that primarily accounted for the young man's and many other Iranians' continued appreciation of the goal-scorers' feat. He acknowledged that many more skillful footballers could probably be found in Iran. What was primarily significant about these goal-scorers was their critical efforts to score goals for Iran, that is to offer Iranians the chance to articulate themselves with *others* in a different way than they were allowed within the Islamicized political space, from which contested representation – a characteristic feature of politics since the French Revolution – had abdicated. Through revisiting the match the young man and his friends reasserted the players' authority by reiterating their participation in the game as members of the audience who watched the playful opening up of the Islamic space. Thus, by authorizing the players' performance as national the young man and his friends were able to claim the space in which performance took place as 'home', a tantalizing, inaccessible place for Iranians inside and outside the country. Beside the goal-scorers, the players who 'rescued' the team from conceding more goals, who tackled the opposition and who showed stamina, were all taking part in the construction of an 'imaginary homeland'; the alternative space to the one in which they lived, and to which they could travel through participation in the global game of football.

Spectatorship and pleasure in Islamic context

The enthusiasm with which the young man asked me if I had seen the goals was an attempt to simultaneously displace a witnessing role on to an interlocutary one, on the one hand, and a performer role on to that of a narrator. The double displacement reduced the role of narrativity in the construction of an 'imaginary homeland'. The authority conferred on the two Iranian football players did not derive from their mere goal-scoring achievement on the pitch but from the verdict of spectators outside of it, whose *presence* rescued the two players from the anonymity of goal-scorers in a game of football and raised them to the status of national heroes. The transformation of the recounted match into a performance-oriented narrative involved a reconstruction of the football players, whose play was governed by the rules of a game of football, within a national cultural context where the players' agency was circumscribed by relations based on class, gender, ethnicity and age.

The popular cultural reconstruction of the players bestowed a critical importance on the articulation of Iranian national identity in a highly ritualized, textualized Islamic space in which human action was forcefully stripped of its contextual social and cultural agency by the state. In order to confer the status of action on their football players' goal-scoring achievement, Iranians had to interact with the players as their *spectators*. The spectatorship, geared to a secular (profane) contextual distance, was scarcely compatible with the textually constructed, ritualized Islamic space in which distance is measured in terms of the sacred/profane polarity and from which pleasure as a profanity had been abdicated. In this space the legitimate form of pleasure was a transcendental one (Kant in Mercer 1986) requiring the suspension of the 'agreeable' and the 'corporeal'.

Within the Islamic space coordinated by the quest for salvation there was hardly any room for play, with its avowed lack of interest in anything beyond itself. Play served no other purpose than providing pleasure for those who took part in it, a provision scarcely compatible with a ritual space polarized along the sacred/profane opposition.

The abdication of pleasure from the textually constructed Islamic space is exemplified in the officially proscribed clapping. Until very recently the audience in Iran were expected to show their appreciation only by shouting 'Allah, the Almighty' while raising their clenched fists in the air. This defiant gesture, originally associated with a secular protest against civil and political exclusions, was adopted by Muslims to express a non-compliance with the seductive earthy world. The realization of joy under Islamic rule was a part and parcel of the mobilization of Muslims to redeem themselves from original sin. A typical demonstration of the Islamic authorities' refusal to allow Iranians to lapse into forbidden joy was the prevention of urban residents from holding outdoor picnics in green public spaces in the evening during hot seasons. The devices used by the Islamic authorities to interrupt this popular habit included flooding the picnic area with water and cutting the electricity supply to the public lighting in the areas where residents spread their mats! The forbidding of pleasure was also the reason why the Islamic authorities imposed a differentiated restriction on Iranian musical instruments. The degree of official restriction on each instrument was proportionate to its role in the generation of joyful pleasure (*jouissance*) as opposed to a meaningful pleasure (*plaisir*) (Barthes 1977).

The street was the space where the conflict between the individual's desire and the 'apparently mysterious processes' which were taking place 'out there' in society, was most acutely experienced (Williams 1961: 112). It was also the place where shops were situated and market forces were most effective in inspiring members of the Muslim community (*ummah*) to cast themselves in the anonymous, 'disenchanted' role of consumer by severing their connection with the *ummah*. The role of the anonymous occupant of urban space driven by a relentless pursuit of desire – represented in the celebrated figure of the *flâneur* – accounted for the prevalent fear experienced by Muslim men of losing control over women. The streets in the Islamic Republic were the arena from which were excluded not only contested representations – unofficial demonstrations, the sale of political newspapers and street debates which normally accompanied the sale – but also lapses into the forbidden experience of joy. The space for individuality created by the market opened up the possibility of a fusion of individuals within a contingent unity, and subsequent undoing of the Islamic project of constituting *a people* in the wake of the revolutionary exercise of power by 'we *the people*' (Balibar 1994). As a prime site of modernity the streets were seen as the place where the Islamic order was threatened by subversion and where Muslims were in danger of becoming 'unhinged'.

More often than not, two forms of 'corruption', political and non-political, were presented by Islamic officials as being identical. 'The bastards' – a 'natural' Islamic reference to atheist socialists but easily extended to include almost all opposition groups – who became involved in political representations were also those suspected of expanding the domain of taste and choice and objectified sexual desire that corrupted the Islamic moral order. In the public space, the Islamic regime denied the user of nationally circulated cultural products not only the autonomy of a consumer but also the status of a customer and the membership of a non-official community (Williams 1961).

The pleasure experienced by a football spectator, on the other hand, was 'real', that is it belonged to history, or its profane realm. It was this profane domain to which the young male Iranian referred when he described the celebrating crowd as overwhelmed by the joy on the streets of Tehran and other places in Iran: 'Everyone expressed the joy using whatever means available to them...even though it was not going to last long the joy was nevertheless a real one'. This football spectator refused the mediation of the sacred/profane dichotomy by considering enjoyment a legitimate phenomenon and thus granting it an autonomous existence *vis-à-vis* the sacred. The independent status of pleasure (enjoyment) in football spectatorship undermined the state's relentless efforts to re-constitute its subjects as Muslim through recourse to the sacred/profane polarity. Pleasure was instrumental in the abolition of the distance between 'representation and the referent', the space the Islamic authorities kept exclusively for the construction of the Muslim subject. Indeed, since the body was considered a major disruptive force in this construction, it became the main target of control under Islamic rule.

Whereas the only form of pleasure allowed under Islamic rule was a transcendental one designed to construct an Islamic identity (*plaisir*), the kind of pleasure permitted in football spectatorship was largely 'corporeal' and instrumental in the pursuit of the 'agreeable' (*jouissance*) (Barthes 1977; Bourdieu 1984). The body, which became the object of the most detailed purification practices when the pleasure of being a Muslim was experienced,[5] was left to the subversive law of desire when enjoyment was sought by spectators. The distance between the subject and its object of desire which was filled by Islamic norms in the first was removed in the second, making it possible for the subject to unite with its object of desire. Thus the unity of subject with its object of desire through enjoyment – in watching, touching or hearing – reduced the space for control by external agencies such as the state. The pleasure generated by football spectatorship subverted the power of the Islamic state, which constituted its subjects through the opposition between sacred and profane. Like other forms of leisure, participation in the game was conducive to an identification between subject and its object of pleasure, an autonomy which severely limited the room for interpretation by the state, which claimed its authority primarily from the sacred text as opposed to the historically shaped Muslim believers.

Game versus socio-cultural play

The marked dramatization in the young football spectator's narrative reflected the critical mediation of the body in simultaneously constructing the national-cultural and deconstructing the Islamic-juridical. Football as a game, a paradigm of competition, a set of rules that determined who was the winner and who was the loser, offered 'certain vantage-points' from which a limited number of Iranians, using a specialized language intelligible to them as spectators, understood the game. In recent years a growing 'connoisseur' interest in football, particularly by Iranian youth of both sexes, has developed. The red or blue shirt-wearing girls and boys can be seen on the streets of major Iranian cities expressing openly their support for the two main national football clubs. Football spectatorship facilitated a cross-gender interaction which is restricted if not forbidden in many other spheres of practice. Football spectatorship's articulation across main sources of social divisions, such as gender, remained partial, however. Despite their informal spectatorship, women were banned from stadia hosting football matches.[6] But those 'spectators' who appreciated the Iranian goal-scorers' feat in the qualifying match against Australia were the ones who actually recognized this feat, that is they authorized it as action (otherwise the players' goal-scoring would have been remained relatively little known). These spectators belonged to a larger community of sign-users than the one in which the game of football was made intelligible in terms of skill and technical ability. The community provided the basis for the construction of a narrative of nationhood in which the players were assigned the status of national heroes. Whereas in a game the signifier 'football' was invested with a determinate, predictable relationship with the signified, both in the areas of game and spectatorship, in the extra-game context the relationship becomes indeterminate and much less predictable. Although as a game football was perceived by Islamic officials as a 'pure waste', the game's potential to articulate the social and the cultural made it a source of threat to Muslim rulers, who regarded their constituency as an homogeneous *ummat* within a space emptied of social and cultural contents. Thus, in its less stable relationship with the signified, the signifier 'football' was susceptible to the articulation of social and cultural parameters and an alternative construction of Iranian identity. In this way, from being a global nuisance football became the means to open up the tightly controlled Islamic space through a diversity of representations and expressions of identity. The spectators, whose competence in football as a game was defined with reference to the game's competitive rules, were later drawn from diverse areas of cultural practices which made varied, heterogeneous sources of competence available to them.

When the young man said that the problem he and other Iranians faced was not entry into the World Cup tournament but to gain self-belief, he acknowledged the fact that the vast majority of Iranians have adopted the role of football spectators on a basis much wider than the game; 'self-belief' referred to a competence accessible outside of the realm of a game. 'Self-belief' did not refer to an individual but to a collectivity capable of an autonomous existence. The existence was geared to the articulation of diverse sources of identity, that is to be Iranian, which had been reduced to an homogeneous Islamic identity: 'You see, we had a feeling, how should I say, a quest which had been suppressed in us. We were in the state of being forgotten'. The global connection mediated by a sport with a worldwide grassroots audience offered a chance to Iranians to rescue themselves from being a forgotten people. The diversely based spectatorship conferred on the football players a general character distinct from what was made available to the spectator in the game of football. It was not, the young man insisted, success defined merely in terms of 'a game of football' which drove thousands of Iranians to celebrate the football victory on the streets and public places of cities, towns and even villages. What these Iranians did, according to him, was to seize an unprecedented opportunity to enjoy themselves, to release the desire they had long suppressed. He then went on to say that unlike so many other official occasions, the anniversaries and celebrations of religious figures' birthdays and victories, in which they had taken part, the football celebrations gave them a unique opportunity to express themselves. 'This was something else', the man said. The conjuncture of a wide-based spectatorship and the general authority conferred on the players turned the goal-scoring into an assertion of national will. The signifier 'football', having been offered the unprecedented chance of becoming articulated with such a wide range of signifieds, became the means of articulation of the national-popular.

It is against the political vacancy and the call for a new Caesar to shatter the 'stifling and ossified state in the dominant camp as well, and introduce into national life and social activity a different and more numerous personnel' (Gramsci 1971: 223), that the popular appreciation of the entry into the World Cup tournament has to be gauged. The new Caesar was sought to mediate between conflicting social forces, different social classes, gender, ethnic and even age groups, so that more room was provided for opposing interests; to represent *a higher level of general* (cultural) interest. The spontaneous popular reaction to Iran's successful qualification for the World Cup disturbed the apparently settled position of Muslim rulers. The unexpected entry created space for the expression of the widening gap between represented Iranians and their Muslim representatives. The authority conferred on the goal-scorers served those who granted the authority to transform themselves as football spectators in contradistinction to their officially prescribed membership of the *ummah*. The spontaneous surge of interest in football was an episodic recourse to a mediating agency, apparently operating outside the abolished domain of politics, to forge a general interest. The use of the body, a notoriously capable means of deconstructing meaning (Barthes 1977), facilitated the mediation through the creation of carnivalesque space.

The ambiguity sustained in the space enabled the participants to reclaim the space they occupied, even if temporarily, as their place – home – by redefining themselves as Iranians, a culturally specific people. Thus, the mediation of enjoyment, *jouissance*, to recapture as their place the territory on which the Islamic state based its power, allowed Iranians to re-enter it as cultural agents.

That the country's organic political crisis was given a non-political expression appeared to have taken even the Islamic rulers by surprise. The use of the national flag by the celebrating crowd was a re-appropriation of the national symbol. The widespread use of the flag in moving cars[7] with lights on and horns sounding enabled the crowd to claim the streets and public places from which they had been hitherto conspicuously absent as national agents. The unity symbol, movement, and the homogenizing sound and light were recruited in the concerted effort to create *we the people* with its indeterminate, and potentially insurrectionary, character. The popular assertion displaced, even if only temporarily, *a Muslim people* constituted by the state with marked brutality in an attempt at restoration beyond the division of space into public and private. Thus the tension arising from the emerging power of *the people* soon surfaced when the regime's law and order agents, overwhelmed by the surging crowd who patently violated the Islamic code of practice of sexual segregation, either avoided or quickly retreated from any confrontation with the celebrating Iranians. Although popular occupation of the public space was short-lived, it nevertheless damaged the credibility of the state's claim to a permanent constitution of *a Muslim people*. The space negotiated by the crowd rendered even less tenable the sovereignty of the state's power, which essentially based its legitimacy on the sacred texts. The secular, even if ephemeral, expression of popular pleasure undermined the avowedly eternal, sacred authority of their Muslim rulers. Thus, despite its 'frontal attack' appearance, the popular occupation of public places during the celebrations would have a more lasting effect on the 'war of position' of the popular classes against their Muslim rulers.

The body and juridical power

The Islamic regime's relation to modern sports is derived from an opposition to the impact of sports, as distinct practices involving the use of the body, on the space between representation and the represented. More often than not this space has been used exclusively by the state to mobilize meaning in order to construct the Muslim subject through a forged cohesion between the Muslim jurist and his followers. By encouraging the subject to unite with its object of desire, sports threatened to undermine the domain in which the state has acted as the sole legitimate agent of interpretation. The more popular sport has become, with the concomitant rise in the mediating role of audience, the more this threat has increased. The involvement of a larger audience made the threat of subversion by the audience all the more serious in terms of the state's control of the space in which its juridical rule rested. That is why the Islamic state's attitude was markedly elitist in so far as it favoured sports which enhanced the regime's prestige in international competition with little domestic audience involvement. The distinction sought by the Islamic state through promotion of sports is geared to the mediation of the body to ensure the 'most distanced relation to the adversary' (Bourdieu 1990: 157). The elitist notion of sport is harnessed to the regime's means-to-end, instrumental rational approach to international relations.[8]

Rationalist discourse, in which mind is accorded mastery over the body through the mediation of the mind/body dichotomy which is ingrained in modern western social and political thought (Hargreaves 1987), remains oblivious to the way in which the body is invested with cultural significance and is incorporated in the social order. Islamic discourse, by contrast, is primarily concerned with a relentless purification of the body, as it is seen as the source of desire and a shelter for the unharnessed forces of nature. The autonomy claimed in the rationalist discourse both for reason and the body, over which the latter seeks control, is sustained by the mind/body dichotomy which is based on the separation between truth and power (Foucault 1996). The separation is premised on the mobilization of truth in pursuit of power. The ideological terrain in which such mobilization has taken place in the West is a developed civil society normally capable of resisting the pressure asserted by the state. In Iran, on the other hand, the Islamic state sought to dissolve an unevenly developed Iranian civil society, which had rebelled against the state, within the textually constructed ritual space of the Muslim community or *ummah* (Sanadjian 1996). In this space, truth is indistinguishable from (the sovereign Islamic) power. Thus the unity forged between truth and power in the Muslim community made redundant the idea of the normality of the body – defined in terms of physical/mental health, medical/hygienic, recreational/enjoyable fashion/choice/desire – which had already taken partial root in Iranian civil society in the wake of capitalist development in the country (Sanadjian 1996). The notion of normality was the outcome of an articulation between truth and power, with an implicit recognition of both parts' distinct existence. The juridical mode of power which secured the Islamic sovereignty was designed to do away with a conception of power which was cognizant of the socially constituted power and granted the notion of legality a relatively independent status (see Foucault 1975). The abolition of the power/truth distinction by the Islamic state also undermined the sustainability of the notion of legal power. The Muslim rulers ruled out in a most dramatic, humanly costly and tragic manner, any challenge by 'truth without power' to their power whose truth became indisputable (Foucault 1996).

The economy of power deployed by the Islamic state in its juridical rule short-circuited the two meanings of subject – to be the subject of the state and to be a Muslim – thus foreclosing the possibility for resistance through keeping the two meanings apart. Ponderous, repressive forms of control exercised by the Islamic state over the body were designed to bypass the expansive – and, inevitably expensive (given the complexity of social organizations involved) – forms of control exercised through schools, hospitals, health and medical institutions, workplace and family through which the individual was disciplined within these institutions of civil society. The state's pastoral power was based on a purely juridical mode of power centred on the representation of 'the Sovereign' (Allah) (see Foucault 1982) who could no more tolerate a dispute over the truth of his words than a quarrel over his power. The new meaning given to the 'Islamic' was designed to reincorporate the partially autonomous individual created within the civil society into an invisible Islamic whole represented by the state (see Williams 1961).[9] The whole notion of society 'as a thing in itself' became redundant in the new, Islamic re-appropriation of individual. Hence the Islamic authorities' sense of contempt for the notion of human rights which is based on the idea of the 'bare human being' abstracted from society.

The mediation denied by the Islamic state to Iranian civil society and its short-circuited power relation with the body enhanced the significance of the body as the contested site of power exercised under Islamic juridical rule. Thus the body in post-revolutionary Iran was the major site of power struggle, the potential source of resistance, and the space in which power was stripped of its social and cultural bearings. The body's deconstructive power bestowed a critical import on the role of the audience, whose presence testified to the abolished social and cultural relations. Hence the potentially subversive role of popularized sports such as football under Islamic rule. Thus the 'ascetic severity' to which the body was subjected by the Islamic regime was threatened by a slackened football spectacle in which the players' close interaction with the audience removed the distance between them, giving way to illicit sensational desires. The screen on which the televised game was shown mediated to draw in the 'incompetent' viewers equipped with a heterogeneous repertoire for action, e.g. the plebeian pursuit of victory at all costs, largely influenced by the social conditions under which they lived. Freed from the constraints of a 'competent' seeing and listening, this 'incompetent' audience was able to mediate through play and to acknowledge social and cultural dimensions of their existence which had been suppressed under Islamic rule.

Islamic/global identities

The ambiguous position of the football spectator is understandable in a 'war of position', in which spectatorship on the terraces or by television viewing in a living room or by demonstrated support on the street were only momentary occupations. The identity of the 'spectators' who poured onto the streets of Iran to celebrate the national team's qualifying match against Australia in November 1997, or the match against the USA in June 1998, far from being fixed, was subject to a changing process of identification (see Nowell-Smith 1980). Involved in this process were the interdependent body, space and time, whose relative significance was determined in the conflict-ridden relationship between the Islamic state and Iranian civil society. The Iranians' celebration of their successful entry into the World Cup tournament involved a re-investing, with a culturally specific import, of the space they inhabited; space which had been emptied of cultural significance by the Islamic state. The masses of celebrating Iranians on the streets created a popular, even if 'illegal', space where they could relate themselves to each other as members of an 'imagined community' moving up in history (Anderson 1991). The competition temporarily suspended Iranians' isolation from other nations, an isolation which was the result of having their faces turned forcefully back towards a pure, uncompromising, belligerent Islamic past. It set Iranians free from this forced isolation and regression which had left them in a wilderness where Iranian identity was synonymous with exclusion. The competition offered Iranians an equal place among other nations in a game of football governed by egalitarian rules.

Thus entry into the tournament temporarily released Iranians from homelessness. Significantly, the source of suffering identified by Iranians in their narrative of temporal release was not primarily Iranians' relationship with other peoples, but their relationship as a nation with the Islamic state which purports to represent them. Evident in Iranians' celebration was their appreciation of the chance offered to them, through the heroic act of the players, to re-assert themselves as a nation free from the Islamic state, which both 're-presented' them as well as 'speaking for' them as a Muslim people. The Islamic state allowed no other agents, either in the civil society or within the political domain, the representation – in both meanings of the word – of its subject. The exclusive use of power by the state to 're-present' as well as to 'speak for' its subject removed the distance between truth and power, a distance sustained, even if partially, by the institutions of the civil society. Since the chance offered to the jubilant Iranians was not conditioned by a prior dispute with other nations, it eliminated the temporal dimension from the international competition, thus contributing to its equalizing effect. Once the opportunity of becoming a nation on equal terms with other nations was offered, Iranians seized the opportunity by claiming the place, especially the public part of it, as theirs, the home. The realization of nationhood, a culturally specific phenomenon, required access to a place, even if an 'imaginary' one. With temporal, narrative, devices of going home having been ruled out, the spatial presence – turning up in the streets and public places – was the most immediate, universal, synchronizing 'home-coming'.

In this way Iranians, as nationals, recaptured, however temporarily, the territory in which the Islamic state based its power when it expropriated absolute sovereignty from the monarchy in the wake of the national-popular movement which toppled the monarchy in 1979. In defining the former monarch's subjects as 'Muslims' the Islamic jurist denied them membership of social and cultural groups. Thus Islamic rule polarized even further the already troubled relation between the 'cultural community and political sovereignty' (Anderson 1995: 71) as the Islamic state refused to be the 'expression of a single nation'. Under this rule, the territory of the nation and that of the state were not identical, even though territory effectively provided the state with its power base. The inhabitants of this territory, however, were not recognized as a nation since the place they occupied was defined as devoid of any historically specific character. The transnational term 'Islamic' connoted sacred pilgrimages beyond any national border inside which secular pilgrimages could take place within the emptied time and space of the 'imagined community' (Anderson 1991). Under Islamic jurisdiction, Iranians were territorially bound to the state but forbidden to define this exclusive territorial tie in cultural terms. Thus the Islamic state, for most of its history, has been involved in a cultural deconstruction of the place over which it rules.

The territorialization of Islam intensified the contest over the control of space. It denied the inhabitants of the state's territory their *uniqueness* as a people who related themselves to the territory as their *place* through historically specific narratives. The history provided the temporal limits within which the inhabitants made, in their capacity as nationals, their secular pilgrimages. The World Cup tournament provided Iranians, now reduced to unspecified Muslim subjects, the opportunity to re-establish themselves as a distinct, unique people with minimum recourse to a narrativized claim to their place. Qualifying for the World Cup enabled Iranians to compete, that is to put themselves on equal terms with other peoples. It secured for Iranians a recognition by others of their distinct presence amongst them. The competition was the means by which Iranians re-imagined themselves as a territorially based community with a specific (unique) history (Anderson 1995). This made the qualifying match against Australia particularly a significant opportunity for Iranians to assert their uniqueness/difference. Unlike the match against the USA, which evoked a narrativized Iranian/American difference centred on a relation of domination/subordination often used by the state to territorialize Islam as a solution to the unequal relationship between the two peoples (Sanadjian 1999), the Australian match de-narrativized the differences between Iranians and others. It was joining the others as opposed to differing from them that made the Australian match a critical point in the assertion of Iranian identity. Whereas the match against the USA represented a competition between two entities, the match against Australia represented, to Iranians, the struggle for survival as a distinct, culturally specific, people. The position fought over in the qualifying match had a more lasting effect for Iranians' secular pilgrimage than the positions lost or gained in the game against the Americans. The USA's participation, as a big player, in the tournament had conferred an added significance on the Iranians' claim to an equal place among other nations. The USA/Iran game, labelled the 'most politicized match of the World Cup', increased the global dimension of the Iranians' quest for identity. The qualifying match against Australia, on the other hand, was geared to a dispute over the viability of the national basis of such global competition. That explains the great resistance shown by so many Iranians to let their victory over the USA – success in competition with a powerful nation – overshadow the prime significance of Iran's participation in the World Cup, which lay in the conflict between the Islamic state and Iranian nation. Thus, in their reference to the USA/Iran match, many Iranians considered the competition as essentially a race between the two nations independent of their respective states. Iranians in particular refused to share the victory of their national team with the Islamic state by highlighting their differences with Islamic officials' reading of the event (Sanadjian 1999). The young Iranian cited above agreed that America had in the past intervened in Iran to help the Shah against the Iranian people's wishes. But, he added that 'we', i.e. Iranians, had done wrong things too, such as seizing the American embassy in Tehran in 1979. This reference to the embassy incident was significant not only because the event was a turning point in the historical trajectory of the Islamic state, but also because it marked an unequivocal statement about the incompatibility of Iranians and Americans; an incompatibility which the Islamic state frequently exploited in order to do away with the institutions of Iranian civil society.

One significant result of the pronounced mediation of audience in the popular response to the football matches cited above, was a reduction in the tension arising from the aim of goal-scoring and the quest for elegant displays of footballing skill (cf. Archetti 1997). Elegant play, a widely recognized aesthetic value in football, lives in continuous tension with the powerful drive towards the 'plebeian pursuit of victory at all costs'. For the Iranian players, however, so long as they were able to represent their people *vis-à-vis* others, the distinction between demonstrations of elegance and the 'plebeian' demand for victory remained relatively insignificant. The players' actions were authorized by spectators who shared with them a contingent interest in their 'exploits'. The egalitarian drive among the spectators to reduce their distance from each other militated against the quest for distinction which rested on such distance (Bourdieu 1984). Even the 'competent' Iranian spectators praised their players primarily for their commitment and dedication in their pursuit of victory. Against the overwhelming 'plebeian' quest for *saviour*, the demand for *genius* was negligible. Thus the 'invidious comparison' and calls for demonstrations of 'exploits' and distinction (Veblen 1924) gave way to the conjunctural surge of a universal interest which called for a new articulation of morality with football (cf. Archetti 1997).

While the Islamic state sought to establish its exclusively territorial power base devoid of any cultural content, it made itself vulnerable to transnational economic and cultural influences, to whose spread the state itself contributed significantly. The effective exclusion by the state of cultural terms in which the inhabitants of its territory were defined as its subjects, drove a large number of inhabitants out of the territory. In diaspora, however, these same Iranian exiles became instrumental in the diffusion of cultural influences over those who were left behind in Iran. The exiled communities kept their fellow nationals at home in tantalizingly close contact with the consumerism and 'decadence' which had been damned by the Muslim rulers. In this way, the more Islamic juridical rule was reinforced at home, the more effectively it was subverted by global cultural and economic influences. The more Islamic rule clung to its *local* base, the more vulnerable it became to those global influences which increasingly 'unbundled' its territoriality (Ruggie 1993). The fact that the state's territory had been emptied of its specific cultural content by the Muslim rulers made this territorial unbundling even more acute. It was not an insignificant fact that the Iranian footballer who played a leading part in the Iranian team's victory was actually living abroad playing in the German league. The heroic status attributed to him was less for his competence as a player than for his ambition to claim back the Islamic state's *territory* as a *place* – a culturally specific one – for its inhabitants, who rallied behind him defining themselves as Iranians.

Islamic rule, which had initially rested on religious practice as a contradictory source of power, subsequently sought to resolve, often through brutally repressive methods, the contradictions in a homogeneous expression of faith (Sanadjian 1997a). This attempted resolution reduced the multiple sources of identification for Iranians, thus increasing the tension between their official definition as Muslims and their becoming, unofficially, Iranians. In this 'war of position' a locally guarded, textually constructed Islamic identity could hardly resist globally generated, heterogeneous cultural influences. Of particular importance in these global influences were the means of communication employed – for example sound, the body and space – which enabled the local actor to resist Islamicization through direct identification with the object of desire. By becoming football spectators Iranians were able to identify directly with a particular player, or a set of players, leaving no room for the Islamic authorities to make their spectatorship meaningful with reference to the sacred texts. This resistance, and the deconstruction on which it rested, offered Iranians the opportunity to reconstruct themselves as members of a cultural community. Although, like other authoritarian states, the Islamic state had abolished politics as the space of contested representations (Sanadjian 1997b), unlike them it could not take part in the construction of the national-popular. The alternative, open to other authoritarian regimes, has been to organize the sport in an attempt to contain its popular character and to neutralize any dissent expressed through it. But in order to do that, the regime has had to do away with the juridical mode of power on which its rule was based. This meant that the Islamic state has had to recognize the social nature of power and the need to organize its rule socially and culturally. It entailed a new economy of power, which is more costly than the juridical one, and calls into question the whole Islamic character of the state.

Conclusion

The mediation of the body to maintain or change the relationship between social groups makes sport, supported by a historicized notion of play, a significant domain of representation. The articulation of the game, as a set of rules governing the relationship between participants and their competition, with social and cultural relations surrounding it, allows for the examination of major areas of the exercise of power within the relationship between represented/representatives. Such an examination is especially necessary when the identity imposed on truth and power, by the state, renders obscure the multiple sources of power which are embedded in social and cultural relations. By revisiting the two distinct meanings of representation – 'to re-present' and 'to speak for' – through an approach to sport which sees it as a contested representation, the 'play' can be linked to the 'war of positions', which characterizes the historically determined, conflict-ridden relationship between the state and civil society (Gramsci 1971). Looked at from this angle, the body is not regarded as 'the instrument *par excellence* of every kind of domestication' (Bourdieu 1990: 167), nor is it seen as the essential object of pleasure which defies the construction of meaning (Barthes 1977). Rather, the body is seen as an articulation, the site of the tension-ridden relationship between two distinct forms of pleasure – *plaisir* and *jouissance* – a multi-accentual 'sign' (Volosinov 1973; Mercer 1986; Hall 1981) conveying different references to the body in practices by a people, and the mobilization of these meanings in a social struggle (see Hall 1981). From this perspective, the body is considered over-determined by economic, political and cultural relations, shaped in the political field (the state) and in civil society and within their conflictual relationship.

By focusing on the upsurge of popular excitement generated in Iran by their qualifying to take part in the World Cup tournament in France and the prospect for progress this promised, the argument here is based on the transformation of an Islamicized public space by football spectators. The spectators' identification with the players removed the space between the represented and representation in which the Muslim subject was constituted by the state. Having abolished politics as the space of publicly contested representations, the Islamic state made every field of popular culture a potential site for the expression of dissent. Compared to the despotic monarchy of the pre-revolutionary period, the guardianship of the Muslim jurist (*faqih*) had a decisive effect on the dissolution of Iran's unevenly developed civil society within the state. The result was the abolition of politics as a distinct domain of practice based on a sustained distinction between civil and political life. A distinguishing feature of Islamic juridical rule's abolition of boundary between the political and the civil was that the aim was not to expand Islamic rule's popular base through negotiation of consent from within civil society. Rather, the aim was to neutralize the fast growing areas of power-exercise in a recently shaken civil society. It was not civil hegemony which lay behind the Islamic abolition of politics, but an absolute political domination.

The Islamicization of politics marked the dialectic of 'revolution/restoration' in a conjuncture dominated by the restoration drive. But, as Gramsci (1971: 219–20) pointed out, 'in the movement of history there is never any turning back, and...restorations *in toto* do not exist'. Like any other form of state, the Islamic one was involved in the construction of a form of civilization. Given, however, the historical conjuncture at which the Islamic state operated the civil construction, this assumed a predominantly negative form. Hence the overwhelming emphasis by the state on punishment, and its primary concern with dangerous elements. The Islamic state's refusal to allow civil society to mediate its rule, through the separation of political and civil practices, made it possible for the state to have recourse to a juridical mode of power which did not require the mediation of social structures. Juridical rule did away with the notion of legality as a form of power considered as action upon other actions (Foucault 1982). The concept of legality required the mediation of society as the space in which such power was exercised. In its capacity as a juridical ruler, the Islamic state refused to be an 'educator' in as much as education involved the creation of a new type of civilization. Under the Islamic juridical rule, the political character of the state collapsed into the ethical. Thus the progressive individuation consequent upon capitalist development was cast into an homogeneous Islamic unit. The growing capacity to reconstruct diverse global processes on its premises has increasingly exhausted the Islamic repertoire for action and, correspondingly, progressively confined the Islamic basis for identity.

Notes

1   An early version of this chapter was read at the conference on Globalisation and Identities, Manchester Metropolitan University, Manchester, 30 June–2 July 1999.
2   The recorded conversation took place in a German city in April 1999. This is the place where I have been doing ethnographic research, over a number of years, among Iranian exiles (Sanadjian 1995). The German data are supplemented by the information I collected in Britain on Iranians' response to the international football events (Sanadjian 1999).
3   The recorded conversation with the young football supporter is used, along with other sources – ranging from recordings of focused discussions and casual talks, direct observation and newspapers – to 'piece together' the 'construable signs' through which human agents make a context (Geertz 1973). The aim is to provide a 'thick description' of an event or action, such as the young supporter's participation in the massive football celebrations in Iran or his narration, by placing them in 'webs of significance' the actor has spun, as a cultural agent, around himself. Thus an ethnographic account is considered here an act of *representation*. The extent, however, by which this representation approximates *reality* depends on how *thickly* a situation or action is described; for without access to different layers of meaning human facts are hardly intelligible.
4   The term, meaning membership of God's Party, was used to refer to those who in defining themselves as members of God's Party, which they often took as synonymous with Khomeini's rule, rejected the legitimacy of any alternative positions adopted in response to change, including conservatism, liberalism and socialism (Wallerstein 1989). The historical trajectory of the term, and the annihilation from the political domain it

promises, has to be traced back to the dialectical relation between restoration/revolution triggered by the popular movement which toppled the Pahlavi regime in 1979 (see Balibar 1994).

5   The shi'a clergy, which included the Muslim rulers in Iran, had a distinguished reputation and could make a claim to the allegiance of followers, or to become a source of imitation (*taqlid*), when they produced a treatise, a large part of which was allocated to very detailed instructions on how to keep the body free from sources of pollution such as sex, food and physical contact.

6   In early December when the Iranian football team was given a heroic welcome home in the fully packed national stadium in Tehran, several thousands of women battled their way into the stadium against the official ban on female presence. The unwanted women were led by the officials to a separate section in the stadium, but their presence put an end to the live television transmission of the event by several Iranian channels.

7   The flags displayed often lacked the Islamic emblem – the intersecting crescents at the centre.

8   A similar pattern is discernible in the Islamic state's promotion of Iranian cinema designed for the consumption of international connoisseur film audiences. This internationally oriented film production happens at a time when the Islamic state's control of its domestic cinema audience remains tight enough to be pushing the business towards bankruptcy (MacDonald and Sanadjian 1999).

9   The 'inseparability' connoted by the term 'individual' in its medieval, as opposed to its modern use (Williams 1961: 99) is pertinent to the context described here, provided the novel way in which the individual is placed within an organic Islamic whole is taken into account. Unlike a fascist state, which is positively involved in the construction of its power networks on the body, in sports and recreation, the Islamic state was predominantly concerned to control the body by divesting it of its socially constituted power relations.

References

Anderson, B. (1991) *Imagined Communities: Reflections on the Origin and Spread of Nationalism*, London: Verso.

Anderson, J. (1995) 'The Exaggerated Death of the Nation-state', in J. Anderson, A. Cochrane and C. Brook (eds) *The Global World: Re-ordering Political Space*, Milton Keynes/Oxford: Oxford University Press/Open University Press.

Archetti, E. P. (1997) 'The Moralities of Argentinian Football', in S. Howell (ed.) *The Ethnography of Moralities*, London: Routledge.

Balibar, E. (1994) *Masses, Classes, Ideas*, London: Routledge.

Barthes, R. (1977) *Image, Music, Text*, London: Fontana.

Bourdieu, P. (1984) *Distinction: A Social Critique of the Judgement of Taste*, Cambridge MA: Harvard University Press.

——(1990) 'Programme for a Sociology of Sport', in P. Bourdieu, *In Other Words: Essays Towards a Reflexive Sociology*, Cambridge: Polity Press.

Foucault, M. (1975) *Discipline and Punish: The Birth of the Prison*, trans. Alan Sheridan. Harmondsworth: Penguin.
——(1982) 'The Subject and Power', *Critical Inquiry*, vol. 8, no. 4, 777–95.
——(1996) 'Truth and Judicial Forms', *Social Identities*, vol. 2, no. 3, 327–41.
Geertz, C. (1973) *The Interpretation of Culture*, London: Fontana
Gramsci, A. (1971) *Selections from Prison Notebooks*, ed. and trans. Q. Hoare and G. Nowell-Smith, London: Lawrence and Wishart.
Hall, S. (1981) 'Notes on Deconstructing "The Popular"', in R. Samuel (ed.) *People's History and Socialist Theory*, London: Routledge and Kegan Paul.
Hargreaves, J. (1987) 'The Body, Sport and Power Relations', in J. Horne *et al.* (eds) *Sport, Leisure and Social Relations*, London: Routledge and Kegan Paul.
MacDonald, R. and Sanadjian, M. (1999) 'Market, Consent and Islamicisation of Film Production and Consumption in the "New Iranian Cinema"', paper presented to the conference on Globalisation and Identities, Manchester Metropolitan University, Manchester, 30 June–2 July 1999.
Mercer, C. (1986) 'Complicit Pleasures', in T. Bennett *et al.* (eds) *Popular Culture*, Milton Keynes: Open University Press.
Nowell-Smith, G. (1980) 'Television–Football–The World', in T. Bennett *et al.* (eds) *Popular Television and Film*, London: BFI/Open University Press.
Ruggie, J. G. (1993) 'Territoriality and Beyond: Problematizing Modernity in International Relations', *International Organisation*, vol. 47, no. 1, 139–74.
Sanadjian, M. (1995) 'Temporality of "Home" and Spatiality of Market in Exile: Iranians in Germany', *New German Critique*, no. 65, 3–36.
——(1996) 'Public Flogging in South-Western Iran: Juridical Rule, Abolition of Legality and Local Resistance', in O. Harris (ed.) *Inside and Outside the Law*, London: Routledge.
——(1997a) 'Islamic Rule and the Strategy for Power: The Recent Presidential Election in Iran', *Social Identities*, vol. 3, no. 3, 385–95.
——(1997b) 'Politicisation of Islam and Islamicisation of Politics: Insurrection by the People and the Constitution of a People', unpublished paper.
——(1999) 'Equality of Game, Abstract Discourse on Asylum Rights and Marginal Position in Diaspora: The World Cup and Iranian Exiles', unpublished paper.
Veblen, T. (1924) *The Theory of the Leisure Class*, London: George Allen and Unwin.
Volosinov, A. (1973) *Marxism and the Philosophy of Language*, New York: Seminar Press.
Wallerstein, E. (1989) *Unthinking Social Science: The Limits of Nineteenth-Century Paradigms*, Cambridge: Polity Press.
Williams, R. (1961) *The Long Revolution*, Harmondsworth: Penguin.

9 Globalization and the underdeveloped Muslim world

A case study of Pakistan

Muhammad Ahsan

> A world-wide phenomenon, globalization is a coalescence of varied transnational processes and domestic structures, allowing the economy, politics, culture, and ideology of one country to penetrate another. The chain of causality runs from the spatial reorganization of production to international trade and to the integration of financial markets....In short, globalization is a market-induced, not a policy led, process.
>
> James H. Mittelman[1]

In every sphere of life, the twentieth century brought rapid changes to the world, especially the globalization processes involved in the geographical extension of economic activities in general, and the functional integration of internationally dispersed activities in particular (Dicken 1988: 5). The degree of interdependence and interconnection within the world economy has increased dramatically (Dicken 1988: 79). One of the main problems for Muslim countries is how to integrate these changes into their system. If the change is not integrated smoothly, it can disrupt the whole process of the development of a country, which leads to political instability, social and religious tensions, and economic imbalances. This chapter is an effort to review the situation of the contemporary world and to try to see where Muslim countries stand on the globalization highway. Are they gaining or losing in the race?

For the past three decades, changes in the global economy have been referred to as a new phase of capitalism involving the globalization of markets, trade and labour.[2] Therefore globalization, as a concept, refers to both the compression of the world and its intensification (Robertson 1992: 8), and this phenomenon applies to a series of developments concerning the world as a whole. Giddens argues that 'the development of the sovereignty of the modern state from its beginnings depends upon a reflexively monitored set of relations between states' (Giddens 1987: 263). In this context, globalization is a process of historical change, and in modern times it is 'the crystallization of the entire world as a single place' (Robertson 1987a: 35–43), and 'the emergence of a global-human condition' (Robertson 1987b: 20–30).

Many sociologists have put forward the notion that religion, in the contemporary Western world, has become increasingly privatized (Beyer 1996: 373–95). This means that, through the process of secularization in the modern world, traditional religion is primarily the concern of the individual rather than a collective matter.[3] With reference to 'the West' the validity of this idea cannot be denied, but 'in the "East"', as Pasha and Samatar argue, the situation is different:

> The insertion of a new Islamic consciousness into the daily political life of many Muslim societies is increasingly becoming an incontestable fact. In countries like Iran, Sudan, and Afghanistan, state power has been captured by Islamic movements. For others, such as Algeria, Egypt, Tunisia, and Turkey, there is deadly intensity with high stakes as numerous civil associations define themselves as Islamic and, as a result, violently challenge the legitimacy of political authority. Even in less contested countries (e.g. Morocco, Pakistan, Indonesia), Islamic consciousness assumes a more prominent place in the articulation and making of political life.
>
> (Pasha and Samatar 1997: 87)

I would like to emphasize that, in economic terms, there are two main aspects of globalization: the global organization of production, and global finance. The first aspect deals with the complex network of transnational systems of production and consumption, while the second aspect is concerned with the transactions of money and lending. Therefore, in this context, there are two major phases of globalization:

(i) the internationalization of the state;
(ii) the restructuring of national societies and the emergence of a global social structure (Cox 1993: 259–89).

For Muslims, these two phases are experienced differently from the rest of the world because the first phase concerns their common history and culture based upon their religion, and the second phase is concerned with the contemporary time period within which they feel

themselves to be alienated. Muslims recognize the need for harmoniza-
tion with the current globalization process, and the emergence of
various modern Muslim organizations is the consequence of this
recognition and of efforts to bridge the gap.

The Muslim world: past to present

It will be useful to briefly review the initiation of the first Muslim state
which was created on the global map in 622 when the Prophet
Mohammad (*pbuh*) migrated from Makkah to Madinah. His ten-year
rule over Madinah was a true reflection of Islamic government. In his
state administration system four points were of key importance:

1   organization and management (Haeri 1993: 14)
2   education and research
3   land consolidation and utilization
4   cooperation and self-reliance

   After arriving in Madinah his first step was to conduct a population
census. This census established the percentage of the labour force and
the number of people who could read and write. On the basis of the
available statistics, he organized his people into a volunteer workforce
and developed the country (Ahsan 1991: 15–16). His model was based
on the concept of *ummah*.[4] By the time the Prophet died, almost the
entire Arabian Peninsula was under the rule of Islam. Following his
death, Abu Bakar became his successor and was called the *Khalipha
tur Rasool*.[5] With few exceptions, Muslims consider the rule of the first
four caliphs as the period of ideal implementation of the concept of
ummah through the institution of the caliphate. This ideal did not last
long, however, as after approximately three decades, the caliphate
became secularized by hereditary succession. Later, multiple political
entities were created within the *ummah* by the members of the *ummah*
themselves (Ahsan 1988: 9). Although Muslims lost the real institution
of the caliphate soon after its inception, a weak caliphate survived in
Islamic history until 1924.

   In spite of the disappearance of the real Caliphate during its early
period, Muslims made progress in pre-medieval and medieval times.
The following example from early Muslim history indicates the level of
development and the efforts towards globalization during that age.[6]

   During the period of Caliph Umar (successor of Abu Bakar), the
Muslim state was divided into eight provinces[7] and many new depart-
ments were established. *Nizart-al-Nafia* (the Department of Civil

Engineering) played a primary role in the enhancement of national and international trade and development. In order to provide facilities to the general public, to traders and to travellers, the department oversaw the construction of bridges, roads, police posts and public lodges. It also prepared a feasibility report and drew up plans to connect the Mediterranean Sea to the Red Sea by a canal. The plan and objective was similar to the present Suez Canal. The report was presented to the Caliph but, after detailed consideration and discussion, the project was not approved due to security reasons.[8] Although the Suez Canal could not be built at that time, its deficiency was countered by the construction of various other canals, some of which were purely for transportation purposes. A major achievement of this department was the construction of the Ameer-ul-Mu'meneen Canal, which linked the River Nile to the Red Sea. Nearly sixty-nine miles long, this canal was constructed for shipping purposes and completed within six months (Ahsan 1992; Hussain 1997).

For almost thirteen centuries, from 632 to 1924,[9] Islam expanded across the globe and the *ummah* remained intact. Eventually, however, rivalries for power within the caliphate eroded its effectiveness, and the *ummah*, as the designation of the political unity of the Muslim world, gradually dissolved. As the caliphate crumbled in the hands of those who paid any price to wield its political authority, the vacuum was increasingly filled by Western powers (Husain 1995: 209). In fact, until the first quarter of the twentieth century, Muslims remained more or less united under the umbrella of the caliphate. After the collapse of this institution, the vast Muslim empire disintegrated into many parts and various independent states emerged on the global map. In this changed environment, a series of efforts were made by these states to establish a central institution to fill the gap left by the collapse of the *ummah*. In August 1969, arson damage to the Al-Aqsa mosque in Jerusalem outraged Muslims all over the world, and two months later a conference of twenty-four Muslim countries was held in Rabat (Morocco). Then, in March 1970, a meeting of the foreign ministers of Muslim countries, held in Jeddah,, directed the creation of the Organization of Islamic Countries (OIC) (Husain 1995: 211; Ahsan 1988: 18). Since its creation, membership of the OIC has doubled (Bhuyan 1996: 233–5). The OIC's charter is said to be based on the concept of *ummah*, but in reality the idea of national sovereignty is borrowed from Western secular thought and the concept of *ummah* is limited to the extent of the mutual cooperation between Muslim countries. This contradiction in its charter is in itself a sign of the weakness of the OIC

(Ahsan 1988: 24), and it is due to this that, in the main, the organization has failed to solve the various political and economic problems of the Muslim world. However, in spite of this weakness, it is a well established institution and provides a base and a sense of solidarity in the fragmented Islamic bloc. Muslims all over the world feel some satisfaction when they see their leaders sitting together to discuss the problems of Muslim *ummah* (Husain 1995: 212).

Three elements play a key role in the process of globalization, which is bringing the global community to the 'global village':

(i) international politics
(ii) international trade and financing
(iii) the media.

In this context, under the framework of the OIC, there are two top-level political institutions, the Islamic Summit Conference and the Foreign Ministers Conference. Two commercial institutions, the Islamic Development Bank (IDB), based in Jeddah, and the Islamic Centre for the Development of Trade (ICDT), located in Casablanca, were established in 1970 and 1981 respectively. With regard to the media, again two institutions, the International Islamic News Agency (IINS) and the Islamic States Broadcasting Organization (ISBO) have also been established (Ahsan 1988: 23–43). The question which must be asked is 'how effective a role do these insitutions play?'.

Muslim political institutions have not been successful in solving any of the major problems of Muslims. From the Soviet invasion of Afghanistan to its civil war, from the Iran–Iraq War to the Gulf War, and from the problem of the Southern Filipino Muslim community (Choudhury 1988: 197) to the Kosovo crises, the failure is clearly apparent. The same is also true of trade among Muslim countries, which constitutes around 10 per cent of total world trade (Choudhury 1988: 196). This situation has gone unchanged for several years. During 1991, intra-Islamic country trade was only between 8 and 9 per cent of their total trade, compared to 60 per cent for the European Community, 34 per cent for US/Canada and 28 per cent for the European Free Trade Association (Shakweer 1996: 131–59). Although a trend towards some improvement has been observed in Muslim countries' real per capita GDP, this healthy sign is neutralized by their dependence on foreign loans. It is estimated that the proportion of external debt to GDP is double that of developing countries in general (Choudhury 1988: 198–9). The media are a major component of globalization and play a key role as a catalyst in moulding global opinion for a particular cause (Uddin 1995), but they are completely neglected by the Muslim world. The IINA has failed to establish its own network, while the ISBO does not broadcast programmes, but rather produces some programmes for member states on a limited scale. In these circumstances, Muslim views and news are either neglected or misinterpreted by Western media, and Muslim countries are totally dependent upon Western media, not only to communicate with the rest of the world but also to communicate among themselves (Ahsan 1988: 109).

Where does the Muslim world stand?

It is estimated that Muslim countries produce two thirds of the world's oil, 70 per cent of its rubber, 75 per cent of its jute, 67 per cent of its spices, two thirds of its palm oil, and half of all its tin and phosphate (Sarwar 1994: 203). In addition to having a vast number of gas reserves, Muslim countries also produce a large quantity of the world's cotton, tea, coffee, wool, uranium, manganese, cobalt, and many other commodities and minerals (Sarwar 1994: 203). Geographically, Muslim countries occupy the most strategically important positions. Nearly 60 per cent of the Mediterranean Sea is bounded by Muslim countries, and the Red Sea and the Persian Gulf are completely within the Muslim region (Sarwar 1994: 203). Moreover, the population of Muslim countries,[10] 1,187 million, is their human capital, and their social capital is a common history and culture. This is the positive side of an otherwise negative picture.

In the context of the above facts, it is important to mention the Human Development Index (HDI) of the United Nations Development Programme (UNDP) which is calculated each year for every country. HDI is an aggregate value of life expectancy, adult literacy, mean years of schooling and per capita income. Although there are criticisms about the validity of HDI, this is the basic indicator which reflects the situation of human development in any country.[11] In this fast changing and competitive world, it seems that Muslim countries are lagging behind in human development. According to the *Human Development Report 1998*, as many as forty out of fifty Muslim countries had a lower value of HDI compared to the world's average. The report also indicates that the four countries (Mali, Burkina Faso, Niger and Sierra Leone) which were at the bottom of the list of 174 countries, also belong to the OIC. In Niger[12] and Burkina Faso, the literacy rates were only 14 and 19 per cent respectively. On the other hand, the Central Asian Muslim states have an excellent literacy record but their GNP per capita was much lower (Azerbaijan 510, Kyrgyzstan 440, Tajakistan 330 and Turkmenistan 630US\$/capita) (UNDP 1998: 128–30).[13] The World Bank's statistics indicate that out of fifty Muslim countries, twenty-four were in the list of 'low income', thirteen in the 'lower middle income' and seven were counted in the 'upper middle income' countries. There were only five small Muslim states (Brunei, Kuwait, Lebanon, Qatar and the UAE) which fell into the category of 'high income' countries (World Bank 1999: 189–91, 232).[14] In Gabon, which is one of the smallest Muslim countries in the world, every child is born in debt to the sum of US\$4,213. Other Muslim countries, such as Jordan, Syria, Mauritania and Algeria, are also heavily indebted to foreign loans (US\$/capita 2030, 1428, 1182 and 1147, respectively). It is estimated that dependency on foreign loans is disproportionately high in Muslim countries, and the proportion of debt to GDP is nearly double that of developing countries in general. This indicator highlights the vulnerability of Muslim countries with regard to the interest rate and exchange rate mechanisms (Choudhury 1998: 198). In these circumstances, what role can Muslim countries play in globalization? This is the reason why the past development experience of the Third World (including Muslim countries) has failed to inaugurate a new era of sustained growth and social welfare (Ahmad 1994). Due to the limited space available in this chapter, the position of just eight Muslim countries, the members of the Developing Eight organization, will be reviewed, and I will then focus on Pakistan.

In June 1997, the eight major Muslim countries – Bangladesh, Egypt, Indonesia, Iran, Malaysia, Nigeria, Pakistan and Turkey – established an organization called D-8 (Developing Eight), with the aim of promoting cooperation and joint efforts in the economic sphere. Since the vast majority of the world's Muslim population lives in these countries, their union into an economic block may be an important step towards the overall unity of the Muslim world. Although it is too early to judge the success of this organization, it is expected that the individual and collective efforts of D-8 will be promising, since they possess diverse economic resources, including oil and gas, jute, non-fuel minerals and trained human resources (*Daily Dawn*, 17 January 1999). In order for the organization to be successful, it is essential that its members acknowledge the benefits of globalization, and also recognize the accompanying risks of destabilization and increased inequities between developed and developing countries, including Muslim countries.

Where do the D-8 countries stand?

The basic data of the D-8 member countries are given in Table 9.1. The importance of this organization can be seen from the fact that 785 million people live in these eight Muslim countries. This is nearly two thirds of the total population of OIC member countries.[15] Like other Muslim countries, the situation of human development in this block is not encouraging. The table below shows that from 1990 to 1998 all these countries have fallen in HDI world ranking, in spite of the fact that they have shown some progress with regard to the value of HDI. In reality their rate of improvement in the value of HDI has been much slower, indicating that it will take centuries before these countries reach the level of industrial countries (Table 9.2). The statistics indicate that although Malaysia and Turkey have a better status of human development and are above the world average, the existing rate of growth will still require a long time to reach the level of industrial countries. In the D-8 group, Pakistan has the worst record in this regard, and if the present growth rate of human development remains, this country needs more than 500 years to reach the existing level of industrial countries. Iran is the only country to show remarkable progress in this field. This progress is mainly due to the allocation of huge financial resources for education and health.[16] It is estimated that Iran requires only a decade to arrive at the level of the world HDI average, and less than a century to reach the status of the HDI average for industrial countries.

Table 9.1 Population and HDI of D-8 countries

Country	Population, millions (1997)	HDI: world ranking		HDI value		Annual percentage growth in HDI
		1990	1998	1990	1998	
(1)	*(2)*	*(3)*	*(4)*	*(5)*	*(6)*	*(7)*
Bangladesh	124	108	147	0.318	0.378	1.98
Egypt	60	86	112	0.501	0.612	2.27
Indonesia	200	77	96	0.591	0.679	1.62
Iran	61	70	78	0.660	0.758	1.62
Malaysia	21	46	60	0.800	0.834	0.51
Nigeria	118	107	142	0.322	0.391	2.21
Pakistan	137	95	138	0.423	0.453	0.83
Turkey	64	59	69	0.751	0.782	0.50

Source: Column 2: World Bank (1990: 190–1, 232). Columns 3 and 5: UNDP (1990: 128–9). Columns 4 and 6: UNDP (1998: 128–30). Column 7: computed from columns 5 and 6.

Table 9.2   The number of years required for D-8 member countries to achieve the level of the world's HDI average and industrial countries' HDI average

Country	World HDI average (index value: 0.772)	Industrial countries'
HDI average (index value: 0.911)		
Bangladesh	199	269
Egypt	71	132
Indonesia	57	143
Iran	9	94
Malaysia	na	152
Nigeria	173	236
Pakistan	386	554
Turkey	na	261

Source: World's HDI average and industrial countries average, UNDP (1998: 128–30ii)
The figures on this table are computed from Table 1, considering the world's and industrial countries' HDI averages, and HDI values for D-8 member countries as the benchmarks.

Notes:
na not applicable
This table is based on the 1998 figures

As mentioned earlier, the D-8 countries, like other Muslim countries, fall under the category of developing countries. According to the *World Development Report 1998–99*, Malaysia and Turkey are considered to be 'upper middle income' countries, Iran and Egypt 'lower middle income', and Bangladesh, Nigeria and Pakistan 'low income' (World Bank 1999: 189). With regard to per capita GNP, Nigeria is one of the poorest countries in this group, occupying the 119th position in the world, followed by Bangladesh (116) and Pakistan (97). Table 9.2 indicates that these countries are spending more money on defence than health, particularly Pakistan, which is top of the list due to the instability of the South Asian sub-continent. The proportion of the health and defence expenditures of Pakistan is 1:7.6 as compared to Nigeria and Bangladesh where the same figures are 1:2.7 and 1:1.4 respectively. These huge expenditures on defence are in spite of the fact that these countries were heavily indebted (Table 9.3). With respect to total foreign debts, Indonesia is the most highly indebted country in this group. However, if we look at the figures of per capita debt burden, then Malaysia is at the top, followed by Turkey. Being 'upper middle income' countries, the debt burden for Malaysia and Turkey is less of a problem than it is for Nigeria, Pakistan and Bangladesh, which fall in the category of 'low income' countries.

In addition, these three 'low income' countries are not only pressed under the burden of external loans and facing the problems of debt

Table 9.3 GNP and government expenditure of D-8 member countries

Country	GNP per capita (1997)			Government expenditure by sector (as a percentage of GNP for education and as a percentage of GDP for health and defence)		
	US$	*World Ranking*	*Growth Rate (%)*	*Education (1995)*	*Health (1990–5)*	*Defence (1995)*
Bangladesh	270	116	3.7	2.3	1.2	1.7
Egypt	1,180	72	3.0	5.6	1.6	5.7
Indonesia	1,110	75	2.8	na	0.7	1.8
Iran	1,780	na	1.2	na	na	na
Malaysia	4,680	35	5.2	5.3	1.4	1.6
Nigeria	260	119	1.2	na	0.3	0.8
Pakistan	490	97	0.0	na	0.8	6.1
Turkey	3,130	48	6.4	3.4	2.7	4.0

Source: World Bank (1999:190-191, 200-203, 222, 223, 232

serving, but they are also unable to attract sufficient foreign investment. This was especially true for Bangladesh where, until 1996, the
per capita debt burden was US$130, while total foreign investment in
that year was only US$15 million (i.e. 12 cents per capita). The same
situation was also reflected in the case of Overseas Development
Assistance (ODA) where, during the same year, Bangladesh received
only US$10 per capita, which was probably less than one hour's earn-
ings of a working-class citizen in the developed countries. Pakistan
and Nigeria received even less money in the form of ODA, i.e. US$7
and 2 per capita respectively (Table 9.4). Although Egypt received a
large amount of ODA compared to the other D-8 countries, it is
common knowledge that this aid is linked to the Middle East's political situation.

   Although there is no question of a comparison between D-8 and G-
8 countries (Canada, France, Germany, Italy, Japan, Russia, the UK
and the USA), it is interesting to see where the eight Muslim countries
stand in the world. The basic indicators of G-8 countries are given in
Table 9.5. With regard to the GNP per capita, Japan (US$37,850) was
at the top in this block as against Malaysia (US$4,680) which held the
highest position among D-8 countries. The proportionate difference of
GNP per capita of these two countries stood at 1:8. On the other
hand, Russia (which, after the fall of Soviet Union, is still passing
through its transitional stage) was at the bottom of the G-8 group as
against Nigeria among D-8 countries. The same differential for these
two countries was 1:11. The huge income differential between Japan
(top in G-8) and Nigeria (bottom in D-8) can be judged from the ratio
of 1:146.

Table 9.4   D-8 member countries: foreign direct investment (FDI), official development assistance (ODA) and external debts

Country	ODA, US$ per capita (1996)	FDI (1996)		Total external debts (until 1996)	
		US$, millions	US$ per capita	US$, millions	US$, per capita
(1)	(2)	(3)	(4)	(5)	(6)
Bangladesh	10	15	0.12	16,083	130
Egypt	37	636	10.60	31,407	523
Indonesia	6	7,960	39.80	129,033	645
Iran	3t	na	na	11,511*	198*
Malaysia	22	4,500	214.28	39,777	1,894
Nigeria	2	1,391	11.78	31,407	266
Pakistan	7	690	5.03	29,901	218
Turkey	4	722	11.28	79,789	1,247

Source: Columns 2, 3 and 5 (except Iran): World Bank (1999: 230–1. Columns 4 and 6 (except Iran): computed from Table 1 (column 2) and columns 3 and 5 of this table. *Iran: based on the year 1991–2 and computed from Amuzegar (1997: 62, 392). Iran (t): based on the year 1995 and computed from UNICEF (1998: 115)

Note: na figures were not available in the original source.

The same situation is reflected by the HDI values. Canada held first position in the world as against 60th position for Malaysia in the D-8 group. At the bottom in the G-8 group was Russia, in 72nd position as against Bangladesh, which was in 147th position in the world ranking. If we consider the G-8 countries, excluding Russia, Italy was at the bottom, holding 21st position in world ranking, as against Malaysia's 60th position, which was at the top of the D-8 countries. Another comparison between G-8 and D-8 countries can be made in terms of government expenditure on health. The G-8 countries are enjoying a far higher standard of health, but proportionately they were also spending far more money in this sector as compared to the D-8 countries. Germany was spending 8.2 per cent of its GDP on health, as against Turkey where the figure was only 2.7 percent. It is evident from Tables 9.3 and 9.5 that both of these countries were at the top in their respective groups and were allocating the maximum resources for the health sector. On the other hand, Russia and Nigeria were at the bottom of the list in their respective groups, and were spending the least proportion of GDP on health. In spite of its serious financial crisis, the percentage figure for Russia's GDP's expenditures on health were 4.1 as against Nigeria, where the figure was only 0.3 percent.

Table 9.5 Basic indicators for G-8 member countries

Country	HDI		GNP		Government expenditure	
	Value	World ranking	Per capita	World ranking	Education (% of GNP)	Health (% of GDP)
(1)	*(2)*	*(3)*	*(4)*	*(5)*	*(6)*	*(7)*
Canada	0.960	1	19,290	18	7.3	6.8
France	0.946	2	26,050	11	5.9	8.0
Germany	0.925	19	28,260	7	4.7	8.2
Italy	0.922	21	20,120	17	4.9	5.4
Japan	0.640	8	37,850	2	3.8	5.7
Russia	0.769	72	2,740	51	4.1	4.1
UK	0.932	14	20,710	15	5.5	5.8
USA	0.943	4	28,740	6	5.3	6.6

Source: Columns 2 and 3: UNDP (1998: 128–30). Columns 4–7: World Bank (1999: 200–3)

Can a nuclear Pakistan play any global role?

There are four main reasons for choosing Pakistan as a case study:

- It is the first country which came into existence on the basis of religion (Ahmad 1991).
- It has an extremely poor human development record.
- It is the only nuclear power in the Muslim world.
- It is one of the architects of the OIC and D-8 organizations, and a main advocator of Muslim unity.

But can it play an active role in globalization, or at least in the OIC? In this section I will explore this question.

The first and foremost factor in this issue is that unless a country is internally stable and strong it has no global voice. In fact, the strength of a country depends upon its internal political and economic stability, its socio-cultural harmony and a mutual tolerance among different segments of society. But this is not the case in Pakistan. During the past half century this Islamic Republic has had twenty-four heads of state and has adopted three constitutions. Half of its period of existence has been under three periods of martial law, and it has gone to war three times with a powerful neighbour, losing half of its territory (Bangladesh). This situation is expressed by a Pakistani thinker in the following way:

> Pakistan is a unique country. Born with its two halves more than a thousand miles apart, it was the only modern nation of its size whose very identity was based on religion. The country experienced a

massive and violent exchange of population with India. It began its
national existence short of any manufacturing industries, bankers
and entrepreneurs. There has been much trauma in the country's
political history – three wars with India, three full-scale military
coups, political instability, a bloody civil war resulting in the separation of Bangladesh and, since 1979, the influx of three million
refugees from Afghanistan. For all the apparent disadvantages
regarding the country's development, Pakistan's economy has grown
more rapidly than the economies of its South Asian neighbours.
Moreover, compared with the parallel experience of other low-
income countries, there has been a fair continuity of growth through
Pakistan's successive regimes....In spite of this commendable growth,
there are some very serious anomalies and drawbacks in the
country's economy. No Asian country with nearly its growth record
has had its bleak record in the development of its social sectors, i.e.,
education, including literacy, health, population programmes and
participation of women in the modernization process.

(Naik 1993: 1–2)

As previously mentioned, Pakistan is considered a 'low income
country' where per capita income is only US$490, and among the fifty
Muslim countries it holds 31st position in this respect (World Bank
1999: 189, 190–1, 232).[17] Nearly 34 per cent of its population lives
below the national poverty line and 45 per cent of the people have no
access to basic health services. One quarter of the inhabitants drink
unsafe water and, due to the lack of social security programmes,
nearly one million people either die or are affected by disasters of
some kind every year (UNDP 1997: 55). The situation in the education
sector is even worse, where 60 per cent of the population is illiterate
(Government of Pakistan 1998: 119). Behind this disappointing figure,
there are large disparities in terms of rural and urban, and male and
female literacy ratios. During 1998, the figures for male and female
literacy stood at 51 and 28 per cent respectively illiterate (Government
of Pakistan 1998: 119). In 1951, female literacy was below 17 per cent,
and after four decades managed to rise to 28 per cent, indicating a
growth rate of only 0.24 per cent per year. It is estimated that, if such
growth rates of literacy continue, it will take 303 years for females and
127 years for males to meet the target of 100 per cent literacy in
Pakistan. Similar views were expressed by Khawaja (1989: 8): 'the past
efforts and present literacy programmes have been able to provide
benefits to only 0.2 million persons on an average per year. If this rate
of progress is considered valid, then Pakistan will achieve universal

literacy in 200 years'. This alarming situation provokes the question 'can an illiterate nation play any role in the modern world?'.[18] However, in addition to the internal factors of poverty and illiteracy, the external factors of international trade and financing also determine the global role of a country. Therefore, the issues of international trade, workers' remittances, foreign debts and debt servicing in Pakistan are briefly discussed in the following sections.

The international trade situation

It is common knowledge that international trade is one of the most important components of globalization (Waters 1995: 4). Unfortunately, the continuing deficit and fluctuating situation of Pakistan's foreign trade during the 1990s shows an unhealthy picture (Table 9.6). During 1995, the country's share in the world export market was only 0.18 per cent (Government of Pakistan 1997: 80). The total exports of Pakistan, worth US$6,131 million during FY 1990–1, increased to US$8,707 million (30 per cent) in 1995–6, then declined, almost to the level of 1990–1, to US$6,294 million in 1997–8. The import market also showed similar trends during these years, and Pakistan continuously faced a deficit in her international trade. This trade deficit has adversely affected the country's overall economic situation, particularly the balance of payments. Another aspect to be considered is Pakistan's percentage share of international trade with Islamic countries. Like other Islamic countries, Pakistan's trade with the Muslim world is comparatively much less than its total international trade (Shakweer 1996: 131–59) (see Table 9.7). During the 1990s the share of its imports was only in the range of 17–28 per cent as against the share of exports, which was in the range of 12–16 per cent. Among the imports to Muslim countries, the lion's share has always been the import of oil from the Persian Gulf states.

Table 9.6   Overall situation of international trade during the 1990s (US$, millions)

Year	Export	Import	Balance
1990–1	6,131	7,619	1,488
1991–2	6,904	9,252	2,348
1992–3	6,813	9,941	3,128
1993–4	6,803	8,564	1,761
1994–5	8,137	10,394	2,257
1995–6	8,707	11,805	3,098
1996–7	6,130	8,750	2,620
1997–8	6,294	7,707	1,413

Source: Government of Pakistan (1997: 145; 1998: 86)

Table 9.7   Situation of international trade with OIC member countries

Year	Total trade (Rs. million)	OIC member countries	
		Rs. million	Percentage share
(1)	*(2)*	*(3)*	*(4)*
1990–1			
Σ export	138,282	17,527	12.67
Σ import	171,114	30,606	17.88
1991–2			
Σ export	171,728	25,058	14.59
Σ import	229,889	37,939	16.50
1992–3			
Σ export	177,028	28,411	16.04
Σ import	258,643	43,740	16.91
1993–4			
Σ export	205,499	28,134	13.69
Σ import	258,250	53,922	20.87
1994–5			
Σ export	251,173	32,316	12.86
Σ import	320,892	68,436	21.32
1995–6			
Σ export	294,741	37,961	12.87
Σ import	397,575	88,892	22.35
1996–7			
Σ export	236,804	27,983	11.81
Σ import	337,962	94,503	27.96

Source: Columns 2 and 3: Government of Pakistan (1997: 170–6). Column 4: computed from columns 2 and 3.

Workers' remittances

The emigration of workers has been an important feature of Pakistan's economy:

> Due to the Middle East oil boom of the early seventies, Pakistan exported its manpower for the absorption of its fast growing labour force and earned foreign exchange in the form of workers' remittances. During the peak period of 1977–83, the country exported about one third of its incremental labour force at an average rate of nearly 137,982 workers per annum, mainly to the Middle East, and the workers' remittances rose from US$578 million in 1977 to the peak of US$2,886 million in 1983.
>
> (Pakistan/Netherlands Project on Human Resources 1991: 57)

Mittleman (1997: 1) points out that '[l]ike many other labour exporting countries, Pakistan in some years has received more capital in migrants' remittances than the state has allocated for national development at federal and local level'. This outflow of workers brought huge socio-economic changes to remote rural areas of Pakistan, and completely changed consumption patterns (Pakistan/ Netherlands Project on Human Resources 1996: 44). Although emigration has been the backbone of Pakistan's foreign exchange resources, remittances now show a declining trend and this is a matter of great concern for the country (Pakistan/Netherlands Project on Human Resources 1993: 69). Table 9.8 shows the amount of workers' remittances and the share from the Middle East. The declining trend in workers' remittances indicates that slowly and gradually Pakistan is losing this major source of foreign exchange. This is mainly due to falling oil prices, competition from other labour-exporting countries, the completion of infrastructural projects in the Middle East, diversification of manpower by labour-importing countries, and indigenous human resources development programmes in the Arab world (Ahsan 1995).

Foreign debts and debt servicing

Many developing countries of the world are crippled under their debt burden and their prospects of development are bleak (Molana 1999). Pakistan is also falling into the debt trap, and is facing severe constraints due to its growing volume of external debts (Ahmad 1996). At the end of every five-year plan, Pakistan found itself deeper in the debt morass, and helpless before international creditors, both bilateral and multilateral (Kardar 1987). The absolute debt burden stood at US$24 million at

Table 9.8 Workers' remittances and the share of the Middle East (US$, millions)

Year	Total remittances	Share of Middle East	
		Amount	*Percentage*
1981–2	2,224.89	1,848.58	83.08
1985–6	2,595.31	2,021.51	77.89
1990–1	1,848.29	1,234.84	66.80
1991–2	1,467.48	985.03	67.12
1992–3	1,562.24	1,097.08	70.22
1993–4	1,445.56	1,070.90	74.08
1994–5	1,866.10	1,440.39	77.18
1995–6	1,461.17	1,053.24	72.08
1996–7	992.47	721.06	72.65

Source: Government of Pakistan (1997: 180–2)

the end of the pre-plan period in 1954–5. It increased sixfold at the end
of the first Five-year Plan in 1959–60, sevenfold over the second Plan,
and threefold over the third Plan. The multiplication rate of debt slowed
after that, to 37 per cent over the sixth Plan period (1983–8) and 47 per
cent over the seventh Plan (1988–93). At the end of the eighth Plan
(1993–8) when the debt burden increased by 20 per cent, Pakistan found
itself completely buried under debt, both in terms of debt service and
the need for more credit. The situation of external debts during the
1990s is given in Table 9.9. The statistics show that during the period
1990–8, the debt burden increased by 63 per cent (nearly 8 per cent per
annum). The same is also reflected by the figures of debt servicing as a
percentage of GDP. During FY 1990–1, the amount of debt servicing as
a percentage of GDP was 2.9, which rose to 3.8 per cent in 1997–8. The
same trend can be identified with regard to export earnings. During
1990–8, the figure of debt servicing as a percentage of export earnings
increased from 21.5 to 27.9 (9.6 per cent per year). A national newspaper report revealed that in December 1998, Pakistan owed a total of
US$26.9 billion against its reserves of only $1,028 million (*Daily Dawn*,
16 March 1999). According to another source, in FY 1997–8, out of
the total government revenue, 26 per cent came from external
borrowing and 24 per cent from internal borrowing. Out of the total
revenue, 41 per cent went on interest payment, 29 per cent on defence
and only 19 per cent was utilized for development purposes
(Government of Pakistan 1998). The most alarming aspect of this
situation is that the country has now reached the stage where it needs
more loans to pay the interest on previous loans.

The state of financial cooperation among Muslim countries and the
role of the Islamic Development Bank (IDB) can partly be judged
from the external debt situation of Pakistan (Table 9.9). The IDB is
considered to be one of the most active and important institutions of
the OIC. After the nuclear test in May 1998, when Pakistan's economy
was close to collapse due to international sanctions, this institution
tried to play a leading role in persuading financial institutions in the
Gulf Cooperation Council (GCC) to give an indicative amount of
US$1.5 billion to Pakistan (*Daily Dawn*, 10 August 1998). However,
the IDB soon found itself paralysed, and looked for the green light
from the International Monetary Fund (*Daily Dawn*, 8 March 1998).
In the present globalization process, this situation can be regarded as
another form of colonization, either 'financial colonization' or 'recolonization'. Is the picture of the 'global village' any different from that of
a Third World village where a feudal lord is the moneylender and the
villagers are bound to him?

Table 9.9 Pakistan's external debts and debt servicing situation in the 1990s

Year	External debts, US$, millions	Debt servicing		
		Amount, US$, millions	Percentage of GDP	Percentage of Export Earnings
1990–1	15,471	1,316	2.9	21.5
1991–2	17,361	1,413	3.1	21.9
1992–3	19,044	1,648	3.2	24.2
1993–4	20,322	1,746	3.3	25.7
1994–5	22,117	2,042	3.4	25.1
1995–6	22,275	2,136	3.3	24.5
1996–7	23,145	2,265	3.7	27.2
1997–8	24,545	2,416	3.8	27.9

Source: Government of Pakistan (1998: 98)

Table 9.10 Year-wise disbursement of foreign debts of Pakistan and share of OIC member countries including Islamic Development Bank (US$, millions)

Year	Total debts	Share of OIC countries and IBD	
		Amount	Percentage
(1)	(2)	(3)	(4)
1989–90	361.90	- (17.7)	4.89
1990–1	149.40	60.80 (17.6)	40.69
1991–2	315.90	12.9 (4.9)	4.08
1992–3	145.40	15.15 (9.9)	10.41
1993–4	164.90	116.90* (-)	70.89
1994–5	298.40	88.00 (65.0)	29.49
1995–6	388.50	33.50 (-)	8.62
1996–7	85.00	- (-)	-

Source: Computed from Government of Pakistan (1997: 199–201)

Notes:
Column 3: Out of total lending from Islamic sources, the figures in parentheses indicate the lending from the Islamic Development Bank.
* Out of a total lending of US$116.90 million from Islamic sources, US$100 million were received from Malaysia and US$16.9 million from Kuwait.

Review and reflections

At the concluding stage of this chapter I would like to summarize this discussion in the words of Abusulayman:

> Internally weak, relatively backward, frustrated, conflict ridden, suffering from internal tensions, and often controlled and abused by foreign powers, the Muslim world is in a state of crisis. For Muslims, all of modern history is a tragedy. At an earlier time, during the sweeping revolution of Islam, Muslims were the custodians of civilisation and both the centre and master of the civilized world. But at present, the Muslim polity is neither master nor partner, and both Muslims and Islam are often regarded in world politics as little more than problematic. How did such a state of affairs come about and in what ways can the Muslim people alter this condition?
>
> In Muslim countries it is customary to blame external powers and imperialism for all manners of ills. Although this habit may point up many of the grievances and obstacles Muslims face, it cannot explain the internal cause of the ills. These ills put in motion a process of decay that dissipated the internal power of the Muslim world. The resultant weakness brought external powers into the picture, complicating the difficulties. The problem of the external factors along with the complications they cause for the Muslim world, cannot be dealt with before the internal factors are fully understood.
>
> (Abusulayman 1994: 1)

So what is the solution to this problem? Choudhury (1988: 204) argues that an Islamic state must take a leading role and initiate the process of restructuring its own system by linking itself with the international politico-economic changes in the Muslim World. Initially this action by a single state may seem insufficient, but it could generate a framework of interrelation within itself and with other Muslim countries, and could then broaden its sphere to the global level. In reality, this approach relies mainly upon government initiatives, and the experience of the past decades shows that, in general, those in power in Muslim countries put their own interests first. Under these circumstances, none of the governments are willing to take such big steps. In the present age of democratization, any feasible approach should be generated from the grassroots level. In fact, the urgent need of the time is for Muslim countries to enable themselves to influence the governance of the global economy and build a partnership of equals with the North. In the present situation, where the Muslim world is divided politically as well as economically, Muslim countries cannot achieve these targets unless they develop their countries individually and collectively.

As emphasized earlier, three important elements – political unification, a sound network of mutual trade and financing, and above all, the establishment of a powerful Islamic news agency – are the key issues which must be addressed if the Muslim world is to play an important role in, and create a state of balance and harmony with, the process of globalization. In order to achieve this, two simultaneous approaches should be adopted. Regarding the internal sector, the most important step is that new evolutionary movements must be developed to eliminate social evils. These movements must emerge through collaboration between the general public and liberal and moderate Muslim intellectuals and politicians, in order to jointly establish pressure groups and win public support across the country. At the level of the *ummah*, such national movements should closely coordinate their actions in order to influence the governments of Muslim countries. The objective of this approach should not be the bringing about of a revolution within the Muslim world which may lead to disaster; rather, the objective should be to start a peaceful and social evolutionary process at grassroots level. Such efforts in various Muslim countries would be helpful in creating internal solidarity and stability, and external coordination and harmony. This process would initiate a new era of globalization. Unless this development takes place, Muslim countries will be unable to play an active role in global processes.

Ironically, the establishment of the OIC at the level of the *ummah* was itself a great achievement of the Muslim world, but there is now a need to strengthen this organization. One of the most important and urgent steps should be the establishment of an Islamic news agency and a communications network within the framework of the OIC. As I have argued elsewhere, unless Muslim countries establish a powerful global news agency they will remain ineffective and neglected in the globalization process (Ahsan 1999). This is of primary importance because it is vital to spread the voice of Muslim countries both internally and externally and, as a further development of telecommunications, they should have their own satellites in space. Some Muslim countries, particularly Pakistan, have gained the necessary technological skills for this but are unable to launch a programme due to the financial constraints. However, this situation can be overcome through the initiation of joint ventures with oil-rich Arab states which lack the technological skills.

On the political front, Muslim countries should strive to solve their problems amongst themselves in order to create a state of political solidarity and stability. The sessions of the Islamic Summit Conference need to be held on a regular basis, preferably every year at the time of the annual gathering of *hajj*. This would provide opportunities for Muslim leaders to concentrate on the common problems of the Islamic world and to make relevant decisions. On the one hand this situation would help to create an environment of mutual trust and confidence within these countries, while on the other, it would ease the job of the United Nations, which would then be able to focus more attention on other global problems. The hand-in-hand partnership of these two organizations would be a healthy sign for global peace and prosperity.

Due to the problems of poverty and debt servicing, many Muslim countries are facing severe financial crises. However, other Muslim countries have large amounts of financial reserves in foreign banks. In the long term, it would be appropriate for some of this money to be used to create a Muslim Monetary Fund under the administrative control of the Islamic Development Bank. This action would be important in making the IDP more effective and independent, and would enable it to provide loans to Muslim countries on easy terms. There is a huge potential for boosting trade among Muslim countries, but due to lack of political will, physical facilities and the large geographical distances, insufficient progress has been made. These problems can be tackled by adopting specific strategies. Lessons can be learned from other global organizations such as the North American Free Trade Association (NAFTA) and the European Free Trade Association (EFTA). Along these lines, various common markets of Muslim countries can be developed at regional and sub-regional levels. In this context, it would be appropriate to strengthen those organizations which already exist but are not working efficiently, for example the Economic Cooperation Organization (ECO),[19] the Arab Cooperation Council (ACC), the Arab Common Market (ACM), the Arab Maghreb Union (AMU) and the Arab Free Trade Area (AFTA). The coordination of local institutions with the Islamic Development Bank, the Islamic Chamber of Commerce and Commodity Exchange (ICCIC) and the Islamic Centre for the Development of Trade (ICDT) is of vital importance in this regard.

In the present fast-changing world, the concept of security has changed shape and broadened its sphere of application, as it is not only limited to the military power of a country but also encompasses socio-economic issues. It is estimated that Muslim countries spend more than US$70 billion on defence every year.[20] These countries should think about saving some of this expenditure by creating an organization along the lines of NATO for their common security. A 10 per cent cut in the defence budgets of Muslim countries would save at least US$7 billion annually. Initially, half of this money would be enough to establish a common security organization and the remaining half could be utilized to create a Human Development Fund for the eradication of poverty and illiteracy in the deprived Muslim countries. I must stress that, although such measures would not be enough to bring about a revolutionary change in the Muslim world, they would be enough to initiate an evolutionary process and to equip Muslim countries for globalization.

Appendix: basic facts about OIC member Muslim countries

Table 9.11 Muslim countries' area, population and HDI

Country	Population 1997 (millions)	HDI 1995	Literacy rate (%) 1995	GNP per capita 1997 (US$)	Defence expenditure 1997 (US$)	External debts 1996 (US$, millions)
(1)	(2)	(3)	(4)	(5)	(6)	(7)
Afghanistan	24	na	31*	na	209 (10)	na
Algeria	29	0.746 (82)	61.6	1,490 (67)	2,114 (73)	33,259 (1,147)
Azerbaijan	8	0.623 (110)	96.3	510 (96)	146 (19)	435 (54)
Bahrain	0.6	0.872 (43)	85.2	7,820 na	364 (608)	na
Bangladesh	124	0.371 (147)	38.1	27 (116)	593 (5)	16,083 (130)
Benin	6	0.378 (145)	37.0	380 (104)	27 (5)	1,594 (266)
Brunei	0.2	0.889 (35)	88.2	25,090 na	353 (1,141)	na
Burkina Faso	11	0.219 (172)	19.2	240 (121)	67 (6)	1,294 (118)
Cameroon	14	0.481 (132)	63.4	650 (90)	240 (17)	9,515 (680)
Chad	7	0.318 (163)	48.1	240 (122)	43 (6)	997 (142)
Comoros	0.5	0.411 (141)	57.3	400 na	308 (7)	na
Djibouti	0.6	0.324 (162)	46.2	na	20 (30)	na
Egypt	60	0.612 (112)	51.4	1,180 (72)	2,743 (45)	31,407 (523)

Table 9.11 continued

Gabon	1	0.568	63.2	4,230	115	4,213
		(120)		(38)	(83)	(4,213)
Gambia	1	0.291	38.6	350	15	na
		(165)		na	(13)	
Guinea	7	0.277	35.9	570	51	3,240
		(167)		(92)	(7)	(463)
Guinea-Bissau	1	0.295	54.9	240	8	937
		(164)		(123)	(7)	(937)
Indonesia	200	0.679	64.0	1,110	4,812	129,033
		(96)		(75)	(24)	(645)
Iran	61	0.758	69.0	1,780	4,695	na
		(78)		na	(68)	
Iraq	22	0.538	58.0	na	1,250	na
		(127)			(56)	
Jordan	4	0.729	86.6	1,570	496	8,118
		(87)		(64)	(105)	(2,030)
Kazakhstan	16	0.695	99.0	1,340	503	2,920
		(93)		(69)	(31)	(183)
Kuwait	2	0.848	78.6	22,110	3,618	na
		(54)		na	(1,681)	
Kyrgyzstan	16	0.633	97.0	440	45	789
		(109)		(99)	(10)	(49)
Lebanon	4	0.796	92.4	3,350	676	3,996
		(66)		(46)	(163)	(999)
Libya	5	0.806	76.2	na	1,250	na
		(64)			(215)	
Malaysia	21	0.834	83.5	4,680	3,377	39,777
		(60)		(35)	(157)	(1,894)
Maldives	0.2	0.683	93.2	1,150	na	na
		(95)		na		
Mali	10	0.236	31.0	260	43	3,020
		(171)		(118)	(4)	(302)
Mauritania	2	0.361	37.7	450	24	2,363
		(149)		(98)	(10)	(1,182)
Morocco	28	0.557	43.7	1,250	1,386	21,767
		(125)		(70)	(48)	(777)
Niger	10	0.207	13.6	200	22	1,557
		(173)		(128)	(2)	(156)
Nigeria	118	0.391	57.1	260	1,965	31,407
		(142)		(119)	(18)	(266)
Oman	2	0.771	59.0	4,950	1,815	3,415
		(71)		(33)	(887)	(1,708)
Pakistan	137	0.453	37.8	490	3,503	29,901
		(138)		(97)	(26)	(218)
Qatar	0.6	0.845	79.4	11,570	1,346	na
		(57)		na	(2,380)	
Saudi Arabia	20	0.778	63.0	6,790	18,151	na
		(70)		(29)	(1,071)	
Senegal	9	0.342	33.1	550	71	3,663
		(158)		(93)	(8)	(407)
Sierra Leone	5	0.185	31.4	200	52	1,167
		(174)		(129)	(10)	(233)

Table 9.11 continued

Somalia	10	na	na	na	40 (7)	na
Sudan	27	0.343 (157)	46.1	280 na	418 (14)	na
Syria	15	0.749 (81)	70.8	1,150 (73)	2,217 (145)	21,420 (1,428)
Tajikistan	6	0.575 (118)	99.0	330 (110)	132 (22)	707 (118)
Tunisia	9	0.744 (83)	66.7	2,090 (59)	334 (35)	9,886 (1,098)
Turkey	64	0.782 (69)	82.3	3,130 (48)	8,110 (131)	79,789 (1,247)
Turkmenist an	5	0.660 (103)	98.0	630 (91)	107 (230)	825 (165)
United Arab Emirates	3	0.855 (48)	79.2	17,360 (20)	2,424 (978)	na
Uganda	20	0.340 (160)	61.8	320 (113)	166 (8)	3,674 (184)
Uzbekistan	24	0.659 (104)	99.0	1,010 (78)	447 (19)	2,319 (97)
Yemen	16	0.356 (151)	38.0	270 (117)	403 (24)	6,356 (397)

Source: Column 1: List of OIC member countries is drawn from Bhuyan *et al.* (1996: 233–5).
Columns 2, 5 and 7: World Bank (1999: 190–1, 232). Columns 3 and 4: UNDP (1998: 118–19, 128–30). Column 6: International Institute for Strategic Studies (1998). * World Bank (1999: 232).

Notes:
Countries listed in the above table together with Palestine become 51 members of the OIC.
Columns 3 and 5: figures in parentheses indicate world ranking.
Columns 6 and 7: The figures in parentheses indicate per capita.
na Figures were not available in the original source.

Notes

1 Mittelman (1997: 3).
2 See Offe (1985); Lipietz (1987); Lash and Urry (1979); Featherstone (1996).
3 Beyer (1996). See also Parsons (1966); Berger (1967: 133); Luckmann (1967: 103); Bellah (1970).
4 In the Islamic context, *ummah* is the aggregate community of Muslims, which took shape under the leadership of Prophet Mohammad. See Ahsan (1988: 1–9); Samad (1992: 342–7).
5 The period of the first four caliphs, Abu Baker, Umar, Usman and Ali, is called *Khilafat-i-Rashida*. The Arabic word *rashid* means true or right. They are called 'right caliphs' because, according to the Muslim belief, they were the true representatives of the caliphate. In Islamic philosophy, the concept of the caliphate is different from traditional and modern governing systems where the ruling class enjoys every facility of life while the working classes face most of the hardships. In the Quran it is said that *Allah* is the ultimate source of power and law (3:154, 12:40, 25:2, 67:1) and man is His representative on earth (2:30, 6.165) who

should obey His order. As he (man) has the choice to obey or disobey, he will be tested on the day of judgement. Therefore, as the representative of *Allah*, the caliph should implement Allah's laws in the country, and day-to-day decisions should be made with the consultation of the people. In this way the caliph is also accountable to God, unlike the present day prime minister, president or king who is only accountable to the public.

6 According to Waters (1995: 4), 'Globalization has been in process since the dawn of history, and it has increased in its effects since that time, but there has been a sudden and recent acceleration'.

7 These provinces were Makkah, Madinah, Syria, Jazira, Basra, Kufa, Egypt and Palestine.

8 During that period there was a danger of attack from the Romans as they had a stronger navy than the Muslims.

9 The institution of the caliphate was established in 632, and it was abolished in 1924 by the Turkish Grand National Assembly. See Sarwar (1994: 129–32); Ahsan (1988: 10).

10 See Appendix.

11 Choudhury (1988: 152–3) challenges the accuracy of the HDI because it lacks a concept of social welfare and therefore only presents a partial picture. He emphasizes the importance of institutional change and argues for the construction of a Social Well-being Index (SWI) rather than the HDI. In Choudhury's opinion, it is the stock market situation which in fact reflects the actual situation of socio-economic stability in a country. As long as the stock market is stable, there will be more investment and social well-being. Therefore, his concept of an SWI is essentially based on the behaviour of the stock market.

It is important to note, however, that an SWI would not be able to present an accurate picture of human development because the emphasis is on economic growth. Haq (1997: iii) argues that economic growth is not an end but merely a means to development, because this growth does not necessarily translate into human development. This is particularly true for countries such as Pakistan where, in spite of reasonable economic growth, benefits have been hijacked by politically influential, wealthy people. Therefore the gap between the different social classes has widened.

12 According to the UNICEF statistics, Niger was top of the list, where the 'per thousand under-five mortality rate' was 320 as against Singapore and Sweden, where the same figure was only 4 (see UNICEF (1988: 93).

13 See also Appendix.

14 In fact, the oil-rich Muslim countries of the Middle East, which have always bought everything with cash, are now themselves under the burden of foreign debts. The prosperity achieved during the 1970s is now at risk. On the other hand, Western countries are gaining more and more financial benefits and they employ long-term planning. In the United States, the cost of one gallon of petrol, imported from thousands of miles away, is only half of the cost of one gallon of locally produced milk. The same is also true for many other products (Rehman 1995).

15 See Appendix.

16 During the First Five Year Plan (1989–94), Iran allocated 20 per cent for the education sector and 5.6 per cent for the health sector out of its total developmental expenditure (see 'Plan and Budget Organization' in Amuzegar 1997: 380

17 See Appendix.

18 An important issue throughout the educational history of Pakistan has been the setting of unrealistic targets which were then changed by future policies. The new targets and deadlines were just as unrealistic as the previous ones. Another important factor is that, despite the adoption of sound strategies, there has been a failure of implementation. From the recommendations of the Commission on National Education (1959) to the National Education Policy (1992), emphasis has been laid on the recruitment of female teachers but much still has to be done in this area. The national five-year development plans followed a similar pattern to the education policies, where unrealistic targets were set and dates were extended from plan to plan. In fact, education has never been given the priority it merits in the economy of Pakistan. During the first Five-Year Plan of 1955–60 only 2.3 per cent of total financial resources were allocated to the education sector. Of this, only 15.4 per cent was earmarked for primary education. In addition, less than half of this (i.e. 7 per cent of total resources allocated for the education sector) was actually spent on primary education. Although, there was an increase in resource allocation to the primary education sector in the seventh Five-Year Plan of 1988–93, this allocation was still only 2.89 per cent of the total Plan allocation. See Government of Pakistan (1956; 1959; 1970; 1990; 1992; 1998); Bray (1983); Ghaffar (1992).

19 ECO: Afghanistan, Azerbaijan, Iran, Kyrgyzstan, Pakistan, Tajikistan, Turkey, Turkmenistan and Uzbekistan.

20 See Appendix.

References

Abusulayman, A. A. (1994) *Towards an Islamic Theory of International Relations: New Dimensions for Methodology and Thought*, Herndon: International Institute of Islamic Thought.

Ahmad, E. (1996) 'Capital Inflow and National Debt', *The Pakistan Development Review*, vol. 35, no. 4, part II, Islamabad, 943–60.

Ahmad, I. (1991) *The Concept of an Islamic State in Pakistan: An Analysis of Ideological Controversies*, Lahore: Vanguard.

Ahmad, K. (1994) *Islamic Approach to Development: Some Policy Implications*, Islamabad: Institute of Policy Studies.

Ahsan, A. (1988) *OIC: The Organization of the Islamic Conference*, Herndon: International Institute of Islamic Thought.

Ahsan, M. (1991) 'Population Administration During the Time of Prophet Mohammad', *We People*, vol. 6, July-December, 15–16 (a biannual journal of the government of Pakistan).

——(1992) 'Population Administration During the time of Four Right Caliphs', *We People*, vol. 7, January-June, 46–8 (a biannual journal of the government of Pakistan).

——(1995) 'Pakistan's Manpower Migration to the Middle East', *Asian Profile*, vol. 23, no. 3, June, 257–69.

——(1999) 'Human Development Strategies and the Muslim World: A Multidimensional Approach', *National Development and Security: Quarterly Journal*, vol. VII, no. 27, February, 53–93.

Amuzegar, J. (1997) *Iran's Economy under the Islamic Republic*, London: I. B. Tauris.

Asian Management Information Resource (TAMIR) (1998) *First Pakistan Almanac '98*, Lahore: Tamir (PVT) Ltd.

Bellah, R. (1970) 'Religious Evolution', in *Beyond Belief: Essays on Religion in a Post-Traditional World*, New York: Harper and Row, 20–50.

Berger, P. L. (1967) *The Scared Canopy: Elements of Sociological Theory of Religion*, Garden City: Doubleday.

Beyer, P. F. (1996) 'Privatization and the Public Influence of Religion in Global Society', in Mike Featherstone (ed.) *Global Culture: Nationalism, Globalization and Modernity*, London: Sage.

Bhuyan, A. R. *et al.* (eds) (1996) *Towards an Islamic Common Market*, proceedings of the international seminar on Islamic Common Market, 18–20 December 1993, Dhaka: Islamic Economic Research Bureau.

Bray, M. (1983) 'Universal Education in Pakistan: A Perpetually Elusive Goal?', *International Review of Education*, vol. XXIX, 167–78.

Choudhury, M. A. (1988) *Studies in Islamic Social Sciences*, London: Macmillan Press.

Cox, R. W. (1993) 'Structural Issues of Global Governance: Implications for Europe', in Stephen Gill (ed.) *Gramsci's Historical Materialism and International Relations*, Cambridge: Cambridge University Press.

Daily Dawn, internet edition (*http://Dawn.com*) 10 August, 27 September, 11 December 1998; 1, 17 January, 25, 26 February, 8, 16, 21, 25 March 1999.

Dicken, P. (1998) *Global Shift: Transforming the World Economy*, London: Paul Chapman.

Featherstone, M. (1996) 'Global Culture: An Introduction', in Mike Featherstone (ed.) *Global Culture: Nationalism, Globalization and Modernity*, London: Sage.

Ghaffar, S. A. (1992) 'Development of Education in the Decade 1980–90 in Pakistan', *Journal of Rural Development and Administration*, vol. XXIV, no. 3, summer, 75–91

Giddens, A. (1987) *The Nation-State and Violence*, Berkeley: University of California Press.

Government of Pakistan (1956) *First Five Year Plan: 1955–60*, Karachi: Printing Corporation of Pakistan.

——(1959) *Report of the National Commission on Education*, Karachi: Printing Corporation of Pakistan.

——(1970) *New Education Policy 1970*, Islamabad.

——(1990) *Seventh Five Year Plan: 1988–93*, Islamabad.

——(1992) *National Education Policy 1992*, Islamabad.

——(1994) *Eighth Five Year Plan: 1993–98*, Islamabad.

——(1995) *Evaluation of Seventh Five Year Plan: 1988–9*, Islamabad.

——(1996) *Social Indicators of Pakistan: 1995*, Islamabad.

——(1997) *Economic Survey 1996–97*, Islamabad.

——(1998) *Economic Survey 1997–98*, Islamabad.

Haeri, S. F. (1993) *The Elements of Islam*, Dorset: Element Books.

Haq, M. (1997) *Human Development in South Asia 1997*, Karachi: Oxford University Press.

Husain, M. Z. 1995) *Global Islamic Politics*, New York: Harper Collins.

Hussain, S. A. (1997) *The Glorious Caliphate*, Lakhnow: Islamic Research and Publications.

International Institute for Strategic Studies (1998) *Military Balance 1998–99*, London: Oxford University Press.

Kardar, S. (1987) *Political Economy of Pakistan*, Lahore: Progressive Publishers.

Khawaja, S. (ed.) (1989) *Report of the National Workshop to Train Planners and Administrators in Integrated Planning and Eradication of Illiteracy*, 21–6 March 1987, Islamabad: Government of Pakistan and UNESCO.

Lipietz, A. (1987) *Miracles and Mirages: The Crisis of Global Fordism*, London: Verso.

Luckmann, T. (1967) *The Invisible Religion: The Problem of Religion in a Modern Society*, New York: Macmillan.

Mittelman, J. H. (1997) *Globalization: Critical Reflections*, Boulder: Lynne Rienner.

Molana, H. (1999) 'The Foreign Debt Problem', *Economic Review*, vol. 16, no. 3, February, 24–8.

Naik, E. A. (1993) *Pakistan: Economic Situation and Future Prospects: South Asia as a Dynamic Partner*, Islamabad: Pakistan Institute of Development Economics.

Offe, K. (1985) *Disorganized Capitalism*, Oxford: Polity Press.

Pakistan/Netherlands Project on Human Resources (1991) *Workforce Situation Report and Statistical Yearbook 1990*, Islamabad.

——(1993) *Workforce Situation Report and Statistical Yearbook 1992*, Islamabad.

——(1996) *Workforce Situation Report and Statistical Yearbook 1995*, Islamabad.

Parsons, T. (1966) 'Religion in a Modern Pluralistic Society', *Review of Religious Research*, vol. 7, 125–46.

Pasha, M. K. and Samatar, A. I. (1997) 'The Resurgence of Islam', in James H. Mittelman (ed.) *Globalization: Critical Reflections*, Boulder: Lynne Reinner.

Rehman, S. M. (1995) 'Social Development: A Case of Fundamental Economic Rights', *National Development and Security: Quarterly Journal*, vol. III, no. 4, May, 129–55.

Robertson, R. (1987a) 'Globalization and Societal Modernization: A note on Japan and Japanese Religion', *Sociological Analysis*, vol. 47, S, 35–43.

——(1987b) 'Globalization Theory and Civilization Analysis', *Comparative Civilization Review*, vol. 17, 20–30.

——(1992) *Globalization*, London: Sage.

Samad, A. (1992) *Iqbal's Concept of State with Reference to the Emergence of Pakistan*, Niigata-ken: International University of Japan.

Sarwar, G. (1994) *Islam: Belief and Teachings*, London: Muslim Educational Trust.

Shakweer, F. (1996) 'Prospects for the Establishment of the Islamic Common Market and the Role of the Islamic Development Bank', in Ayubur Rahman Bhuyan *et al.* (eds) *Towards an Islamic Common Market*, proceedings of the international seminar on Islamic Common Market, 18–20 December 1993, Dhaka: Islamic Economic Research Bureau.

Uddin, M. (1995) 'Role of Uncontrolled Media in a Controlled Society: The Case Study of Iranian Revolution', *National Development and Security: Quarterly Journal*, vol. III, no. 4, Islamabad, 101–28.

UNDP (1990) *Human Development Report 1990*, New York: Oxford University Press.

——(1991) *Human Development Report 1991*, New York: Oxford University Press.

——(1994) *Human Development Report 1994*, New York: Oxford University Press.

——(1997) *Human Development Report 1997*, New York: Oxford University Press.

——(1998) *Human Development Report 1998*, New York: Oxford University Press.

UNICEF (1997) *The State of the World's Children 1997*, New York: Oxford University Press.

(1998) *Annual Report 1998*, New York: UNICEF.

——(1998) *The State of the World's Children 1998*, New York: Oxford University Press.

Waters, M. (1995) *Globalization*, London: Routledge.

World Bank (1995) *Priorities and Strategies for Education: A World Bank Review*, Washington DC: World Bank.

——(1997)*The World Development Report 1997*, New York: Oxford University Press.

——(1999) *The World Development Report 1998–99*, New York: Oxford University Press.

10 Tradition versus ideology as a mode of political communication in Iran

Ali Mohammadi

This chapter centres on sociological distinctions between tradition and ideology which focus not only on the differences of formal content but also on differences in the relationship between those who articulate and those who listen. Tradition suggests certainty and compulsion, whereas ideology implies openness and choice. Using ideas drawn from Gouldner (1976) and Germani (1981), this argument is developed within the context of the Iranian situation in order to explain the continuing force of Shi'ism and its political involvement of the masses, as opposed to the structural difficulties of developing secular, ideological politics. Communiqués of the revolution are analysed to show how political involvement is presented as religious duty, and how the hegemony of the theocratic state can be seen in the dynamic of the popular movement itself. This chapter argues that the central step of political development, that is the transition to ideological politics, has yet to be permanently taken in Iran. However, after twenty years, the clash between traditional and modern forces emerged and manifested itself through student unrest in Tehran University during July 1999.

A theoretical discourse

> In the society we propose to establish, the Marxists will be free to express themselves because we are convinced that Islam contains the answer to the people's needs. Our faith is capable of standing up to their ideology.
>
> Ayatollah Khomeini[1]

> The ideological mobilization of masses (like the use of ideology as a basis for social solidarities) premises a detraditionalization of society and of communication, of what is allowed to be brought into open discussion, to be sought and claimed...ideology is a very special sort of

rational discourse by reason of its world-referring claims. It defends its policies neither by traditionalistic legitimation nor by invoking faith or revelation. As a historical object then, ideology differs from both religion and metaphysics in that it is concerned to make 'what is' in society a basis for action.

Alvin Gouldner[2]

Ideology is a slippery concept. Each of its multiple meanings carries a weight of intellectual baggage constituted from the crystallization of numerous intense debates on the role of ideas in human action. The very familiarity of the term allows for an evocative usage that rarely demands definition anymore, since that is left to the many rigorous works devoted solely to the topic.[3]

Ideology is one of the most used and abused concepts in social science, and has been wielded with panache in attempts to make sense of the popular movement that overthrew the despotic monarchy in Iran. The Iranian Revolution, it is claimed, vindicates the notion of the power of ideas in the welding of social solidarities and thus in the making, rather than the occurring, of revolutionary movements (Skocpol 1982). Differences in opinion amongst the Shi'ite masses (Hegland 1983); differences of orientation amongst the *ulema* (Akhavi 1983); the existence of pro-constitutionalist and nationalist sentiments (Tabari 1981); and the power of revolutionary Shi'ism (Floor 1983) have all been described as 'ideologies'. The problem is that the concept loses all definitional power and thus it loses both the possibility of helping to distinguish between narrow and broad differences of opinion within a broader framework, and the possibility of helping to indentify differences between frameworks. It is at once an(y) idea, a delimited system of thought and an over-arching conceptual framework. It seems to signify at once too little and too much and, like Iranian politics, it is everywhere and nowhere.

This chapter seeks to re-establish the centrality of the area of analysis demarcated by the problematic of 'ideology', but in a very specific way: it views ideology as a particular form of modern political discourse, most usefully contrasted to traditional political discourse, and which is most conspicuous in the Iranian context by its relative absence.[4]

Here my attempt is to set out a communications model, derived from work by Gouldner (1976), Pye (1961) and others, which provides a means for distinguishing between traditional communication and ideology, and so for constituting religion and ideology in the Iranian context as different modes of political discourse. This difference is determined not by differences in formal content but rather by differences in the relationship between those who articulate and those who listen, that is, in the differences that exist in the relationships between spiritual as opposed to secular leaderships and their respective followings. Constructed as ideal-types, religion and ideology differ as much in their telling as in what they tell. They are different models of communication, of leadership and of participation. As such these notions are evocative for unravelling some issues that pertain to political mobilization and political development in Iran.

The lack of political development in Iran has been most often analysed in terms of the inadequate institutionalization of channels of participation and their lack of autonomy from the despotic state.[5] The implications are that there is a poorly developed party political structure and an absence of a 'public sphere' of political debate.[6] Thus issues of political organization cannot easily be separated from issues of political communication and its particular form and orchestration in Iran.

I would not wish to claim that either socio-economic or political development in the Third World recapitulates the stages of development of Western societies, which occurred in very different epochs and international contexts. However, I do wish to argue that the testing out and development of social scientific language on the nature of the modernization process, in which the political dimension is central, still remains an important task. This task is simply avoided by recourse to cultural relativity and arguments about historical uniqueness. It is in the creative play between an abstract typology, here of traditional political discourse versus contemporary ideological discourse, and the specific case, here of the popular mobilization in Iran, that the validity of the former and the social features of the latter can be delineated.

Tradition versus ideology

There is substantial agreement amongst sociologists, even of widely differing perspectives, that the emergence of the 'age of ideology' was a part of the broader process of modernization and secularization of Europe around the time of the French Revolution. The change that occurred involved a shift from the idea of politics as merely the concern of rulers to being the concern of the public. A 'public' became possible with the development of the means of mass communication, particularly with the spread of printing and the rise of mass literacy (Speier 1950). In traditional societies information was essentially spread by word of mouth in context-sustained, face-to-face conversation which allowed for immediate feedback and questioning (Lerner

1958; Pye 1961). With the development of the modern media of mass communication, information became decontextualized and presented in a way that had to be intelligible, interesting and convincing to persons of diverse background and interests. This in itself promoted more talk amongst strangers who shared information but needed to develop social consensus over its meaning (Gouldner 1976).

Traditional face-to-face communication is multi-modal. Personal presence and social status, dress, gesture and other non-verbal signs all provide the context within which talk is interpreted. The ethos of the speaker is often as important as his argument, and the emotive response from the crowd can also effect what is being said. Print, in particular, with its finished decontextualized product and non-present author, demands a different mode of approach from the reader. One that stresses privatization, rationality and individualized interpretation.[7]

The post-Enlightenment concern with the development of science and the growth of reason was best helped by 'the creation of a class of intellectuals no longer dependent exclusively on patronage or inheritance for their livelihood' (Shils 1972: 49). It was the liberal, middle-class backgrounds of the emergent intelligentsia that determined the non-religious nature of the new ideologies, so that 'the language, the symbolism, the costume of the French Revolution are purely non-Christian' (Hobsbawm 1977: 269). Hobsbawm goes on to argue that if the intellectual leadership of the French Revolution had stemmed more from the masses who actually made it, then doubtless its ideology would have shown more signs of traditionalism. Essentially ideology is seen as playing a role of breaking down and breaking away from the power of 'tradition', which in Western Europe meant both the power of the church and the monarchy.

Gouldner (1976) has argued that what distinguishes traditionalism from ideology is both the nature of the claims that could be made under each system as well as the manner in which they could be justified. In traditional societies only relatively fixed and limited claims could be made. Ideology conjured up abstract ideas and new solidarities, often of nation or class, beyond the ordinary experience of everyday life and the particularist ties of family, religion and locality:

> Ideology serves to uproot people; to further uproot the uprooted, to extricate them from immediate and traditional social structure...thus enabling persons to pursue projects they have chosen. Ideologies thus clearly contribute, at least in these ways, both to rational discourse and rational politics.
>
> (Gouldner 1976: 25)

Another distinguishing factor between tradition and ideology is the nature of the authority vested in the speaker in the former with the de-contextualized argumentation of the latter. In traditional communications, those who participate do so on the basis of their social and political position in the community, and information flows along the lines of the social hierarchy or according to the particular-istic patterns of social relations in each community: 'thus the process [of communication] in traditional societies was not independent of either the ordering of social relationships or the content of the communication' (Pye 1961: 21).[8]

Yet another distinguishing factor is the manner in which content is arrived at. Germani (1981) maintains that it is not the content of thought which is the distinguishing criterion but the manner in which the content is arrived at; an argument which echoes Gouldner (1976). Germani (1981) conceives of secularization as a multi-faceted process in which one central trait is the supercession of prescriptive action by elective action. In both contexts a normative framework regulates ends, means and the relation between them, but whereas this is rigid and strictly determined in the first case, there is a certain degree of choice for the actor in the second (Germani 1981: 118). The ability to exercise some level of individual choice becomes the critical criterion for all kinds of secular activity, leaving open the question of whether the choice is made in a manner that can be typified as 'rational'.

Thus traditional modes of communication are strongly context- and speaker-specific, deriving their meaning and power from known phys-ical and social locations. They are 'time-binding', as Innis (1951) called them, reflecting a strong sense of continuity and community, transmit-ting, alongside tradition, a notion of an unchanging social order.

Tradition works with a restricted linguistic code in which assertions can be justified in terms of the speaker's societal status, on authority *per se* rather than on the justifiable content of what is said. Ideology has to develop a more elaborated reflexive linguistic code in order to provide rational argument and convincing evidence to entice people away from non-reflexive acceptance of traditional viewpoints.[9] Traditionalism demands the continuation of order and accepted meaning. Ideologies, however, create profound linguistic and epistemo-logical anxiety (Gouldner 1976).

Thus such an approach provides two polar types of (political) communication. Tradition begins to appear as a model of communica-tion in which pre-determined actors issue directions which by dint of their authority produce compulsion in the audience which is addressed. Ideology as a model of communication depends upon competition between would-be leaders for persuasive argument and methods of communication that cajole publics into forming opinions.

Essentially, as ideal-types, tradition is a model of compulsion; ideology a model of persuasion. Tradition is based on certainty and closure, whereas ideology fosters doubt and openness. Tradition is a power game; ideology is a language game. Tradition interpolates existing, long-established, primordial identities.[10] Ideology tries to interpolate identities precipitated by a changing social structure, and these are most frequently those of nation or class or interest group.[11] The definition being used here is clearly a very strong and specific application of the notion of ideology. The essential concern in delineating such a bipolar model is not with the validity or even the rationality of one position or viewpoint over another, but rather to develop an argument about the preconditions for and the nature of ideological politics. Typically, it is openness and argumentativeness by unknown speakers which is the basis of ideological politics. Tradition, on the other hand, works through accepted meanings voiced by authoritative speakers, on certainty and closure and on the elimination of alternatives. Ideological politics depend on certain structural prerequisites for social development and political possibility, which include a broad level of literacy. A public sphere within which autonomous groups can organize and speak through channels of communication, print and other media, enables an independent intelligentsia to emerge within a non-repressive, modern political environment.[12] I would like to argue that this is an evocative approach for an analysis of both the dynamics of the Iranian mobilization and the subsequent political events under the Islamic Republic. It can help to explain the phenomenon of rapid and radical political mobilization in a population unused to political participation, and help to explain the limited role of secular intellectuals in the revolutionary process. My argument is that the popular movement was precipitated onto the streets through the coercive persuasion of the traditional religious leaders.[13]

The Iranian revolution: a model of tradition

In the Iranian situation the focus is too frequently on the content of ideology (as a systematic political outlook) at the expense of examining how 'ideology' works, how it has power, why it resonates (or not) amongst a population. Such an approach shifts the focus from, for example, the exegesis on the finer points of Shi'ite jurisprudence (let alone arguments amongst Feday infractions about the true nature of the Iranian bourgeoisie) to the manner in which a popularly accessible viewpoint was used to mobilize a crowd not familiar with political activity.[14] More specifically, in Iran, this implies a focus on the continued relevance of Shi'ism in social life, the particular relationship between the Shi'ite clergy and the people, and the language used by the former to address the latter. Political communication in Iran has been dominated by traditional forces, channels and contents controlled either by the monarchy, which was the dictatorial (and by the 1970s increasingly despotic) lynch-pin of the political system, or by the clergy.

In Iran the clergy maintained their institutional independence from the state by surviving on the financial contributions from religious taxes and support from the other traditional social force, the bazaar (Akhavi 1980). The clergy also possessed the only independent network of social spaces not incorporated by the regime: the religious network of mosques and meeting halls. They were not only the priestly carriers of the religio-cultural tradition but also the organic intellectuals of the traditional social classes, who were being forced onto the defensive as modernization and secular decline threatened to undermine their traditional social influence. As declining strata, the clergy needed to act dramatically to preserve their status. Also, the particular implementation of mass media in Iran and the nature of the nonparticipatory political system, meant that the media did not act as a multiplier of political modernity, as suggested by Lerner (1958).[15] Instead the mass media was readily incorporated by the regime as a modern facade for essentially hierarchical, top-down communications based on attempts to legitimize one traditional form of authority: the monarchy. It was non-participatory, uncritical and ultimately repressive, providing limited choice in the area of entertainment while strictly controlling political expression. The result was the growth of a cultural dependency in which all contemporary materials were brought from the West while internal voices were silenced. This produced deep feelings of inferiority and loss of cultural identity.

Autonomous political activity in Iran has flourished in only brief and discontinuous periods, and these were typically periods of regime weakness: the time of the Constitutional movement of 1905–11; the period of Reza Khan's coup in the early 1920s; the period of Allied intervention; the forced abdication of Reza Shah and the rule of the young Mohammed Reza in 1941–53, during which Mossadegh managed to develop a concern not only with the nationalization of internal resources but also with the establishment of the institutional framework of democracy. The period until 1953 is essentially the last period of competitive ideological politics (with autonomous party organizations, unions and a free press) in contemporary Iranian history up to the time of the popular movement in 1978. In the twenty-five years between 1953 and 1978, the political system suffered a regression. There was increasing regime repression, particularly after 1963, with censorship, regime orchestration of political parties, a non-participatory political environment, and the arrest and torture of political prisoners. In 1975, the director of Amnesty International named Iran as the country with the worst human rights record in the world.

Given that two thirds of the Iranian population is under thirty years of age, there is little collective memory of an open political system or practice in political debate. Given also that two thirds of the Iranian population is functionally illiterate, and that the press and other forms of publishing are strongly controlled, the extreme difficulties of establishing the forms of ideological discourse that have been outlined become more readily apparent. This lack of political development has served only to reinforce the traditional authority and reactionary demagogy of the fundamentalist clergy.

Under the Pahlavi regime, radical politics, with both Marxist and Islamic roots, went underground in guerrilla formations. Exile politics and publications grew, and radio stations beamed into Iran. But these would-be political leaders lacked any direct contact with the Iranian masses and lacked any political practice other than the language-play of political opposition. Yet, even in its language, secular politics was unevocative to many Iranians as radical groups played on statuses, in particular those of class, that the Iranian masses did not identify with. Instead, the simple bipolar world of the *mostazafin*, the disinherited, versus the *mostakbarin*, the oppressors, proposed by the populist rhetoric of the religious leaders, was easily to assimilate. The religious leaders also reduced imperialism and dependency to the notion of a conspiracy against Iran, and alienation was explained through loss of faith. The language of nationalism had been co-opted and corrupted by the regime, along with notions of development, revolution and progress. Thus the ideological space of the lay/radical leadership was effectively eroded because their rhetoric lacked appeals that were accessible to and assimilable by the masses. The lay/radical leadership also lacked social standing and the automatic respect paid to religious figures. In addition, they lacked unity, a charismatic leadership, organizational practice, and, most of all, they lacked the social space in which to grow. Thus the gap between secular ideologies (and ideologists) and the masses grew, rather than diminished.

Instead, the political mobilization of the Iranian popular movement provides an almost classic model of the power of traditional communication, here based on the power of religious affiliation and religious leaders. The ideational content of the movement centred on the politicization of a primordial identity, Islam, overlaid with populist appeals against a much-disliked despotism. This was expressed by the *ulema*, who explicitly drew upon their continuing social status and authority in the community. This status and authority is based on a number of factors: the *marji-taglid* are the intercessors between the masses and God. They legitimate Shi'ite worship and practice and are a supreme source of emulation for others. As Cole has argued:

> While the *ulema* remained a rather loose and unstructured body of experts, the institution of a supreme source of emulation introduced the possibility of a strong centralized leader…the idea that all Shi'ite laymen owe allegiance to one Shi'i jurisprudent, and that the local *ulema* were to be judged on how faithful they were to the rulings of this supreme exemplar, provided an ideological underpinning for the social and political power of the *ulema*.
>
> (Cole 1983)

The *marji-taglid* alone possess the right to make religious interpretations, and since Islam is conceived as a complete and totalizing system, there is an asymmetry in the right to interpret ideology since Shi'ism has no need to confront other systems (Fischer 1980). The *marji-taglid* are traditionally educated men, *alim*, with access to esoteric knowledge, who wear special garb. They could dismiss ideological challenges from people like Ali Shariati as the work of unschooled outsiders, one who is not *alim* (Enavat 1982). As revered elders of the community, they form a gerontocracy of practised professional communicators who possess a language honed on years of intimate contact with popular audiences (Fathi 1979).

The summons of the religious leaders to religio-political mobilization can be clearly apprehended from an examination of the *elamiyeh* or communiqués of the revolution. This was the main method through which high *ulema* orchestrated the popular movement, and will be briefly examined in the following section.

Compelling a revolution: religious authority and political mobilization

From the start of the street demonstrations in January 1978 to the final achievement of an Islamic Republic in February 1979, the grand ayatollahs orchestrated the popular movement through live sermons in mosques, through tape-recorded speeches and through brief Xerox communiqués. Building on the seven-day and forty-day mourning cycle of Islam, the religious pulse of the movement also had religious direction.

The religious leaders addressed the people from the beginning as though they expected them to follow their instructions. The language was one of command, not exhortation; one of direction, not persuasion. For example, the *ulema* informed the nation that a certain fortieth day was proclaimed a national day of mourning; in which they expected the entire Muslim community to participate. The active subject which the religious leaders called upon to participate was either the entire Iranian nation or more often the Muslim community, which is almost coterminous with the nation, given the fact that 98 per cent of Iranians are Muslim.[16] Thus the nationalist appeals of the democratic liberal politicians represented by the National Front are already incorporated in the appeals of the religious leaders. The left, on the other hand, scrambled for a language to address its would-be constituencies: as *kargaran* – workers, *zahmatkeshan* – toilers, *khalgh* – nation, *tudeh* – the masses. Again, the religious leaders succeeded with the simple appellation of *mostazafin*, the oppressed, broadly inclusive and in polar opposition to the *mostakbarin*, the oppressors, a limited and identifiable coterie of elite families and chosen individuals around the Shah.

Participation in the popular movement was constructed by the religious leadership as an extension of a broader religious duty and commitment. The same phrases are repeated time and again, particularly in statements from Khomeini but also from other leading ayatollahs: 'This is an Islamic duty and must be followed', 'This is a godly duty and it is incumbent upon the Iranian people (*Bar Mellat ast*)'. Such language is especially evident in Khomeini's statement for the start of the month of *Muharram*, 23 November 1978. The powerful rhetoric welcomes the opportunity that this symbolic period provides, since '*Muharram* is like a divine sword in the hands of the soldiers of Islam'. In this communiqué, Khomeini sets out explicit political acts that will bring down the tyrannical regime. These all share a similar construction:

> It is the duty of the entire nation that has now risen in revolt to pursue and broaden its struggle against the Shah with all its strength and to bring down his harmful, disastrous regime....The military government is usurping and contrary to both the law of the land and the *sharia*. It is the duty of everyone to oppose it....It

is the duty of all oil company officials and workers to prevent the export of oil....Advance together with a single voice and a single purpose, to the sacred aim of Islam....There is no excuse for any class of people in the nation to remain inactive today: silence and apathy mean suicide, or even aid to the tyrannical regime.

(Khomeini 1981: 34)

The movement is presented as having an explicitly religious purpose for God and Islam, not for anything as immediate or mundane as economic betterment. Khomeini rapidly dispelled that notion by saying that the revolution was not made for bigger melons and better houses. This later became a rationalization for the evident inability of the movement to solve deep-rooted economic problems. The movement would only succeed, so the rhetoric went, with total solidarity in Islam. Khomeini used the expression *vahdat-e-kalameh*, which literally means unity of the word (of the Quran), but became a rubric for the suppression of dissent (Rose 1983). In this way, from early on in the popular movement, the notion of religious hegemony and interpretative dominance over all and any other theories and viewpoints was clearly established and enforced. Thus the subsequent repression of political groups and other orientations, including those who participated in the popular movement, would not have been so surprising if the true nature of the fundamentalist orientation was understood.

Clearly, in the real world, the two ideal-types of discourse I have identified are not so far apart, but rather, they overlap and function to address different social groups. Different perspectives contaminate each other, language overlaps and rationalizations have to be made, particularly in addressing the group of transitionals for whom simple, traditional appeals were not enough. Thus, while the status, authority and religious commands of the *ulema* were probably enough to mobilize the recent rural migrants, the popular urban classes and those social elements still deeply embedded in traditional culture, for groups moving further in to the modern sector, with higher education and external contacts, a more rationalized, more justificatory, 'ideological' approach was needed.

The recognition of ideological conflict by the religious leaders was dealt with in three main ways. First, the argument was so constructed as to render the alternative perspectives unnecessary in the light of the complete and totalizing perspective of Islam/Quran. So, for example, those who demanded a 'democratic republic' were fobbed off with the response that 'Islam is, in fact, superior to all forms of democracy' (Khomeini 1978). Second, there was the labelling and ridicule of the other speakers, which, by implication, devalued their speeches. Thus intellectuals were labelled as *fokul-kerevati*, 'the tie-wearers', that is Westernized and therefore inauthentic. Other labels were *taghuti* – 'oppressor', *zede-enghelab* – 'anti-revolutionary', or*kafer* – 'atheist'. By being so labelled, the persona was erased, so there remained no necessity to do battle with the arguments raised. Third, the central 'ideological' argument was a return to nativism, through the construction of an authentic Islamic cultural identity which was being eroded by foreign agents. This justified the appeal for retraditionalization as a defence against modernizing forces which had undermined the pristine and wholly adequate religious culture. This approach again revoked the need to engage in argument about alternative ideas, since these were simply rejected as foreign, corrupt and contaminated.

In much of the literature on political development, the notion of a form of political activity/communication which does not fit into the contemporary 'ideological' institutional mould reoccurs. It is called pre-democratic (as opposed to anti-democratic) politics by Apter (1965), or pre-politics by Hobsbawm (1959). Here, I suggest the notion of pre-ideological, or rather traditional political communication, as a rubric to explain the nature of political discourse and the dynamic of the popular political mobilization in Iran. It seems clear that Iran's popular mobilization was based on the power of traditional communicators, not simply on the availability of traditional networks. The religious leaders were and are the demagogues of a traditional people, able to call upon and politicize a deeply held collective identity. If 'the greatest menace to the development of the new states is demagogy', old states are not free of traditionalist demagogy either (Shils 1972). Authoritarian populism is a far cry from democratic participation.

That few other identities reverberated with any strength, that other ideologies had little power and that secular intellectuals played little role in the popular mobilization is a function of the lack of political development under the Pahlavi regime. The establishment of a 'public sphere' of unconstrained participation and debate which fosters contemporary ideological debate, speakers and contents, remains one of the central challenges for Iranian political development.

All revolutions are made in the 'name of the masses', and in the Iranian case, all classes did participate in the rituals of demonstrations. But the structure of the theocratic state that emerged rapidly recreated a hierarchy of 'experts' to determine the new constitution in a country with seventy years secular experience.

There have now been twenty years of preaching a return to nativism. This is one of the slogans of the revolution which revitalized

Islamic identity but did not contribute enough to Iran's development – on the contrary, it had the opposite effect by overemphasizing undefined religious commitment and neglecting professional integrity. The student unrest at Tehran University in July 1999 provides clear evidence in support of President Khatami's programme for bringing Iran into the globalized world and, furthermore, for activating the debate between Islam, modernity and civil society discourse. It is crucial, at the very beginning of this millennium, that the debate on civilization is activated in order to address some of the important issues of modernity and religion. It is especially crucial to bring the traditional faction into the debate to establish what it has to offer for the ills of mankind, particularly in the world of Islam. At the same time, with unleashed and unfettered consumer market capitalism, we must ask: where are moralities and human values?

Notes

1 Ayatollah Khomeini in an interview with *Le Monde*, 6 May 1978, published in English in *MERIP Reports*, 69, p. 20.
2 Gouldner (1976: 23–31).
3 Two recent works are Larrain (1979) and Therborn (1980).
4 Thus, from this point on in the paper, this notion of a particular contemporary form of political discourse is signalled as ideology, while any different meanings/uses of the concept are indicated by 'ideology'.
5 See the discussions in Zonis (1971) and Abrahamian (1982).
6 For elaboration of the idea of a 'public sphere' as an area of autonomous debate independent of the state, see Gouldner and Habermas (1962); on its importance in the development of public opinion in the West, see Speier (1950).
7 It is here that the relevance of the arguments about 'stages of media development' lies, for it appears that without the widespread development of literacy/print, a population is ill equipped to resist either the influence of traditional authority or the power of broadcast media.
8 Pye's failing is an underestimation of the nature of professional traditional communiators and their continuing influence.
9 The notion of restricted and elaborated codes comes from Bernstein (1972).
10 The notion of primordial identities and their role in national integration is discussed by Geertz (1974).
11 The notion of ideological interpellation is developed by Althusser (1971); see also Therborn (1980).
12 Using this model, it becomes possible to argue that there is a process within which 'ideology' so institutionalizes itself as to become a new state religion, blocking dissent and effectively retraditionalizing the nature of political discourse. This might be an effective way of examining the nature of political discourse in state socialist societies, amongst others.

13   The notion of coercive persuasion is developed by Simon (1976).
14   It has been argued that the Islamic movement be seen as a 'counter-mobi-
     lization' to the mobilization under the Shah. I would argue that no such
     political mobilization occurred, it being the very thing the Shah was most
     scared of. See Green (1982).
15   Lerner suggested that the development of mass media would act as a
     multiplier: both of economic participation, essentially through increased
     consumption, and political participation, essentially through participant
     voters.
16   Differences between Shi'ite and Sunni interpretations, and the importance
     of other social categories such as ethnic or linguistic divisions, were played
     down.

References

Abrahamian, E. (1982) *Iran Between Two Revolutions*, Princeton: Princeton
     University Press.
Akhavi, S. (1980) *Religion and Politics in Contemporary Iran*, Albany: SUNY
     Press.
——(1983) 'The Ideology and Praxis of Shi'ism in the Iranian Revolution',
     Comparative Study of Society and History, vol. 24, no. 2.
Althusser, L. (1971) 'Ideology and Ideological State Apparatus', in *Lenin and
     Philosophy*, London: New Left Books.
Apter, D. (1965) *The Politics of Modernization*, Chicago: University of
     Chicago Press.
Bernstein, B. (1972) *Class, Codes and Control*, London: Routledge and Kegan
     Paul.
Cole, J. (1983) 'Imami Jurisprudence and the Role of the *ulema*: Morteza
     Ansari on Emulating the Supreme Exemplar', in Nikki Keddie (ed.) *Reli-
     gion and Politics in Iran*, New Haven: Yale University Press.
Enavat, H. (1982) *Modern Islamic Political Thought*, London: Macmillan.
Fathi, A. (1979) 'The Role of the Islamic Pulpit', *Journal of Communication*,
     vol. 29, no. 3.
Fischer, M. (1980) *Iran: From Religious Dispute to Revolution*, Cambridge
     MA: Harvard University Press.
Floor, W. M. (1983) 'The Revolutionary Character of the *ulema*: Wishful
     Thinking or Reality?', in Nikki Keddie (ed.) *Religion and Politics in Iran*,
     New Haven: Yale University Press.
Geertz, C. (1974) *The Interpretation of Culture*, New York: Basic Books.
Germani, G. (1981) *The Sociology of Modernization*, New Brunswick NJ:
     Transaction Press.
Gouldner, A. (1976) *The Dialectic of Ideology and Technology*, London:
     Macmillan.
Gouldner, A. and Habermas, J. (1962) *Structurwendel der Offentlichkeit*,
     Luchterhand.
Green, J. (1982) *Revolution in Iran*, New York: Praeger.

Hegland, M. (1983) 'Two Images of Husain: Accommodation and Revolution in an Iranian Village', in Nikki Keddie (ed.) *Religion and Politics in Iran*, New Haven: Yale University Press.

Hobsbawm, E. (1959) *Primitive Rebels*, New York: Norton.

——(1977) *Age of Revolution*, London: Sphere.

Innis, H. A. (1951) *Bias and Communication*, Toronto: University of Toronto Press.

Keddie, N. (ed.) (1983) *Religion and Politics in Iran*, New Haven: Yale University Press.

Khomeini, R. (1978) interview, *Le Monde*, 6 May, published in English in *MERIP Reports*, 69, p. 20.

——(1981) 'Muharram: The Triumph of Blood over the Sword', in Imam Khomeini (ed.) *Islam and Revolution*, trans. H. Algar, Mizan Press.

Larrain, J. (1979) *The Concept of Ideology*, London: Hutchinson.

Lerner, D. (1958) *The Passing of Traditional Society: Modernizing the Middle East*, Chicago: Free Press.

Pye, L. (1961) 'Models of Traditional, Transitional, and Modern Communications Systems', in Lucien Pye (ed.) *Communications and Political Development*, Princeton: Princeton University Press.

Pye, L. (ed.) (1961) *Communications and Political Development*, Princeton: Princeton University Press.

Rose, G. (1983) 'Velayat-e Fagih and the Recovery of Islamic Identity in the Thought of Ayatollah Khomeini', in Nikki Keddie (ed.) *Religion and Politics in Iran*, New Haven: Yale University Press.

Shils, E. (1972) 'Demagogues and Cadres in the Political Development of the New States', in Edwards Shils (ed.) *The Intellectuals and the Powers*, Chicago: University of Chicago Press.

Shils, E. (ed.) (1972) *The Intellectuals and the Powers*, Chicago: University of Chicago Press.

Simon, H. (1976) *Persuasion: Understanding, Practice and Analysis*, New York: Addison-Wesley.

Skocpol, T. (1982) 'Rentier State and Shi'a Islam in the Iranian Revolution', *Theory and Society*, vol. 11, no. 3.

Speier, H. (1950) 'Historical Development of Public Opinion', *American Journal of Sociology*, vol. LV, no. 4.

Tabari, A. (1981) 'Role of the Shi'i Clergy in Modern Iranian Politics', *Khamsin*, vol. 9.

Therborn, G. (1980) *The Ideology of Power and the Power of Ideology*, London: New Left Books.

Zonis, M. (1971) *The Political Elite of Iran*, Princeton: Princeton University Press.

Bibliography

Abdullah, Aslam (1997) 'Shaving Is His Protest against Coercion', *Los Angeles Times*, 10 May.

Abootalebi, A. R. (1995) 'Democratization in Developing Countries, 1980–1989', *Journal of Developing Areas*, vol. 29, no. 4, 507–29.

Abrahamian, E. (1982) *Iran Between Two Revolutions*, Princeton: Princeton University Press.

Abu-Lughod, L. (1997) 'Dramatic Reversals: Political Islam and Egyptian Television', in Joel Beinin and Joe Stark (eds) *Political Islam*, London: I. B. Tauris.

Abusulayman, A. A. (1994) *Towards an Islamic Theory of International Relations: New Dimensions for Methodology and Thought*, Herndon: International Institute of Islamic Thought.

Afkhami, M. (ed.) *Faith and Freedom: Women's Human Rights in the Muslim World*, Syracuse NY: Syracuse University Press, 51–60.

Ahmad, E. (1996) 'Capital Inflow and National Debt', *The Pakistan Development Review*, vol. 34, no. 5, part II, Islamabad, 943–60.

Ahmad, I. (1991) *The Concept of an Islamic State in Pakistan: An Analysis of Ideological Controversies*, Lahore: Vanguard.

Ahmad, K. (1994) *Islamic Approach to Development: Some Policy Implications*, Islamabad: Institute of Policy Studies.

Ahmed, A. S. (1992) *Postmodernism and Islam: Predicament and Promise*, London: Routledge.

Ahmed, A. S. and Donnan, H. (eds) (1994) *Islam, Globalization, and Postmodernity*, New York: Routledge, 1–20.

Ahsan, A. (1988) *OIC: The Organization of the Islamic Conference*, Herndon: International Institute of Islamic Thought.

Ahsan, M. (1991) 'Population Administration During the Time of Prophet Mohammad', *We People*, vol. 6, July–December, 15–16 (a biannual journal of the Government of Pakistan).

——(1992) 'Population Administration During the Time of Four Right Caliphs', *We People*, vol. 7, January–June 46–8 (a biannual journal of the Government of Pakistan).

——(1995) 'Pakistan's Manpower Migration to the Middle East', *Asian Profile*, vol. 23, no. 3, June, 257–69.

——(1999) 'Human Development Strategies and the Muslim World: A Multi-dimensional Approach', *National Development and Security: Quarterly Journal*, vol. VII, no. 27, February, 53–93.

Akhavi, S. (1980) *Religion and Politics in Contemporary Iran*, Albany: SUNY Press.

——(1983) 'The Ideology and Praxis of Shi'ism in the Iranian Revolution', *Comparative Study of Society and History*, vol. 24. no. 2.

Al-Alili, A. A. H. (1974) *Al-Huriyyat al-ommah filfikr-wal Nidham al-Siyasi Fil Islam* (Public Liberties in Thought and Political Systems in Islam) Cairo.

Al-Faqih, S. (1997) personal interview, London: March.

Al-Mass'ari, M. (1995 and 1997) personal interviews, London: June 1995, March 1997.

Al-Qaradawi, Y. (1998) 'Mr Anwar Ibrahim Fatwa', 10 September, *http://www.qaradawi.net/english/fatwa/Mr_anwar_fatwa.htm*.

Al-Rashid, I. (ed.) (1976) *Documents on the History of Saudi Arabia*, vol. 3, Salisbury NC: Documentary Publications.

Alibhai-Brown, Y. (1998) 'God's own Vigilantes', *Independent*, 12 October.

Althusser, L. (1971) 'Ideology and Ideological State Apparatus', in *Lenin and Philosophy*, London: New Left Books.

Amin, S. (1989) *Eurocentrism*, New York: Monthly Review Press.

Amnesty International (1987) *Iran Violations of Human Rights*, London: Amnesty International Press.

Amuzegar, J. (1997) *Iran's Economy under the Islamic Republic*, London: I. B. Tauris.

An-Na'im, A. A. (1998) 'Does Culture Matter?', *Human Rights Dialogue*, vol. 11, June, 22–3.

An-Na'im, A. A., Gort, J. D., Jansen, H. and Vroom, H. M. (eds) (1995) *Human Rights and Religious Values: An Uneasy Relationship?*, Michigan: William B. Eerdmans Publishing.

Andersen, R. R., Seibert, R. F. and Wagner, J. G. (1998) *Politics and Change in the Middle East: Sources of Conflict and Accommodation*, 5th edn, Engle-wood Cliffs: Prentice-Hall.

Anderson, B. (1991) *Imagined Communities: Reflections on the Origin and Spread of Nationalism*, revised edn, London: Verso.

——(1994) 'Exodus', *Critical Inquiry*, 20.

Anderson, J. (1995) ' "Cybarites", Knowledge Workers, and New Creoles on the Superhighway', *Anthropology Today*, 11.

——(1996) 'Islam and the Globalization of Politics', paper presented to the Council on Foreign Relations Muslim Politics Study Group, New York City: 25 June.

——(1997) 'Cybernauts of the Arab Diaspora: Electronic Mediation in Transnational Cultural Identities', paper presented at the Couch-Stone

Symposium on 'Postmodern Culture, Global Capitalism and Democratic Action', University of Maryland, April.

Anderson, J., Cochrane, A. and Brook, C. (eds) (1995) *The Global World: Reordering Political Space*, Milton Keynes/Oxford: Open University Press/Oxford University Press.

Appadurai, A. (1990) 'Disjunction and Difference in the Global Cultural Economy', *Theory, Culture and Society*, vol. 7, 2–3, reprinted in M. Featherstone (ed.) *Global Culture*, London: Sage.

——(1996) *Modernity at Large: Cultural Dimensions of Globalization*, Minneapolis: University of Minnesota Press.

Apter, D. (1965) *The Politics of Modernization*, Chicago: University of Chicago Press.

ArabiaTech (1998) 'Egypt Tops Arab PC Markets', 19 November, *http://www.arabia.com*.

——(1998) 'Iran Reviews the Global Picture', 29 June, *http://www.arabia.com*.

Arabshahi, Payman (1996) 'The Internet in Iran: a Survey', last updated 1 October, *http://www.Iranian.com*.

Arkoun, Mohammed (1994) *Rethinking Islam: Common Questions, Uncommon Answers*, Boulder: Westview Press.

Asian Management Information Resource (TAMIR) (1998) *First Pakistan Almanac*, Lahore: Tamir (PVT) Ltd.

Atiyeh, G. N. (ed.) (1995) *The Book in the Islamic World: The Written Word and Communication in the Middle East*, Albany: SUNY Press.

Azmeh, A. (1993) *Islams and Modernities*, London: Verso.

Balibar, E. (1994) *Masses, Classes, Ideas*, London: Routledge.

Banton, M. (1998) 'Islamophobia: A Critical Analysis', *Dialogue*, December.

Barber, B. R. (1995) *Jihad vs. McWorld*, New York: Times Books.

Barthes, R. (1977) *Image, Music, Text*, London: Fontana.

Bauer, J. R. and Bell, D. A. (eds) (1999) *The East Asian Challenge for Human Rights*, New York: Cambridge University Press.

Bauman, Z. (1998) *Globalization: The Human Consequences*, Cambridge: Polity Press.

Bellah, R. (1970) *Beyond Belief: Essays on Religion in a Post-Traditional World*, New York: Harper and Row.

Bennett, T. *et al.* (eds) (1980) *Popular Television and Film*, London: BFI/Open University Press.

Bennett, T. *et al.* (eds) (1986) *Popular Culture*, Milton Keynes: Open University Press.

Berger, P. L. (1967) *The Scared Canopy: Elements of Sociological Theory of Religion*, Garden City: Doubleday.

Bernstein, B. (1972) *Class, Codes and Control*, London: Routledge and Kegan Paul.

Bhabha, H. (1994) *The Location of Culture*, London: Routledge.

Bhuyan, A. R. *et al.* (eds) (1996) *Towards an Islamic Common Market*, proceedings of the International Seminar on Islamic Common Market, 18–20 December 1993, Dhaka: Islamic Economic Research Bureau.

Bickers, C. (1998) 'Reality Bytes', *Far Eastern Economic Review*, March, 19, 27.

Binder, L. (1961) *Religion and Politics in Pakistan*, Berkeley: University of California Press.

Bogert, C. (1995) 'Chat Rooms and Chadors', *Newsweek*, 21 August.

Boli, J. (1998) 'World Culture, World Cultures, and Human Rights Ideology: An Islamic Alternative?', unpublished paper, table 1.

Boli, J. and Thomas, G. M. (eds) (1999) *Constructing World Culture*, Stanford: Stanford University Press.

Bourdieu, P. (1984) *Distinction: A Social Critique of the Judgement of Taste*, Cambridge MA: Harvard University Press.

——(1990) *In Other Words: Essays Towards a Reflexive Sociology*, Cambridge: Polity Press.

Bourdieu, P. and Coleman, J. S. (eds) (1991) *Social Theory for a Changing World*, Boulder: Westview Press.

Bowen, J. R. (1993) *Muslims Through Discourse*, Princeton: Princeton University Press.

Bray, M. (1983) 'Universal Education in Pakistan: A Perpetually Elusive Goal?', *International Review of Education*, vol. XXIX, 167–78.

Brecher, J., Childs, J. B. and Cutler, J. (eds) (1993) *Global Visions: Beyond the New World Order*, Boston MA: South End Press, 103–11.

'British Mosques on the Superhighway' (1996) *http://www.malaysia.net/muslimedia/*, 30 June.

Browning, D. (1998) *Building Bridges Between Islam and the West*, Wilton Park Paper 138.

Calhoun, C. (ed.) (1992) *Habermas and the Public Sphere*, Cambridge MA: MIT Press.

Carroll, L. (1997) 'Muslim Women and "Islamic Divorce" in England', *Women living under Muslim laws*, dossier 19, October.

Castells, M. (1996a) *The Information Age, Volume 1: The Rise of the Network Society*, Oxford: Blackwell.

——(1996b) *The Information Age, Volume 2: The Power of Identity*, Oxford: Blackwell.

——(1998) *The Information Age, Volume 3: The End of the Millennium*, Oxford: Blackwell.

Choudhury, G. W. (1967) *Documents and Speeches on the Constitution of Pakistan*, Dacca: Green Book House.

Cheah, P. and Robbins, B. (eds) (1986) *Cosmopolitics*, Minneapolis: University of Minnesota Press.

Choudhury, M. A. (1988) *Studies in Islamic Social Sciences*, London: Macmillan.

Cohen, M. (1996) 'Modern Times: Islam on the Information Highway', *Far Eastern Economic Review*, 29 August.

Cohen, R. (1997) *Global Diasporas: An Introduction*, Seattle: University of Washington Press.

Cole, R. (1997) 'Islamic Terrorists Organize, Raise Funds in U.S. while Plotting Attacks', *Associated Press*, 24 May.

Daftary, F. (1998) *A Short History of the Ismailis*, London: I. B. Tauris.

Daily Dawn (1998, 1999) internet edition, *http://Dawn.com*, 10 August, 27 September, 11 December 1998; 1, 7, 25 January, 26 February; 8, 16, 21, 25 March 1999.

Dakar Declaration on the Internet and the African Media, 10 July 1997, for hyperlink mail to: *Devmedia*

Davis, C. (ed.) (2000) *Identity and Social Change in Postmodern Life*, Baltimore.

Decalo, S. (1992) 'The Process, Prospects, and Constraints of Democratization in Africa', *African Affairs*, vol. 91.

Del Valle, A. (1997) *Islamisme et Les Etats-Unis: Une Alliance contre l'Europe*, Lausanne: L'Age d'Homme.

Dicken, P. (1998) *Global Shift: Transforming the World Economy*, London: Paul Chapman.

DITnet (1998) 'Internet Boom: Double Digit Growth Rates for Internet Users in the Middle East', *http://www.ditnet.co.ae*, accessed 25 November.

Egyptian Organization for Human Rights and International Freedom of Expression Exchange Clearing House (1997) 'University Professor Branded an Apostate', *http://www.ifex.org/alert/00001971.html*.

Eickelman, D. F. (1999) 'The Coming Transformation of the Muslim World', *Middle East Review of International Affairs*, vol. 3, no. 3, September, *http://www.biu.ac.il/SOC/besa/meria/journal/1999/issue3/jv3n3a8.html*.

——(1989) 'National Identity and Religious Discourse in Contemporary Islam', *International Journal of Islamic and Arabic Studies*, vol 6, 1–20.

——(1998) 'Inside the Islamic Reformation', *Wilson Quarterly*, vol. 22, 80–9.

Eickelman, D. F. and Piscatori, J. (1996) *Muslim Politics*, Princeton: Princeton University Press.

Eide, A. and Hagtvet, B. (eds) (1992) *Human Rights in Perspective: A Global Assessment*, Oxford: Blackwell, 3–30.

Enavat, H. (1982) *Modern Islamic Political Thought*, London: Macmillan.

Engineer, A. A. (1990) *Islam and Liberation Theology*, New Delhi: Sterling Publishers.

Esack, F. (1997) *Qur'an, Liberation, and Pluralism*, Oxford: Oneworld.

Esposito, J. L. (1988) *Islam: The Straight Path*, New York: Oxford University Press, 116–61.

Esposito, J. L. and Voll, J. O. (1996) *Islam and Democracy*, New York: Oxford University Press.

Evans, K. (1996) 'Thoroughly Modern Mullahs', *Guardian*, 16 March.

Fakhry, M. (1983) *A History of Islamic Philosophy*, New York: Columbia University Press.

Falk, R. (1995) *On Humane Governance: Toward a New Global Politics*, University Park PA: Pennsylvania State University Press.

——(1999) *Predatory Globalization: A Critique*, Cambridge: Polity Press.

Fathi, A. (1979) 'The Role of the Islamic Pulpit', *Journal of Communication*, vol. 29, no. 3.

——(2000) 'Archiving Cultures', *British Journal of Sociology*, special issue on the millennium, vol. 51, no. 1, January.

Featherstone, M. (1991) *Consumer Culture and Postmodernism*, London: Sage.

——(1995) *Undoing Culture: Globalization, Postmodernism and Identity*, London: Sage.

——(2000) 'Globalization and the Problem of Ethics in a Multicultural World', paper delivered to the 'Merging Mosaic? Facing the Ethical Challenge of the Global Community' conference, College Women's Association of Japan, Tokyo, mimeo.

Featherstone, M. and Lash, S. (eds) (1999) *Spaces of Culture: City, Nation, World*, London: Sage.

Featherstone, M. (ed.) (1990) *Global Culture: Nationalism, Globalization and Modernity*, London: Sage.

Featherstone, M., Lash, S. and Robertson, R. (eds) (1995) *Global Modernities*, London: Sage.

Fischer, M. (1980) *Iran: From Religious Dispute to Revolution*, Cambridge MA: Harvard University Press.

Fischer, M. and Abedi, M. (1990) *Debating Muslims: Cultural Dialogues in Postmodernity and Tradition*, Madison: University of Wisconsin Press.

Forsythe, D. P. (1991) *The Internationalization of Human Rights*, Lexington: Lexington Books.

Foucault, M. (1975) *Discipline and Punish: The Birth of the Prison*, trans. Alan Sheridan, London: Penguin Books.

——(1982) 'The Subject and Power', *Critical Inquiry*, vol. 8, no. 4, 777–95.

——(1996) 'Truth and Judicial Forms', *Social Identities*, vol. 2, no. 3, 327–41.

Frank, A. G. (1998) *ReORIENT: Global Economy in the Asian Age*, Berkeley: University of California Press.

Fraser, N. (forthcoming) 'Recognition', *Theory, Culture and Society*.

Friedman, J. (1994) *Cultural Identity and Global Process*, London: Sage.

Geertz, C. (1974) *The Interpretation of Culture*, New York: Basic Books.

Gerges, F. (1999) *America and Political Islam: Clash of Cultures or Clash of Interests?*, Cambridge: Cambridge University Press.

Germani, G. (1981) *The Sociology of Modernization*, New Brunswick NJ: Transaction Press.

Ghaffar, S. A. (1992) 'Development of Education in the Decade 1980–90 in Pakistan', *Journal of Rural Development and Administration*, vol. XXIV, no. 3, summer, 75–91.

Giddens, A. (1987) *The Nation-state and Violence*, Berkeley: University of California Press.

——(1990) *The Consequences of Modernity*, Cambridge: Polity Press.

— (1991) *Modernity and Self-identity*, Cambridge: Polity Press.

Gill, S. (ed.) (1993) *Gramsci's Historical Materialism and International Relations*, Cambridge: Cambridge University Press.

Golding, P. and Harris, P. (eds) (1997) *Beyond Cultural Imperialism: Globalization, Commuincation, and the New International Order*, London: Sage, 49–68.

Gouldner, A. (1976) *The Dialectic of Ideology and Technology*, New York: Seabury Press.

Gouldner, A. and Habermas, J. (1962) *Structurwendel der Offentlichkeit*, Luchterhand.

Government of Pakistan (1956) *First Five Year Plan: 1955–60*, Karachi: Printing Corporation of Pakistan.

——(1959) *Report of the National Commission on Education*, Karachi: Printing Corporation of Pakistan.

——(1970) *New Education Policy 1970*. Islamabad.

Government of Pakistan (1990) *Seventh Five Year Plan: 1988–93*, Islamabad.

——(1992) *National Education Policy 1992*, Islamabad.

——(1994) *Eighth Five Year Plan: 1993–98*, Islamabad.

——(1995) *Evaluation of Seventh Five Year Plan: 1988–9*, Islamabad.

——(1996) *Social Indicators of Pakistan: 1995*, Islamabad.

——(1997) *Economic Survey 1996–97*, Islamabad.

——(1998) *Economic Survey 1997–98*, Islamabad.

Gramsci, A. (1971) *Selections from Prison Notebooks*, ed. and trans. Q. Hoare and G. Nowell-Smith, London: Lawrence and Wishart.

Green, J. (1982) *Revolution in Iran*, New York: Praeger.

Habermas, J. (1987) *The Theory of Communicative Action*, 2 vols, Boston MA: Beacon.

——(1989) *The Structural Transformation of the Public Sphere*, Cambridge: Polity Press.

Haeri, S. F. (1993) *The Elements of Islam*, Dorset: Element Books.

Hafez, K. (ed.) (1997) *Der Islam und der Westen: Anstiftung Zum Dialog*, Frankfurt am Main: Fischer Verlag.

——(ed.) (1999) *Islam and the West in the Mass Media: Fragmented Images in a Globalizing World*, Cresskill: Hampton Press.

Halliday, F. (1992) *Arabs in Exile: Yemen Migration in Urban Britain*, London: I. B. Tauris.

——(1996) *Islam and the Myth of Confrontation*, London: I. B. Tauris.

Haq, M. (1997) *Human Development in South Asia 1997*, Karachi: Oxford University Press.

Harootunian, H. and Myoshi, M. (eds) (1989) *Postmodernism and Japan*, Durham NC: Duke University Press.

Harris, O. (ed.) (1989) *Inside and Outside the Law*, London: Routledge.

Haynes, J. (ed.) (1999) *Religion, Globalization, and Political Culture*, New York: St Martin's Press.

Henderson, H. (1999) *Beyond Globalization: Shaping a Sustainable Global Economy*, West Hartford: Kumarian Press.

Hiebert, M. (1998) 'Reality Bytes', *Far Eastern Economic Review*, 27 August, 17.

Hobsbawm, E. (1959) *Primitive Rebels*, New York: Norton.

——(1977) *Age of Revolution*, London: Sphere.

Horne, J. *et al.* (eds) (1987) *Sport, Leisure and Social Relations*, London: Routledge and Kegan Paul.

Howell, S. (ed.) (1997) *The Ethnography of Moralities*, London: Routledge.

'Human Rights in Islam' (n.d.) Washington DC: IFTA Office, Islamic Series, no. 5.

Human Rights Watch (1996) *Events of 1995*, World Report, New York: Human Rights Watch.

Hunter, S. T. (1998) *The Future of Islam and the West: Clash of Civilizations or Peaceful Coexistence?*, Westport: Praeger.

Huntington, S. (1997) *The Clash of Civilizations and the Remaking of World Order*, London: Simon and Schuster.

Husain, M. R. (1995) *Global Islamic Politics*, New York: Harper Collins.

Hussain, S. A. (1997) *The Glorious Caliphate*, Lakhnow: Islamic Research and Publications.

Innis, H. A. (1951) *Bias and Communication*, Toronto: University of Toronto Press.

International Institute for Strategic Studies (1998) *Military Balance 1998–99*, London: Oxford University Press.

Jameson, F. and Miyoshi, M. (eds) (1998) *The Cultures of Globalization*, Durham NC: Duke University Press, 273–90.

Jones, S. G. (1997) *Virtual Culture: Identity and Communication in Cybersociety*, Thousand Oaks: Sage.

Jones, S. G. (ed.) (1995) *CyberSociety: Computer-Mediated Communication and Community*, London: Sage.

Kamil, A. H. (1952) *Fundamental Human Rights*, Lahore: Mohammad Ashraf Darr.

Kardar, S. (1987) *Political Economy of Pakistan*, Lahore: Progressive Publishers.

Karim, K. H. (1996) 'Internecine Conflict and Planetary Homogenization: The Only Two Games in the Global Village?', *Islam in America*, vol. 3, no. 2, 10–17.

——(1997) 'Relocating the Nexus of Citizenship, Heritage and Technology', *The Public: Journal of the European Institute of Culture and Communication*, vol. 4, no. 4, 75–86.

——(1998) 'From Ethnic Media to Global Media: Transnational Communication Networks Among Diasporic Communities', SRA Reports, Ottawa: Canadian Heritage.

Karim, K. H., Smeltzer, S. and Loucheur, Y. (1998) 'On-line Access and Participation in Canadian Society', SRA Reports, Ottawa: Canadian Heritage.

Keddie, N. (ed.) (1983) *Religion and Politics in Iran*, New Haven: Yale University Press.

Kepel, G. (1997) *Allah in the West: Islamic Movements in America and Europe*, Cambridge: Polity Press.

Khawaja, S. (ed.) (1989) *Report of the National Workshop to Train Planners and Administrators in Integrated Planning and Eradication of Illiteracy, 21–26 March 1987*, Islamabad: Government of Pakistan and UNESCO.

Khomeini, R. (1978) interview, *Le Monde*, 6 May, published in English in MERIP Reports 69, p. 20.

——(1981) 'Muharram: The Triumph of Blood over the Sword', in Imam Khomeini (ed.) *Islam and Revolution*, trans. H. Algar, Berkeley: Mizan Press.

King, A. D. (ed.) (1991) *Culture, Globalization and the World-System*, London: Macmillan.

Kirmani, M. N. I. (1968) *Tarikh-i Bidari-i Iranian* (History of the Awakening of the Iranians) Tehran: Intisharat-i Bunyad-i Farhang-i Iran.

Kurzman, C. (ed.) (1998) *Liberal Islam: A Source-Book*, New York: Oxford University Press.

——(in preparation) 'Who Are the Islamists? A Literature Review', paper in preparation.

Lapidus, I. (1988) *A History of Islamic Societies*, Cambridge: Cambridge University Press.

Larrain, J. (1979) *The Concept of Ideology*, London: Hutchinson.

Lasch, C. (1996) *The Revolt of the Elites*, New York: Norton.

Latham, R. (2000) 'Sovereignty', *Theory, Culture and Society*, vol. 17, no. 4.

Lerner, D. (1958) *The Passing of Traditional Society: Modernizing the Middle East*, Chicago: Free Press.

Levitt, T. (1983) 'The Globalization of Markets', *Harvard Business Review*, May–June, 92–102.

'Liberty Warns Against Repercussions of De-Democratisation in Malaysia', 24 September, *http://www.lmw.org*.

Lipietz, A. (1987) *Miracles and Mirages: The Crisis of Global Fordism*, London: Verso.

Little, D., Kelsay, J. and Sachedina, A. A. (1988) *Human Rights and the Conflict of Cultures*, Columbia SC: University of South Carolina Press.

Loader, B. D. (ed.) (1997) *The Governance of Cyberspace*, London: Routledge.

Luckmann, T. (1967) *The Invisible Religion: The Problem of Religion in a Modern Society*, New York: Macmillan.

Luhmann, N. (1998) *Observations on Modernity*, Stanford: Stanford University Press.

MacDonald, R. and Sanadjian, M. (1999) 'Market, Consent and Islamicisation of Film Production and Consumption in the "New Iranian Cinema"', paper presented to the conference on Globalisation and Identities, Manchester Metropolitan University, Manchester, 30 June–2 July.

MacFarquhar, N. (1996) 'With Mixed Feelings, Iran Tiptoes to the Internet', *New York Times*, 8 October.

Mahmutehaji, R. (1995) *Living Bosnia*, trans. Spomenka Beus and Francis R. Jones, 2nd edn, Ljubljana: Oslobopenja International.

Martin, H-P. and Schumann, H. (1997) *The Global Trap*, London: Zed Books.

Mawdudi, S. A. A. (1939) *The Political Theory of Islam*, Lahore: Markazi Maktaba Jamaat-i-Islami, Pakistan.

——(1975) *Human Rights in Islam*, trans. Kurshid Ahmad and Ahmed Said Khan (1976) Leicester: Islamic Foundation.

——(1991) [1936] *West versus Islam*, New Delhi: International Islamic Publishers.

Mayer, A. J. (1967) *Politics and Diplomacy of Peacemaking: Containment and Counterrevolution at Versailles, 1918–1919*, New York: Alfred A. Knopf.

Mayer, A. E. (1999) *Islam and Human Rights*, 3rd edn, Boulder: Westview Press.

Mazlish, B. and Buultjens, R. (eds) (1993) *Conceptualizing Global History*, Boulder: Westview Press.

McGrew, A. G. and Lewis, P.G. (eds) (1992) *Global Politics: Globalization and the Nation-State*, London: Polity Press.

McLuhan, M. (1960) *Understanding Media*, London: Routledge.

MEED Special Report (1996) 'Region Joins the Global Revolution', 1 March.

Mehrpour, Hossein (1996) *Human Rights as International Instrument and the Position of the Islamic Republic of Iran*, Tehran: Ettela't.

Mestrovic, S. G. (1994) *The Balkanization of the West*, London: Routledge.

Meyer, W. H. (1998) *Human Rights and International Political Economy in Third World Nations: Multinational Corporations, Foreign Aid, and Repression*, Westport: Praeger.

Midlarsky, M. J. (1998) 'Democracy and Islam: Implications for Civilizational Conflict and the Democratic Peace', *International Studies Quarterly*, vol. 42, no. 3, September, 485–511.

Mittelman, J. H. (ed.) (1996) *Globalization: Critical Reflections*, Boulder: Lynne Rienner.

Mittelman, J. H. and Pasha, M. K. (1997) *Out from Underdevelopment Revisited: Changing Global Structures and the Remaking of the Third World*, New York: St Martin's Press.

Mohammadi, A. (1998) 'Electronic Empires: An Islamic Perspective', in Daya Kishan Thussu (ed.) *Electronic Empires: Global Media and Local Resistance*, London: Arnold.

——(1997) *International Communication and Globalization*, London: Sage: 67–89.

Monshipouri, M. (1997) 'State Prerogative, Civil Society, and Liberalization: The Paradoxes of the Late Twentieth Century in the Third World', *Ethics and International Affairs,*, vol. 11, 233–51.

——(1998a) 'The West's Modern Encounter with Islam: From Discourse to Reality', *Journal of Church and State*, vol. 40, no. 1, winter, 25–56.

——(1998b) *Islamism, Secularism, and Human Rights in the Middle East*, Boulder: Lynne Rienner.

Morewedge, P. and Jackson, K. (eds) *Hope and Challenge: The Iranian President Speaks*, Binghampton: Binghampton University: Institute of Global Cultural Studies.

Mowlana, H. (1979) 'Technology versus Tradition: Communication in the Iranian Revolution', *Journal of Communication*, vol. 29, no.3, 107–12.

——(1996) *Global Communication in Transition: The End of Diversity?*, Thousand Oaks: Sage.

——(1999) 'The Foreign Debt Problem', *Economic Review*, vol. 16, no. 3, February, 24–8.

Mozaffari, M. (1998) 'Can a Declined Civilization be Reconstructed: Islamic Civilization or Civilized Islam?', *International Relations*, vol. XIV, no. 3, 31–50.

Mulgan, G. (1998) *Connexity: Responsibility, Freedom, Business and Power in the New Century*, London/New York: Vintage.

Murad, A. H. (1997) 'Dancing with Liberalism', *Q-News International*, (Great Britain) nos. 264–5, May, *http://muslimsonline.com/bicnews/BICNews/Qnews/qnews2.htm*.

Muslimedia (1999) June 16–30, *http://www.muslimedia.com/archives/editorial99/editor64.htm*.

Naik, E. A. (1993) *Pakistan: Economic Situation and Future Prospects: South Asia as a Dynamic Partner*, Islamabad: Pakistan Institute of Development Economics.

Naipaul, V. S. (1991) 'Our Universal Civilization', *New York Review of Books*, vol. 38, no. 3, Jan. 31, 22–5.

Nasr, S. V. R. (1994) *The Vanguard of the Islamic Revolution: The Jama'at-i Islami of Pakistan*, Berkeley: University of California Press.

——(1996) *Mawdudi and the Making of Islamic Revivalism*, New York: Oxford University Press.

Nordenstreng, K. and Schiller, H. I. (eds) (1993) *Beyond National Sovereignty: International Communication in the 1990s*, Norwood NJ: Alex Publishing, 397–417.

Nowell-Smith, G. (1981) 'Television–Football–The World', in T. Bennett, S. Boyd, C. Mercer and J. Woolcott (eds) *Popular Television and Film*, London: British Film Institute and Open University.

Nua Internet Surveys (1998) 'How Many Online?', accessed 25 November, *www.nua.ie*.

Offe, K. (1985) *Disorganized Capitalism*, Oxford: Polity Press.

Pakistan/Netherlands Project on Human Resources (1991) *Workforce Situation Report and Statistical Yearbook 1990*, Islamabad: PNPHR.

——(1993) *Workforce Situation Report and Statistical Yearbook 1992*, Islamabad: PNPHR.

——(1996) *Workforce Situation Report and Statistical Yearbook 1995*, Islamabad: PNPHR.

Parsons, T. (1966) 'Religion in a Modern Pluralistic Society', *Review of Religious Research*, vol. 7, 125–46.

Patomäki, H. (2000) 'The Tobin Tax', *Theory, Culture and Society*, vol. 17, no. 4.

Pelletreau, R. H. Jr, Pipes, D. and Esposito, J. L. (1994) 'Symposium: Resurgent Islam in the Middle East', *Middle East Policy*, vol. 3, no. 2, 1–21.

Peterson, R. D., Wunder, D. F. and Mueller, H. L. (1999) *Social Problems: Globalization in the Twenty-First Century*, Englewood Cliffs: Prentice-Hall.

Pope, N. and Pope, H. (1997) *Turkey Unveiled: Ataturk and After*, London: John Murray.

Pye, L. (ed.) (1961) *Communications and Political Development*, Princeton: Princeton University Press.

Rathmell, A. (1997) 'Netwar in the Gulf', *Jane's Intelligence Review*, January, 29–32.

Rehman, S. M. (1995) 'Social Development: A Case of Fundamental Economic Rights', *National Development and Security: Quarterly Journal*, vol. III, no. 4, May, 129–55.

Reich, R. (1992) *The Work of Nations*, New York: Vintage.

Renteln, A. D. (1990) *International Human Rights: 'Universalism' versus 'Relativism'*, London: Sage.

Reuters (1998) 'Turkish Police React to Online Dissent', 5 June, *www.arabia.com*.

Richer, S. (1996) 'The Phenomenon of Information Highways in the Francophonie', *International Information and Library Review*, vol. 28, 289–301.

Robbins, T., Shepherd, W. C. and McBride, J. (eds) (1985) *Cults, Culture and the Law*, Chico: Scholars Press.

Robertson, R. (1987a) 'Globalization and Societal Modernization: A note on Japan and Japanese Religion', *Sociological Analysis*, vol. 47, summer, 35–43.

——(1987b) 'Globalization Theory and Civilization Analysis', *Comparative Civilization Review*, vol. 17, 20–30.

——(1992a) 'Globality and Modernity', *Theory, Culture and Society*, vol. 9, no. 2, 151–61.

——(1992b) *Globalization: Social Theory and Global Change*, London: Sage.

Robertson, R. and Lechner, F. (1985) 'Modernization, Globalization and the Problem of Culture in World-Systems Theory', *Theory, Culture and Society*, vol. 2, no. 3, 103–17.

Robinson, F. (1993) 'Islam and the Impact of Print', *Modern Asian Studies*, vol. 27, 229–51.

Roff, W. R. (ed.) (1987) *Islam and the Political Economy of Meaning*, London: Croom Helm.

Rosenthal, J. H. (ed.) (1995) *Ethics and International Affairs: A Reader*, Washington DC: Georgetown University Press, 236–56.

Ruggie, J. G. (1993) 'Territoriality and Beyond: Problematizing Modernity in International Relations', *International Organisation*, vol. 47, no. 1, 139–74.

Runnymede Trust (1997) *Islamophobia: A Challenge for Us All*, London: Runnymede Trust.

Ruthven, M. (1995) 'The West's Secret Weapon against Islam', *Sunday Times*, 1 January.

Sabri Zain's Reformasi Diary (1999) 'Changing Times', 2 February, *http://www.geocities.com/CapitolHill/Congress/5868/change.htm*.

Sadri, M. and Sadri, A. (forthcoming) *Reason, Freedom, and Democracy in Islam: Essential Writings of Abdolkarim Soroush*, trans. Mahmoud Sadri and Ahmad Sadri, New York: Oxford University Press.

Said, B. S. (1997) *A Fundamental Fear: Eurocentrism and the Emergence of Islamism*, London: Zed Books.

Said, E. (1978) *Orientalism*, Harmondsworth: Penguin.

Said, E. and Mohammadi, A. (1978) 'Human Rights: An Islamic Context', paper to the International Studies Association Annual Meeting.

Saif, W. (1994) 'Human Rights and Islamic Revivalism', *Islam and Christian/Muslim Relations*, vol. 5, no. 1, 57–65.

Sakamoto, R. (1996) 'Japan, Hybridity and the Creation of Colonialist Discourse', *Theory, Culture and Society*, vol. 13, no. 3.

Salam, H. (ed.) (1991) *Expressions of Islam in Buildings*, Geneva: Aga Khan Trust for Culture.

Samad, A. (1992) *Iqbal's Concept of State with Reference to the Emergence of Pakistan*, Niigata-ken: International University of Japan.

Samuel, R. (ed.) (1981) *People's History and Socialist Theory*, London: Routledge and Kegan Paul.

Sanadjian, M. (1995) 'Temporality of "Home" and Spatiality of Market in Exile: Iranians in Germany' *New German Critique*, no.65, 3–36.

——(1997) 'Islamic Rule and the Strategy for Power: The Recent Presidential Election in Iran', *Social Identities*, vol. 3, no. 3, 385–95.

——(1997) 'Politicisation of Islam and Islamicisation of Politics: Insurrection by the People and the Constitution of a People', unpublished paper.

——(1999) 'Equality of Game, Abstract Discourse on Asylum Rights and Marginal Position in Diaspora: The World Cup and Iranian Exiles', unpublished paper.

Sardar, Z. (1993) 'Paper, Printing and Compact Disks: The Making and Unmaking of Islamic Culture', *Media, Culture and Society*, vol. 15, 43–59.

Sarwar, G. (1994) *Islam: Belief and Teachings*, London: Muslim Educational Trust

Sassen, S. (2000) 'Electronic Space and Sovereignty' *Theory, Culture and Society*, vol. 17, no. 4.

Saudi Arabia (1992) Saudi Arabian Constitution, March 1992, International Constitutional Law website (ICL document status, October 1993) *http://www.uni_wuerzburg.de/law/sa00000_.html*.

Saudi Gazette (1994) 'Bin Baz calls on Muslims to Ignore Bulletins Seeking to Split Their Ranks', 12 November.

Schimmel, A. (1975) *Mystical Dimensions of Islam*, Chapel Hill: University of North Carolina Press.

Schramm, W. (1964) *Mass Media and National Development*, Stanford: Stanford University Press.

Schwartz, P. and Leyden, P. (1997) 'The Long Boom', *Wired*, July: 115–22.

Scott, A. (1997) introduction to A. Scott (ed.) *The Limits of Globalization*, London: Routledge.

Shari'ati, A. (1971) *Tashayyu'i 'Alavi va Tashayyu'i Safavi*, Tehran: Intisharat'i Husayniyah Irshad.

Shariffadeen, T. M. A. (1992) 'Information Technology and the Malaysian Development Paradigm', paper presented at the Kongres Menjelang Abad 21: Islam dan Wawasan, 3 July, Kuala Lumpur.

Shils, E. (ed.) (1972) *The Intellectuals and the Powers*, Chicago: University of Chicago Press.

Shiva, V. (1999) 'Diversity and Democracy: Resisting the Global Economy', *Global Dialogue*, vol. 1. no. 1.

Silk, M. (1995) *Unsecular Media: Making News of Religion in America*, Chicago: University of Illinois Press.

Simon, H. (1976) *Persuasion: Understanding, Practice and Analysis*, New York: Addison-Wesley.

Skocpol, T. (1982) 'Rentier State and Shi'a Islam in the Iranian Revolution', *Theory and Society*, vol. 11, no. 3.

Smeltzer, S. (1997) 'Government Responses in the Information Society: A Comparative Analysis of 6 Asian Countries', SRA Reports, Ottawa: Canadian Heritage.

Smith, D. E. (1970) *Religion and Political Development*, Boston MA: Little, Brown.

Soroush, A. K. (1993) 'The Democratic Religious Rule', *Kiyan*, vol. 3, no. 11, March-April, 12–15.

Speier, H. (1950) 'Historical Development of Public Opinion', *American Journal of Sociology*, vol. LV, no. 4.

Sreberny-Mohammadi, A. and Mohammadi, A. (1994) *Small Media and Big Revolution*, Minneapolis: University of Minnesota Press.

St Clair, J. (1999) 'Seattle Diary', *New Left Review*, no. 238, 81–96.

Tabari, A. (1981) *Role of the Shi'i Clergy in Modern Iranian Politics*, vol. 9, London: Khamsin.

Thapisa, A. P. N. (1996) 'The Impact of Global Information on Africa', *Internet Research: Electronic Networking Applications and Policy*, vol. 6, no. 1, 71–8.

Therborn, G. (1980) *The Ideology of Power and the Power of Ideology*, London: New Left Books.

Thomas, G. M., Meyer, J. W., Ramirez, F. O. and Boli, J. (1987) *Institutional Structure: Constituting State, Society, and the Individual*, Newbury Park CA: Sage.

Thompson, J. B. (1995) *The Media and Modernity: a Social Theory of the Media*, Cambridge: Polity Press.

Thompson, J. H. and Reischauer, R. D. (eds) (1966) *Modernization of the Arab World*, Princeton: Van Nostrand, 26–33.

Trompenaars, F. (1993) *Riding the Waves of Culture: Understanding Cultural Diversity in Business*, London: Nicholas Brearley.

Uddin, M. (1995) 'Role of Uncontrolled Media in a Controlled Society: The Case Study of the Iranian Revolution', *National Development and Security: Quarterly Journal*, vol. III, no. 4, Islamabad, 101–28.

UNDP (1990) *Human Development Report 1990*, New York: Oxford University Press.

——(1991) *Human Development Report 1991*, New York: Oxford University Press.

——(1994) *Human Development Report 1994*, New York: Oxford University Press.

——(1997) *Human Development Report 1997*, New York: Oxford University Press.

——(1998) *Human Development Report 1998*, New York: Oxford University Press.

UNICEF (1997) *The State of the World's Children 1997*, New York: Oxford University Press.
——(1998a) *Annual Report 1998*, New York: UNICEF.
——(1998b) *The State of the World's Children 1998*, New York: Oxford University Press.
Veblen, T. (1924) *The Theory of the Leisure Class*, London: George Allen and Unwin.
Volosinov, A. (1973) *Marxism and the Philosophy of Language*, New York: Seminar Press.
Wahid, A. (1998) 'Anwar, Mahathir, dan Kita di Indonesia', 3 October, *http://www.muslims.net/KMNU/nu/1998/981003b.htm*.
Wallerstein, E. (1989) *Unthinking Social Science: the Limits of Nineteenth-Century Paradigms*, Cambridge: Polity Press.
Waters, M. (1995) *Globalization*, London: Routledge.
Williams, R. (1961) *The Long Revolution*, Harmondsworth: Penguin.
Wilson, R. A. (ed.) (1997) *Human Rights, Culture, and Context: Anthropological Perspectives*, London: Pluto Press.
Witte, J. Jr and van der Vyver, J. D. (eds) *Religious Human Rights in Global Perspective: Religious Perspectives*, The Hague: Martinus Nijhoff, 387–453.
World Bank (1995) *Priorities and Strategies for Education: A World Bank Review*, Washington DC: World Bank.
——(1997) *The World Development Report 1997*, New York: Oxford University Press.
——(1999) *The World Development Report 1998–99*, New York: Oxford University Press.
Yar, M. N. (forthcoming) 'The Politics of Recognition', *Theory, Culture and Society*.
Zonis, M. (1971) *The Political Elite of Iran*, Princeton: Princeton University Press.

Index